And It's Only Monday

A memoir by Michigan native
Sharon Roslund.

Copyright © 2017 by Sharon Roslund.

All rights reserved. This book or any portion thereof may not be reproduced or used in any manner whatsoever without the express written permission of the publisher except for the use of brief quotations in a book review or scholarly journal.

Cover design by Sharon Roslund. Book design by Meg Irish.

Second Printing: October 2017

ISBN: 978-0-692-88312-9

Acknowledgments

Making a living at art had worn me down. Lugging heavy boxes, setting up a booth, driving hundreds of miles for thirty years, were over. I needed a lightweight career. Paper was not heavy. I called the famous Vedic astrologer Chakrapani Ullal in Los Angeles, whom I had once seen for my life reading. He had been astoundingly correct. For sixty dollars he would now answer one question. I phoned him.

"Do you think I could write?" I asked. "Yes," he said, matter of factly. That was not good enough for all that money, nearly a sixty-four dollar question, so I asked him again. "Yes!" he said, more sternly, and with more force, and hung up.

I checked out the Washington Post for suggestions on how to begin and noted the Writer's Center was having a reading event, to introduce their teachers. Bill O'Sullivan read. He was the star of my evening. I said, "I want to learn from you," and proudly added, "I used to be editor of the high-school paper." He graciously did not roll his eyes. He became my mentor. He has had a hand in editing the first drafts of many of these stories, which I wrote in his workshops. Thank you, Bill. My gratitude is fathomless.

It truly was a lazy June day in my hometown of Alma, Michigan, when I asked my cousin Melody to drop me off at the Alma Library. I had no car. What could I do for excitement?

"May I see the head Librarian?" I asked, with no goal in mind. "Yes. However, Mr. Dinwoody has only ten minutes to spare. He is a very busy man." Our ten minutes grew to two hours, and by then Mr. Dinwoody and I were great friends. He even knew a Roslund cousin that I had never met! In the middle of our fun chat, he said, "Why don't we publish your stories in a book, since you are local?" Then he gave me a ride up Superior Street and dropped me at a coffee shop. Thank you, Bryan Dinwoody. You changed my life!

My editor, Meg Irish, just happened to be an expert on more than friendship. She guided "the book" expertly from beginning to completion. She is humble (and secretive) about how many hundreds of hours she has worked on this. A thousand peony bouquets could not begin to show my love and gratitude.

Rin Saunders who proclaimed himself a snob about "amateur" writing and home movies, ended up being a brilliant reader to check my poor spelling, strange wording, and a million wrong uses of the semicolon and colon. Our many erudite discussions at "Woodlands" over Mysore coffee lifted my spirits... always. I owe you, Rin!

Janice Thompson was my "ethical" editor. She encouraged me to write my truth without rancor. If I failed in this, it is not her fault. I am beyond happy for her amazing friendship.

Momi and Harry Sekhon "took me in" literally, gave me dinner immediately, and in time included me as a genuine "Auntie" in their holiday gatherings. Such love! Momi introduced me to her Keytaab Book Club friends, where Brijeet Aulakh was the first to produce a collection of my essays. *Mere piyare dost!*

Now I must speed up. I want to thank my friends and family, who offered valuable advice, shared their knowledge, fed me, and cheered me on. Every person here did their loving part: Lynne Atherton-Dat, Tracy Braun, Richard Roslund, John Roslund, Ike Roslund, Gerald Roslund, Karen Goetz, Larry Houghton, Linda and Nels Roselund, Nancy Post, David and Frieda Bruton, Linda Mc Allister, Dan Roslund, Marilyn Bahena, Elaine Crawford, Donna Bebow, Donna June Crumbaugh, Linda Gittleman, Mary Ann and Nick Boyer, Mary Jane and Bryan Ross, Elaine Chen, Sharon Donovan, Thomas O'Shae, Jane Huff, Irma Lou Galt, Virgie Bieski-Mitchell, Bob Hetzman, Jean Bolean, Sara Bennett (who was bribed with food to come down the street and hear me read my stories out loud for her approval), Howard Driscoll (who kept my pick-up trucks purring for four decades), Shirley Wiitanen (co-editor/pal for our "Summer Snoops Subscription" paper in 1949); David McMacken, Gabor Tiroler (who translated "Dad's Gift" into Swedish), and Eva Forsberg, who traveled with me down the left-handed roads of southern Sweden to find my lost cousins, Gun and Doris. Tears of gratitude to my Uncle Bud.

A fond salute to my children: Amelia (Amy), Adam and Alexander (Zandy). And pets: Tonkatsu, Midnite and Sister Cat.

And to all the little ones, now or then or someday: Keval, Nalin, Nimrit, Seerit, Jadd, Sammy, Autumn, Meadow, Ethan and Noah.

Table of Contents

Saginaw Street (1940 – 1945) 1
California (1940's) 15
Mr. Button (June 1954) 27
Deliver Me (Fall 1954) 31
Criminal Magnetism (starting 1950) 39
The Sailing Summers (1956 & 1957) 47
Short Skirts – High Manners (1967 – 1968) 67
Development (starting 1968) 87
The Tree on Gallows Road (1982) 99
The Bandidos (1987) 105
An Angel in August (1991) 111
Dad's Gift (1996) 117
Apartment for Rent (starting 1985) 127
How I Almost Got New Nipples (2009) 137
I Frame My Friends 145
Yes, You Can Go Home Again (2011) 163
An Invitation (to the Big Party) 165
Maggie Soule's Cabinet (2005 auction) 173
The Roslund Clan 187
Roslund Family Tree 254
Map – St. Louis, Michigan (1940) 257
Map – Alma, Michigan (1950) 258
Map – Emerson Township Farms, Gratiot County, Michigan 259

Saginaw Street

"Smile, Everett!" Mother said as she took a slight step back. "Sharon, straighten your dress."

Mother was holding the little box camera. Dad was beside me, standing tall and handsome in his Texaco cap, smelling slightly of grease and gasoline. I was seven, dressed in my faded plaid dress, which rode high above my bony knees. Thank goodness it was in its last days. I had worn my dress too long for six months, then just right for three and too short for another four. Every dress had to be worn two days in a row. I loved the way it smelled on its first day... fresh from the clothesline plus starch from Mother's fastidious ironing. On day two, it hung limp and dingy on my skinny body. It smelled like pencil shavings and white paste and peanut butter and whatever else I got into. I can see from the photo it was on day two.

"Finally life is going to get better!" I said to myself. The past three years had seemed to last forever. Out in the country with no playmates, my only pet an ornery banty rooster, I wondered, "Will I ever get out of this desolate place?" I was forced to take up lengthy conversations with two imaginary ladies who came into the farmhouse parlor to visit with me. Except for the relief of the Church of God Sunday School or a box social at the Grange Hall with Aunt Bonnie, or Sunday potlucks at Grandpa Roslund's farm with cousins, I had been alone. Now on Saginaw Street, in town, I had a sidewalk to roller skate on and friends. "Olly, Olly in free," was a nightly ritual. The can was kicked, a hiding place was sought, the heart beat faster, and as dusk grew into darkness, we all reluctantly went home when called.

Sharon Roslund, 1940.

I didn't care that I was older, having been kept back from the one-room schoolhouse I could see across the field. "Verneal, you can't send that skinny little thing to school. Walk all that way down a dirt road?" the older farm wives warned my mother. But now I was going to kindergarten. Real life was about to begin!

"At last I will learn to read!" I thought with a private happiness. My half day started at eight. "You morning children will do music," the teacher briskly announced. Milk was delivered in a wooden crate and served at nap time. It was white and room temperature in a glass bottle with a cardboard cap.

There was no alphabet in sight.

Soon I discovered the "afternoon children" were crowned with the better half of the day. They got *chocolate milk* and *art*. That should have been a clue to me that I was going to be an artist because knowing that spoiled the entire school year for me... going without art. Each morning I went across the room to inspect the "afternoon" children's project from the day before... a miniature city of cardboard houses and trees built in a large raised sandbox.

"Oh, why am I a morning girl?" I thought, tasting the first bitter aspects of jealousy. "I hate the triangle. The tambourine hurts my ears. Clicking wooden sticks together to a loud nursery school tune on an upright piano is a sad substitute for learning to read." There was no beauty in the noise we made. My favorite color was yellow, and I could not think of a way to create it with musical notes. And, chocolate milk was my favorite!

The really good thing Dad did was buy a house on Saginaw Street, the best street in St. Louis, Michigan. Well, it must have been the best: the two doctors and the banker lived within a few houses of each other at this location. And, we happened to be there, too, in our simple clapboard house with its tiny screened in porch and little wooden steps.

Saginaw Street bordered on one side of Clapp Park, which held a granite marker that stated, "This marks the middle of the mitten." The shape the state of Michigan's lower peninsula makes looks exactly like a wool mitten, the kind we wore to build snowmen. Printed below the words was a flat copper design of a mitten with a star in the center. Walking home from school I would cross the park so I could study the marker and run my fingers over its raised lettering. "I'm living in the center of the world!" I thought with fascination.

Not everyone knew we were the center. This was not the big famous St. Louis in the state of Missouri readily known in the United States; it was a little town called St. Louis, population 3,000, in mid-Michigan. Many immigrants, like my Great Grandfather Justus Meyer, who came to Ellis Island in 1895, were first incorrectly sent out to St. Louis, Missouri, only to sadly have to find their way (with precious little money to spare) back up to Michigan to their correct "St. Louis" home.

Across from the park was the high school and the Conery, our sweet shop, and a few yards away, the blacksmith. Education, ice cream and fire; all side by side on our street.

Up at the very top of our street hovered the massive sugar beet factory. The piles of rotting sugar beets and potatoes, being processed for the War effort, gave off a terrible stench. The process itself can smell bad. You wanted to plug your nose! The factory's coal furnaces belched sooty smoke that put a fine black powder on every piece of furniture in town. The teeth in our combs were always black.

A few blocks down, the chemical plant shot waste into Pine River and on a windy day sent an unpleasant smell our way. The waste was pink like Pepto-Bismol. Research was being done there to start making DDT for the men in the war, like my Uncle Quenten in the Army, who went to India and China: both insect-ridden places. In the middle of all that, we planted victory gardens in our front yards and flowers out back. The flowers put up a defense with their sweet fragrances. But, I do not remember the doctors or the banker planting a garden. They were probably too busy.

The banker, Veer Nunn, and his wife Edith lived straight across the street from our small house... their rich green back yard dropped gently down to Pine River. Doctor and Mrs. Waggoner also lived on the river, three houses down from the Nunns. Their house seemed the grandest of all with its upstairs ballroom. To our left was Doctor and Mrs. Robinson's three-story, castle-like house. These three sets of prosperous and successful grownups in their wonderful houses, provided me with my first playmates. They were the parents of my three best friends: Janet Nunn, Jacky Robinson, and Bill Waggoner.

Janet Nunn, the banker's daughter, was extremely smart; brainy in fact, and two grades ahead of me. She could read. She knew very big words (like excellent) and used them a lot. Her black hair was parted in an exact straight line, centered as though her mother used a ruler, and pulled severely back into two tight braids.

I knew Janet as an only child. I am sure everyone did, as well as Janet herself. However, unbeknownst to her (I am presuming), she had a half-sister named Vera, five years older, who lived a few blocks away. One evening her adoptive mother Stella was combing her hair. "Why are you dressing me up, Mommy? It's not Sunday," asked little Vera.

"Mr. Nunn from the bank is coming to visit us." she answered. Stella was fond of the banker, tickled she could show off her new adopted daughter. A generous and loving young woman who worked at the bank had given her baby daughter to Stella, wishing for little Vera a loving two-parent home. Then she left town.

Mrs. Nunn was grey, thin, and twenty years older than my mother. She kept a quiet, hushed house due to the thick oriental rugs in the drawing rooms. In awe, I tiptoed on them. Magical! There were refined pieces of furniture in mahogany, carved walnut, and teak. Our house rattled with a hollow sound. It was probably due to the oak floors... and simple un-upholstered furniture. I remember our house as cold and bare but it may have been in part because Mother was too busy vacuuming, dusting, wiping, scrubbing, sewing, mending, cleaning out sooty combs, washing clothes, hanging out laundry, ironing, shopping, cooking, baking a pie or cake from scratch every single night for dinner, growing a little garden, and taking great care of my new baby sister Linda. She did not have time for me. She was distracted. Mother worked all day, all evening; her apron on, her hands chapped.

She did find time to look lovely with powder and lipstick. She was pretty. That I liked. Prettier than the other mothers, always, I believed. Yet, I did wish she could find some time to stop and look at me. To just be with me.

414 East Saginaw Street

While my Mother was on one side of the street working, Janet's mother was on the other side of the street playing bridge. Mrs. Nunn wore one of her best dresses on weekdays, not just for church, and invited other women over. The cards they played with looked uninteresting, but the tallies were exquisite. They were cut out of heavy rippled papers, embossed with sparkling inks of violet, yellow and rose, edged in gold. From each one hung a pure silk tassel. I had never seen anything so beautiful. Mrs. Nunn allowed Janet and me to collect them. They were my first collection, kept in a cigar box, and admired often. The day our new kitten got sick all over the box was as devastating as the day our puppy got run over. Mother threw the tallies out. Dad buried the dog.

One Sunday Janet invited me to go with her and her parents to the Park Hotel. Janet and I sat in the back seat of her father's new black Chevrolet, my first ride in a new car. Too nervous to lean back, I sat up rigidly and looked at Janet in her delicate white organdy dress, and then down at my new pink cotton dress Mother had sewn. "We both look nice," I thought.

The car was filled with cigar smoke and Mr. Nunn's laughter. Behind the wheel, Mr. Nunn was short and small boned with a big belly. He looked very important in his three-piece suit with his pocket watch but he also looked old to me. He had just become the bank president after working his way up from janitor. He had started lugging silver dollars from his bank to the other bank on Main Street in 1909, the year my father was born. He carried $1,000 at a time, weighing sixty pounds a bag, and they helped toughen him up, as he was slight and thin. He ran errands, tended the boiler, and shoveled the street gutters of manure from the customers' horses tethered in front. It had taken him thirty-two years to move up; the same amount of time it took my father to reach his current age.

The Park Hotel was a grand and sprawling place at the north end of Mill Street on the banks of Pine River. Folks drove from as far away as Grand Rapids and Detroit for their famous duckling dinners and to bathe in the hotel's mineral springs. My father went there just once, to bathe, when he nearly died with yellow jaundice.

"Come now, eat a little," Mr. Nunn said, smiling at me while he cut his duck carefully with his knife. How could I? My stomach ached. I liked the heavy silverware and the thick damask cloths but I had never seen a formal waiter. Or heavy white napkins. Before this, I had only sat on a high stool with Dad at the Conery's marble counter and eaten a five-cent single-dip cone. I liked Mr. Nunn, as most people in town did. He laughed a lot and smiled often; even at me. His warmth mixed with the strong cigar smoke put me at ease and made up for Janet and her mother's quiet reserve. I ate enough to earn desert: ice cream in a cold silvery dish with a little pitcher of chocolate on the side. "Oh, I wish Mom and Dad were here," I thought. I was certain they would never get to eat at the Park Hotel.

My other girlfriend, two houses down, was Jacky Robinson. Her father was a doctor, destined in time to operate on me, and also the town mayor. They too ate at the Park Hotel.

My cute little sister Linda and I on Mrs. Gilmore's porch, 1943. The Gilmore house sat between our place and Jacky Robinson's.

I knew a little about how Dad felt about his surroundings. He had graduated two blocks up the hill at St. Louis High as valedictorian of his class. Dad was the best Charleston dancer and could still do the knee moves perfectly in his 80's. He loved his French classes. Learning was a joy for him. He had walked in from the country, five miles on gravel roads to go to school and often against the criticism of Papa, my Grandpa Oscar, who needed his help on the farm. At night, he cut new cardboard soles for his worn-out shoes, for the next day's trek to town. On a lucky day, he got to ride one of Papa's work horses. He loved learning.

But Papa had eight other sons and two daughters, he was barely getting by, and there was no known way Dad could go on to college. "I always wanted to go," I heard Dad tell Mother in too quiet a manner, but repeated enough times for me to sense his pain.

Here he was in the middle of the world, living among achievers, greasing cars and pumping gas. I just wanted to hug him.

7

Years later, when my father was sixty-nine, he wrote a letter to his niece living in St. Louis:

> When I started school in St. Louis in 1923 so much of what was going on at that time in the town impressed me. I was fourteen years old.
>
> The Old Exchange Hotel was still in business. The livery stable was a thriving business, and you could go to six or seven car dealers — Chev, Ford, Buick, Overland, Star and Dodge.
>
> Besides the Fire Engine which was a four wheel drive Bostrom, (Bolstrum), the sugar factory had four or five big solid tire five-ton trucks. The names of the Elite of the town are familiar to me, and I knew many of them by sight.

On the first Monday in October, when I was seven, I was to have my tonsils out by Dr. Robinson. "I'm going to stay home from school and help my Dad with your operation," proclaimed Jacky, my second-best friend. I admired her. She was a year older like Janet and equally smart. Her father had met her beautiful red-headed mother in France and she spoke with an exotic accent, unlike the new Swedish and German immigrants living as farmers around Gratiot County whose accents were not admired. My Grandma Roslund sounded sweet with her kindly Swedish accent but she was out in the country wearing feed-sack dresses with big aprons. Her high society was the Swedish Aid.

In earlier escapades, Jacky, her little sister Coreen, then four, and I had scouted her Dad's clinic, situated in the back part of their house. For some unknown reason, he was not allowed to join the Michigan Medical Association, so he performed his surgeries at home. We girls had giggled with delight when we removed the skeleton in his closet (a cabinet) and counted its bones. We had even opened the "Do Not Enter" door with our grubby little hands and peeked into the operating room.

The Monday morning of the operation I felt sick. Scared. Ill. I sensed a deep foreboding I could not explain. I hadn't insisted on anything so strongly in my life but I begged to wait a day. "Please.

Wait! Help me," I wept. I pleaded with my father and mother. Begging had never worked before but this time it did.

Mother quietly took my small limp hand and said, "Honey, it's OK." She had stopped and looked at me. Deeply looked. Dad was silent and gently patted my arm. They had never seen me this way. I was given a twenty-four-hour reprieve to work up my nerve and calm my unexplained fears. The doctor and Jacky just had to wait.

Very early Tuesday morning we walked past Mrs. Gilmore's house, which was the only house that stood between our places…to get to the doctor's office. Mother and Dad handed me over to Dr. Robinson, and his nurse/assistant/wife, Mrs. Robinson, and their enthusiastic daughter Jacky, who had stayed home from third grade as promised. My Mother and Dad sat tensely on the screened-in porch, remodeled into a waiting room. They waited.

The doctor gave me ether. To his surprise during the operation I started to come to. He added more ether. Too much. I stopped breathing. Silence. Fear. "Come quick!" Doctor and Mrs. Robinson called out to my parents to hurry into the operating room. Now there were six of us. Jacky was running in circles around the table wailing! After frantic maneuvers, never exactly explained or understood, I started to breathe again. I awoke and returned to this world to everyone's great relief. I had a very sore throat.

"You can have *all* the ice cream you want," said Dr. Robinson, beaming over his newly revived patient. I was too sick to smile.

My parents changed doctors. I still liked Jacky.

* * * * *

At school, I made a wonderful new friend, Kay Wells. She was pretty and sweet. When we started second grade our mothers let us walk across town, nearly a mile, to play at each other's houses. She happily wore her Aunt Doris's hand-me-downs and I was content in the cotton dresses Mother sewed.

Our mothers each had treadle sewing machines, where their best scissors were kept in the little side drawer. With permission, we used them for our favorite pastime: paper dolls! We each chose a doll from the Sears Roebuck Catalog and cut her out. The lady model was dressed only in her *"underwear."* Then she was given a paper and crayon wardrobe, more fanciful than any lady shopping on Mill Street could ever imagine.

Kay's father Norman worked as a fireman at Dow Chemical, a huge plant thirty-five miles down the old winding River Road to Midland. He worked "shift work" (seven days on days, three days off; seven days on afternoons, three days off; seven days on midnight shift, three days off) and often the days were twelve to sixteen hours long. Kay rarely saw him. They celebrated Christmas whenever he could be home — usually not on Christmas.

* * * * *

Back then, everything was directed at the War. At home, we were pulling the shades for "blackout." Watching the dark skies, I would ask, "Will the planes bomb us?" I had heard that planes might fly down over Canada to bomb Detroit's auto factories... or even Dow Chemical. We were in the flight path.

In 1941 Dad got a night watchman's job (a security guard) at Dow Chemical, where Kay's father worked. The guards were connected with the FBI... like a deputy sheriff, and were investigated before they were hired. Dad was trained to be a marksman. He learned well and shot his own quota — and everyone else's pheasants and deer if they requested it. He kept his gun in his top dresser drawer with his black silky calf-length socks. I could scare myself by climbing on a chair, and peeking at it, but I never touched it.

Dad drove the same winding road thirty miles to Midland as Kay's father did, working the midnight shift for a year, but was chagrined when he was caught sleeping. Holding down two jobs was challenging.

More dramatic though were the papers I found recently showing Dad had been an FBI agent for "St. Louis, Michigan" during those years. They must have really trusted him!

Pretty exciting, except it was a shame that he never got to tell anyone.

Everett and Verneal, married July 7, 1934. Clapp Park, St. Louis.

In the words from a letter written sometime later by my mother Verneal: "Everett came down with hepatitis and was in such bad shape the doctors thought he would die as they had no drugs available to treat it with. The drugs were all being used for the soldiers. They sent him to the Park Hotel for some mineral baths. I don't know if the baths helped any, but he didn't die! Thank God for that!"

I recall when I was six and Mother allowed me to go into their bedroom and take a peek at my Dad. *He is so yellow.*

Kay and I had a lot in common. We both had our tonsils out. But Kay's blood would not clot and so her tonsil operation had to be moved to a different doctor and out of town. Our fathers worked long hours for small wages with little time for their daughters. Our mothers whose names both started with a "V" were farm girls. In order to attend high school (in the 1920's there were no school buses), they were forced to live in town with a family. Vera Louise Miller lived in St. Louis with the Dr. Hobbs' family, helping them in exchange for her room and board. My mother, Verneal Sandy, lived with her girlfriend Lila Pidcock in Breckenridge. I do not know if she did chores or paid the Pidcocks money in exchange for her lodging. There must have been different arrangements, depending on finances, for the various students all over the village.

Eva Hetzman, an enterprising widow, lived one block from Breckenridge High. Each year she took in two or three girls whom she welcomed as 'family.' They ate dinner together each evening around her large oak dining table. The girls were dropped off at her home on Sunday evening by horse and buggy, and picked up on Friday afternoon.

*****

It was a wintry Friday when Janet Nunn's mother walked across the street for a one time visit to our house. She did not come to invite Mother to play bridge. She didn't come to ask Mother to sit on a carved wooden chair with a needle-point cushion at a dainty card table and eat tiny sandwiches with no crusts. She was carrying a stack of white organdy dresses infested with pounds of lace, ruffles, gathers, and ribbons. Dresses that Janet could no longer wear. They were for me.

Birthday Photo: Who are my two smiling girlfriends on the left with their similar curls? Kay Wells with long dark hair stands behind me, Janet Nunn is next to her on the right with her dark hair in braids, and Jackie Robinson is on the far right. looking down at me. I am seated. It is September 8, 1943. I see my mother put pretty flowers in the vases and someone didn't drink their milk! I remember we played "drop the clothes pin in the bottle."

Mother, loving beauty and not being able to afford such superb quality as these lovely store-bought fineries, was pleased. Excited, really. I was not. My taste ran clean and simple. Clean lines, no frills, and the simple dresses Mother sewed for me were fine. I also suspect the fact Janet had worn them added a bit to my rebellion… perhaps I sensed negative vibrations or maybe it was a combination of my strong developing taste as an artist seasoned with a dab of pride. I learned years later that friendships sometimes required sacrifice, but at that young age I was ignorant. Janet and I were not alike.

I wore one of the dresses once, to placate my mother, and then they disappeared. Maybe my little sister Linda wore them.

My other friend, Bill Waggoner, was cute and blond and had the most fun-to-play-at house on the street because it had an upstairs ballroom (for his parents' dancing parties). His older brother had a grown-up real live drum set. Banging on drums was more fun than the tambourine… or anything kindergarten ever thought of offering. But, when Bill wanted to take after his Dad and "play Doctor," I ran home. I never told my mother.

Author's Note: The houses of Janet, Bill and Jacky still stand as of 2017. All that remains of my house is memories: 414 East Saginaw Street was torn down in 2013 and is now a paved parking lot.

California

Dad made himself a junkyard car. It was free, which was mandatory.

During the Depression, my father needed transportation. He went to the county junkyard and gathered enough parts to put a car together. The only item he couldn't find was a front passenger seat, so Mother in her fur-trimmed galoshes and I in my ever-hated brown shoes rode in the back. Sometimes Mother wore a snazzy hat with a pheasant feather. We felt quite silly, having a driver.

We rented a small apartment in the rear of Kaiser's unpainted clapboard farmhouse, south of Alma, Michigan on a dusty road. When I was old enough to start school, I was not sent. From our bare dirt backyard I could see the one-room schoolhouse far across the flat field. I could hear the yells and squeals of the school kids and yearned to race the half mile, between the rows of beans, and join them. After a while, the shrill clanging bell would call them in from recess and my world turned silent. I was left alone among the clucking, wandering chickens and my only playmate, an ornery banty rooster. He had exquisite feathers but was impossible to pet. I had to be careful where I stepped to miss the hundreds of little white smelly manure piles. "No," Mother said with firmness, "You cannot go to school yet. The ladies down the road say you're too skinny and frail." But I was not at all sick... unless you call boredom an illness.

Mother washed on Mondays, boiling the water on the stove. She stirred the laundry with a stick. She then put the clothes through a hand-turned wringer into a large shiny galvanized tub. I trailed after her carrying the clothespin bag as she lugged the wicker basket of clothes outside. As she hummed her favorites, "Bye Bye Blackbird" or "My Blue Heaven," she tried not to let any clothes touch the ground.

And It's Only Monday

Mother and I with Dad's "junkyard car" at Keiser's, 1939

    Like a dutiful daughter, I handed her one wooden clothespin at a time. The final touch was propping up the wire line even higher with a tall clothes pole. As the clothes fluttered high in the breeze I was already looking forward to the sweet fresh smell of my sheets that night. If we had to hang them out in freezing weather, that was good, too. They froze stiff as boards, and the action bleached them white as snow.

But whatever Mother was doing, she dropped it all to rush to the little wooden radio at 12:45 p.m. Wiping her red, chapped hands on her apron, leaning close, she soaked up every murmur, word, and sigh uttered on her soap opera, "Our Gal Sunday." I always wished I could give her that much happiness.

My mother Verneal's parents: Amelia Meyer, born 1886, died January 22, 1972 and Archie Sandy, born March 15, 1882, died September 11, 1958.

Mother ironed on Tuesdays. Even Dad's oily truck-driving work clothes were pressed to perfection.

On Wednesdays, the dirt road out front gave her a reason to dust. She cleaned everything. She cleaned what was clean. We could have eaten off the oak floor.

Mother herself had been held back from school. It was quietly suggested (an unproven rumor) that she had had a spell — a small mental breakdown — as a young child, so she started school late. If so, she must have studied and progressed fast because at sixteen Mother graduated as valedictorian from tiny Breckenridge High, six-and-a-half miles from St. Louis.

Mother had longed to go to college. "I knew better than to hope," she would say sadly. There was no money. "Even beauty school would have been heaven," she lamented her entire life. She was naturally talented with her own hair and my sister Linda's curls. My scraggly hair was one of her lifetime disappointments.

After graduation, she moved with a girlfriend to Kalamazoo, Michigan, to work as a nurse's aide in the Kalamazoo State Hospital, better known as an insane asylum. It was grim. She lasted about as long as it took for her to pose in her uniform for a photo. Then she quit.

My father first saw my mother in the Breckenridge Post Office when she was sweet sixteen. On the spot, he decided, *"I am going to marry her."* It took him five years.

Mother did talk about the beaus she had before Dad, especially Basil McKenzie. They attended a one room school together outside of Breckenridge. One Valentine's Day he gave her her first box of chocolates. The box was beautiful and she was delighted! She carefully selected a chocolate for herself and then realized she should share them with her classmates... Everyone got a piece but when the box returned to her, it was empty.

Mother and Dad married, midsummer, at the peak of the growing season. Her second most important life-lasting disappointment was her father's unawareness of how much his daughter wanted his attention. Especially at her wedding! As she and Dad drove off down the country road to their justice-of-the-peace wedding on July 7, 1934, they passed her father (my Grandpa, Archie Sandy). He was out in the field, plowing, his mind intent on his crops.

"He didn't even look our way or wave," Mother told me, many times. Following the ceremony, Mom and Dad posed in Clapp Park, across from the high school, in St. Louis with their friends, Lila Pidcock and Howard Presler, who stood up with them. That evening, Grandma and Grandpa Roslund gave a little celebration dinner at their farmhouse. I know Grandma Sandy and Great Grandpa Meyer attended. Where was Grandpa Archie? Was he plowing in the dark? Or had he milked the cows early, washed up, shaved, and come across the county to eat with the rest of them? I believe he did not attend.

"That's just a man for you," Mother would say over the years about many similar incidents.

My great grandfather Justus Meyer, July 31, 1937, celebrating his 80th birthday.

The Stork Cometh

I expected it would be just the three of us, Mom, Dad and me forever: tedious, but dependable.

Too soon I learned that nothing remains the same. One hot August Thursday they sent me off to Grandma and Grandpa Sandy's house, just a half mile down the road, to stay over-night. Grandma tucked me in under her hand-stitched quilt, in the narrow daybed in the dining room, blew out the kerosene lamp, and tiptoed off into the dark in her long flannel nightgown. Their large mantle clock hung high on the wall above my bed. The pendulum swung, and ticked away the minutes that sent me into my last innocent sleep.

When Dad picked me up to take me home the next morning he explained, "The stork came while you were gone... in fact, just before midnight." I followed him into the bedroom, where the three of us had been sleeping for two years, my crib still in the corner. "*A stork?*" I wondered.

Mother had changed. She lay in bed, smiling. She was beaming! I had never seen her in such a blitz of happiness. She cradled a tiny curly-haired baby, who, from that day forward, became her constant joy. Their connection stayed that way until a few years before Mother died.

The War had just begun with Germany; it foreshadowed the arrival of my sister Linda. She came without warning. It was as though a bomb had secretly dropped in the night on a quiet meadow and when the sun appeared in the morning, there lay the destruction.

They had not told me. Either they did not appreciate that a five-year-old was "old enough," and intelligent enough, to understand, or they meant well and didn't know any better. I believe it was the latter.

Mother was even happier now than when listening to soap operas on the radio. She poured her love and attention upon Linda, her beautiful chubby baby. I still can see her laying baby Linda on the kitchen table to pat her dry from her bath and shaking sweet-smelling talcum powder everywhere. I felt unprepared, suddenly left out of the inner circle. Mother's words about my "scraggly straight hair" and skinniness settled in a little deeper.

My pet banty rooster was replaced by my little sister Linda. I learned in time that she was no less ornery or any more cuddly. I cannot explain why we were never close. I heard vague family comments, such as, "Oh, what a shame they were not born closer together." But that idea did not make sense. Many sisters are close and yet far apart in age.

I have only one memory that gives me a clue. Linda was five and I was ten. Linda was in the far corner of the room and something broke at her feet. I have no clear image of what it was. I was ten feet away, across the room. Mother entered and asked, "What happened?" Linda, tossing her adorable curls and batting her eyes, pointed at me and said,

"Sharon did it." I got the spanking. It was pretty maddening and I had no clue how to save myself. Linda and I grew up in the same house but under different management.

A possible explanation is supplied in the doctrine of reincarnation. It helps some puzzling stories make sense. We reap what we sow, good or bad, in the present or from the past. All of our actions have a consequence. It is quite possible I was getting my due; that I had mistreated her on some forgotten occasion from a past lifetime. That idea is not far-fetched.

We lived almost four years in St. Louis on Saginaw Street.

After I finished second grade, we moved the three miles to Alma and rented the Zeta Sigma Fraternity house for one year; the boys had vacated and gone off to war. I snuck down to the basement's full-sized pool table, playing all alone and honing my skill. No one ever asked where I was.

Linda tiptoed up to the third floor and found beds, dressers and desks, stacked high in storage, waiting for the boys to come marching home. In the bathroom were strange looking little bathtubs hung on the wall. She never asked anyone what they were for.

It must have been a tough move for my parents. I felt miserable. I hated third grade at Wright Avenue School and I blamed it all on Elsie McClure, whom I detested. I still do not know why. The teacher asked for a volunteer to share a double seat with one of the girls who smelled bad and wet her pants. I luckily balanced my dislike for Elsie with compassion, and volunteered. I had done this before, back in second grade. My missionary zeal from my Church of God Sunday School class held some weight.

One day I begged, "Mother, don't make me go to school!" I screamed and pounded on our front door. She locked me out. I went.

In my loneliness, I wandered into the small house that was the Alma Library, just across the street from the Zeta Sigma house and close to the Gulf station.

Just a bit too old to serve in the war, Dad ran the Gulf Station one block away down Superior Street, serving the college professors and

And It's Only Monday

prosperous undraftable (4-F) college boys. He greased their cars, repaired flats, pumped gas, and washed their windshields. Any car Dad worked on inside the station's garage was returned whiskbroom-swept and hand-washed. Dad was proud of that.

To heck with reading. I kept practicing pool. This secret sport served me well with the boys in high school. Little did they guess they were out a nickel when I challenged them to a game of pool. "I'll bet you a coke I can beat you!" was my standard ploy.

We left the pool table behind when we moved to Walnut Street, just in time for Carol Blanck to walk me to fourth grade and introduce me to Miss Crum. She taught us geography by connecting each of us with a pen pal in England. The war had ended and thin little air-mail letters began to fly across the sea. We were thrilled. Joyce Clampit Barnes and I wrote in ink for sixty years until we switched to email.

Easter Sunday, April 21, 1946. Back Row: Gail Glendenning, Clarence Blanck, Kathy Blanck. Front Row: Linda Roslund, Sharon Roslund, Carol Blanck.

* * * * *

California

The day World War II ended, Dad put his name in for a new car, a black Hudson.

It would be his first new automobile. And even better, he was driving us to California for a genuine vacation.

My very plain life was suddenly taking on an illustrious sheen. For eleven years, each Sunday and holiday, we had driven *three miles* to spend the day with our multitudinous family. Sundays gave the relief that kept me sane. Grandparents, uncles, aunts, and most of my thirty-eight first cousins were mixed in with Chinese checkers, comic books, softball, frog catching, Old Maid card games, creek minnow fishing, photo albums of strange looking kin from the Old Country, mounds of food, and competitions to play the pump organ.

Most of my friends disappeared every summer and went to their lake cottages. We always stayed in town. Only once had we gone thirty miles and rented a cottage at Crystal Lake. It rained all six days. As we packed to come home, the sun came out and waved us goodbye.

Now we would far surpass the three-mile range... and drive three thousand miles.

It took almost a year for the Hudson to arrive. The neighbors said it looked like a hearse.

While it sat in the driveway waiting to be packed I went out and climbed in the back seat. It was so still inside. I sat there a long time, running my fingers over the nubby pile on the cushions and breathing in the tantalizing factory smells. It reminded me of a new wool sweater and Grandpa Sandy's wet shaving strap.

We went for the entire month of March. Dad did all the driving. Mother sat up front beside him, looking pretty. She had a flair for clothes. and her fancy hair-dos and makeup added to her beauty. Her perfume floated to the back seat. Finally setting off in such a big splash way, must have made them feel giddy... I rarely saw them have fun and be lighthearted. I was proud of our whole family.

In the back seat, I sat with my little sister Linda and Grandma Sandy, who seemed very, very old to me with her silky, drooping double chin. We passed real Navajo Indians, walking along the roadside. We collected petrified wood that lay beside the highway, years before it became the Petrified Forest National Park, and illegal to take away even a sliver. We drove all the way to glittery Los Angeles to visit Dad's sister, Aunt Hulda (and Uncle Jim), and his brother, Uncle Art (and Aunt Gladys), and to meet even more cousins. Nels and Karen were special, as we were close in age.

My father and mother were ecstatic like any small-town tourists. The adults went out one evening to the Cocoanut Grove night club, where movie stars like Bette Davis, Jean Harlow and Sonja Henie dined and partied. Mother showed off that evening's professional photo for years. She could have been called "Ms. California" herself. My parents were just as hungry to expand their horizons as I was. Again, they did not understand that a six-year-old could have gone to Lux Radio Theater and enjoyed it.

"I had to stay at Aunt Hulda's with a baby sitter," Linda said. "I wanted to go with you."

A month later, in April, back home in fourth grade, my eagerness to talk about my trip was obsessive. My classmates began to avoid me, and my teacher Miss Crum was losing her patience. They nicknamed me "California."

Over the summer my star-struck obsession did not fade. In September, Ms. Eberspeaker, our fifth-grade teacher, set up an easel in front of the classroom, with me facing it. While they went on with their lessons, she let me relive my trip, and paint my heart out. It might have been called "art therapy," but that term did not exist. It was loving understanding. She knew I was an artist.

Back in second grade, when I was seven, our teacher Mrs. Cresswell asked us to bring our big fat awkward pencils (during the War that is all we got) and a sheet of scratchy manila paper outside to the bronze statue at "the point" in St. Louis.

"You are all going to draw him," she said. This soldier was on a raised pedestal, holding a gun, looking very serious, probably because he remembered that World War I had killed him. He was the memorial. I looked up and started to sketch him. The silhouette of his dark metal body took shape on my paper. Amazing! Mrs. Cresswell walked by each of us to scan our work.

"Oh my, Sharon!" she exclaimed. My classmates followed her lead. "You can draw!" they murmured. "It really looks like him."

I was shocked more than I was pleased. How could I draw when I had never drawn before? It was fifty years later that I learned about reincarnation and carrying skills over from one lifetime to another. It seemed a possibility.

So now Ms. Eberspeaker was encouraging me to do what I loved. Watercolors were perfect for showing the Grand Canyon, the Painted Desert, the Petrified Forest, and the Indian women in their long skirts with babies in their papooses, who had thrilled me on Route 66.

After I had exhausted my illustration project, she assigned me to write a report. I wrote about Pike's Peak and the Mt. Wilson Observatory. And proudly I told about seeing Ronald Colman and Heather Angel standing on a darkened stage in the center of a circle of light, reading "A Tale of Two Cities" into a microphone for Lux Radio Theater. As I sat in that opulent hall with the grownups it was hard to believe that all over America people had their ears to their radios, even back in Alma, listening to what I was seeing in person. It was live, heard once, never to be replayed. Life was becoming more splendid and more magical than I had imagined.

Mr. Button

We left town the same week. Mr. Button died and I graduated from high school. On my last day in Alma, my first independent act as a graduate was to go to his funeral.

There were four of us, including the minister, so we moved out of the large sanctuary and into the church parlor. While we solemnly sang every verse of The Old Rugged Cross, I thought, "So sad. So few people." Could this be a sign of a failed life?

I realized not once in the ten years I had known him had we talked. Our only words were "Hello," and "Hello." That was it.

Mr. Button spent his days walking the town. Endlessly. He was a giant to me, over six feet tall, massive and muscular, and often grimy, rough, unshaven, shabby, and smelly. But he wasn't like a bear, standing powerfully on his hind legs looking down. Mr. Button was more like a large animal on all fours. He shuffled along bent far over in a perfect right angle, his hands clutched together behind his back. I never knew if his posture came from his years wielding a spike hammer for the railroad, or because he was a "lifter." A lifter, as in holding up a Model A Ford so his brother could work under it... or saving the cast-iron stove from his burning house by carrying it out into the front yard.

He was a bachelor, alone in a small unkempt house on the edge of town. I pictured him eating cold cereal for dinner with no one to bake him a pie. I never saw him with a friend or talk to anyone. I saw loneliness.

In his walks, he passed by our front steps a thousand times in every kind of weather. He smiled. I smiled. Sometimes "Hello." "Hello!"

"Mom," I asked, more than once and usually around holidays, "Can't we have Mr. Button to dinner?"

My fastidious Mother always gave me a firm "no." I guessed he might have messed up our too clean, too neat "boring" house.

In my Junior year, I got a job selling movie tickets at the Strand Theater. My bonus? Regular free movie tickets! I knew exactly what I was going to do! On school nights I sat in the glass booth under the blazing marquee, doing my homework and scouting out Mr. Button. "He'll come by."

Sooner or later Mr. Button would surely come by.

Sure enough, he did.

"Ssshhhh!" I said, smiling, and without a word I slipped him a ticket. To my relief he took it, barely giving me a glance as he shuffled through the lobby, headed for the large padded doors.

A few nights later a giant calloused hand with dirty fingernails moved hesitantly past the ticket window and pushed a box into the half-moon-shaped hole in the glass... chocolate-covered cherries. I didn't like them. I ate them to be polite.

Over time Mr. Button saw a lot of movies that I selected: Million Dollar Mermaid, Gentlemen Prefer Blondes, and Singing in the Rain — and I ate a lot of chocolate-covered cherries. I never stopped wishing they were assorted chocolates with a few hard centers or chewy nuts.

He probably never stopped wishing for a John Wayne thriller.

Sixty years later, I understand. Mr. Button's funeral wasn't just for show. No one was there to be seen; there was no church full of folks to see. No one was there out of duty. Those three other adults probably cared. That's the way I want my funeral. If you didn't love me in life, don't come see me in death.

Three real genuine friends would be just fine.

Mr. Button

The Strand Theater on Superior Street in Alma, Michigan, where Mr. Button delivered chocolate-covered cherries, 1950.

Deliver Me

The Buick was stuffed. Everything I owned was crammed in and Dad was about to drive me to college. An early frost had infused the leaves with a sudden burst of color as though they were giving me a brilliant explosive send off. "Goodbye, Michigan!" I shouted back at the sky.

I waited impatiently as Dad carefully raked the newly fallen leaves and burned the essence of summer. Mother, surrounded by an invisible mist of Shalimar perfume with her neatly set hair and perfectly blended makeup stood on the porch watching, aware of her prettiness. She gave me a goodbye kiss with orders, "Be good, be neat, study hard."

As we climbed into the car I could feel Dad's disapproval. He couldn't see out the back window because of the bulging cardboard boxes on the floor and covering the entire back seat. A battered hand-me-down suitcase held my sweaters, each with a name tag neatly sewn in. Tucked inside my large hooded hair dryer were my garter belts, seamed hose, and a pair of spike-heeled dancing shoes.

My makeup carrying case was filled with lipsticks to match each sweater (hot pink, burnt orange, bright red), bobby pins, hair rollers, white and black shoe polish and my new hair brush from the Fuller Brush man. A wooden orange crate held my high school yearbook, a 1952 Revised Standard Version of the Bible, hair scissors, my new fountain pen from Aunt Bonnie, a bottle of black ink and a box of scented flowered stationery that Grandma Sandy had given me with my initials printed in gold script. Wrapped in newspaper was my very own tin of McConnon's black ointment, a gift from Grandma Roslund. On top of everything, piled clear to the ceiling so they wouldn't get wrinkled were my high school formals: strapless, voluminous satin with multi-layered underskirts of crinoline and netting.

During that summer, my college plans had totally reversed. "Come be my roommate in Indiana!" coaxed Herthol in her loud raspy voice. Herthol was a bubbly extroverted redhead, a rambunctious preacher's kid I knew slightly from our week at Methodist church camp each summer. She had raved, "Taylor is a great school and you would love it." I did not need convincing. What appealed to me above all else was the tantalizing thought of going to college *out of state*. It sounded dramatic and daring. No one in my entire graduating class that I knew of was leaving Michigan.

"It will be far more educational to go away," I told Dad. After what seemed like hundreds of hours of applying for a badly needed scholarship, the University of Michigan, Alma College and Central Michigan were all offering me the honor. Now I was turning all three down. Neither Dad nor Mother argued with me about this decision, or I do not recall that they did. Perhaps because I was paying my entire way. Perhaps because Dad was preoccupied with making a living. Or was I determined and didn't listen?

Driving along passing the endless bean fields, I noticed that the geese flying overhead seemed to be going our way. Like them, I felt free, but tinged with a sense of regret. I smoothed my broomstick skirt nervously, watching Dad's handsome profile as he drove and smoked his Camel, wishing he was easier to talk to. I wanted to think he was enjoying the trip, so rare had our times together been.

For the last three years of high school I had begged, "Please go to the game with me; my treat." Coach Hicks had traded me double season tickets for every football and basketball game. In return I drew giant cartoon posters for the boy's locker room. (I remember one of a tall hairy-legged guy dribbling a ball, with a big clock hanging on the wall behind him. The caption read "Get 8 hours of sleep.") Not once did Dad have time to go to a game with me.

I tried to engage him by talking (which was not smart, as he always said I talked too much). Twisting my clumsy class ring, which

I planned to remove the first day of classes, I softly said, "Boy, what a relief I saved enough, at least for this semester. When I think about all those jobs selling men's coveralls, movie tickets, women's dresses — oh, and picking beans at 5:00 a.m., and those crazy junkyard books I re-copied down, cooking them as they said!" The memory of all that work rushed at me like it was last week. Patting my pocketbook with the earnings inside, I talked on, partly to myself, partly for Dad's benefit, "All those school nights, weekends, holidays, summers: four years of endless saving." As I looked his way for a sign of approval, a modicum of realization crept in: the money was going to be spent all at once. "Was that a smile?" I wondered, glancing at him out of the corner of my eye.

We finally found the tiny town of Upland. We drove right through it and then headed on into the countryside on its further side. Was there a mistake? I thought it was in town. Further down the country road appeared a few quaint buildings situated on a small grassy campus. As far as I could see in all four directions were cornfields. No town, no shops, no drugstore with a soda fountain, no movie theater, no stadium. Just corn.

We pulled up to Swallow dorm where a few girls and their parents were lugging in bags and boxes. Herthol and my other roommate, Peggy Ann, had started to settle in our barren room. The walls were a sickly green, a color I could suddenly use to describe myself. Friendly and smiling, they greeted me and pushed aside their suitcases and boxes to make room for mine. Tossing her curly red hair, Herthol gushed, "What did I tell ya? Great place, huh?"

Peggy Ann was tan and daintily thin with light brown hair that hung below her waist. In her sweet soft voice, she asked, "What are these dresses for?" as she carefully inspected the beads and sequins on my favorite formal.

"For the dances!" I answered with a surprised look.

"What dances?" Herthol shot back loudly. "They don't dance here!"

Peggy Ann, with childlike curiosity added, "Have you really been to a dance? My parents would kill me!"

Just then, as if to save me from answering, there was a knock on the door. Miss Burress, our house mother, wearing a prim grey dress with her hair in a tight permanent with rolled bangs, peered in to say, "Girls, don't be late! Supper at five, prayer meeting at seven."

College had begun.

Art was my only release and escape. Professor Patton wore a very worn white shirt, fraying at the collar, a skinny tie, brown pants and a heavily rumpled tan tweed blazer. In time, I decided it was likely his only one. His wavy pale red hair topped a tall lanky frame and gentle face. After passing out Conté crayons that first day, he leaned against a peeling gray wall and asked us to draw him. "Oh good" I thought, "I am going to learn something new." I had never drawn from a live model. (At that time I had no idea that art schools existed, and that most colleges offered life drawing with unclothed models.) On my first try I drew a perfect likeness of Professor Patton. He was pleased; maybe flattered. "Oh, how I love art," I thought, discovering my surprising new ability. I began feeling like his "teacher's pet," which seemed more appropriate for grade school but enjoyable anyway.

Then came my big art break. Following class one day Professor Patton asked, "How would you like to do a back-drop for the stage?" Missionaries from China were coming for a witnessing weekend sponsored by the Holiness League.

"Of course I would love that!" I agreed in an instant. I had never painted anything larger than the billboard for our high-school homecoming weekend. When I was finished, Jesus appeared eighteen feet high and twenty-five feet wide in a million brilliant colors, smiling down on the entire school body.

Professor Patton may have sensed my relief and happiness to be in his class, where I felt comfortable. Within a month he invited me to a Choral Society concert.

I finally found Herthol in the dining hall and half whispered, "I've got a date with Professor Patton!"

"Are you crazy? He's fourteen years older than you!" she almost yelled. Everyone heard.

"Yes, I know. Old, but nice," I answered, planning what I would wear.

My Christian dorm mates were fascinated and horrified, which made it all the more exciting. Excitement was scarce.

Because most of us could not leave campus and only a few students owned cars (and there was nowhere to go anyway), almost all of the five hundred members of the student body attended the Choral Society concert in the auditorium. Being faculty, Professor Patton had prominent seats for us up front and I dared wear my slender red satin dress, short slit on the side, and my long-neglected bright red lipstick. Herthol and Peggy Ann (really, most of the dorm) watched our every move from the balcony. Looking up, I wanted to wave. As we walked to our seats I sent them a quick smile and then looked straight ahead, trying to act serious and mature.

The concert ended on a lovely note. The fall evening was brisk with a black sky, and stars like rhinestones were scattered across the heavens. Nature had set the perfect stage for a romantic evening. We could have walked hand-in-hand and wandered down a corn row to sit beside the creek bed. But this was not a romance. It was a delicate friendship in a closed setting. "What a lovely evening, Mr. Patton. I enjoyed the concert very much," I said.

"You are welcome," he said, walking stiffly beside me. It would be unthinkable to break the rules and take my hand. I almost felt nervous for him; really, for both of us. "Goodnight, goodnight," we said to each other. On my part, I didn't dare tell him I was wishing for a milkshake. It was an absurd idea even to dare the thought of driving to town to scout one up. I was not allowed off campus.

Our first six weeks on campus were arranged to help us orient ourselves to college life. We could not leave campus, nor were we permitted any visitors. It was set up to give us time to adjust. Being locked in by 8 p.m. each night felt like prison. I was burning with restlessness. The silence was deafening. One evening, in desperation, I called into the hall, "Anyone want a haircut?"

Immediately from next door, almost skipping, came Veneta, who plunked her plump self down on my desk chair. "I've never had it cut in my entire life," she sighed, as she threw back her long black mane, not questioning my ability. "Just cut it short!" she giggled nervously.

"Are you sure?" I asked, the full impact of what I was about to do dawning on me.

"Yes, I've secretly wanted to have it cut for years," Veneta insisted, glancing into the mirror at eighteen years of obedience and seeing for the last time her luscious locks, her symbol of religious purity.

Peggy Ann, always helpful, rushed up with a hand mirror. Herthol looked down from her top bunk with raised eyebrows, attempting to quote the Bible, "Thou shalt not... Oh, you know, just remember what happened with Samson and Delilah!" Herthol's disapproval was drowned out by the laughter of three more girls who had wandered in to watch.

Creativity flowed through my scissors. I had a mission! I could be a missionary like many of my classmates were studying to be. I was needed. After Veneta came Eileen with her never-cut dark brown curls. After Eileen came Rowena and her feather-fine honey-blonde frizz. With a few weeks of in-house practice, my skill at cutting became an art. Word spread to the other dorm. I was exhausted. Not only was I the dorm barber, I cleaned the johns at 50 cents an hour. It never occurred to me to charge for the haircuts, even 25 cents, which would have removed the necessity of bathroom duty.

The weekend we were considered "adjusted" and set free, some of the newly-shorn girls were excited to show their parents. Veneta insisted, "Come meet Mums and Dad." Mums and Dad were not as elated as Veneta. "Did *you* do this?" asked Mums with a look of disgust that she shot squarely at me. "Nice to meet you," I nodded with a nervous smile as I walked backwards up the steps, almost knocking over Rowena, who was smoothing away her tears. "Mother wasn't consoled by the envelope of curls I saved for her," she said.

I was paying the price of rebellion. It was time to clean the johns.

Some days I tried to fit in. For a few brief moments, I felt I could make it. Sitting in the large sedate library, with its huge windows and its heavy oak tables, I felt at peace, especially when it snowed. The corn fields for miles in all directions looked like a giant white grid punctuated with the small black spikes of dried cornstalks. It was perfect for studying the Old Testament and writing poetry. But my spirit felt crushed. I yearned to drive a car, see a movie, sip a malted, and kiss a boy goodnight. Here on campus, the senior couple most admired were Lloyd and Jewell, engaged now for one year. They had not yet kissed.

God was not becoming more real to me. Morning and evening prayer meetings, hall prayer meetings, evangelists, revivals, and testimonials began to weigh heavily, like a bag of groceries that gets heavier the further you carry it. God seemed so sad and far away, without a sense of joy and humor. *How could He not like dancing?* Everything else was OK. If you had never had them you didn't miss them... nicotine, caffeine, alcohol, sex. I didn't know how God might feel about those. But dancing was another thing!

Near the end of the semester Herthol rushed into our room, stomping the snow off her boots and pulling off her earmuffs, as she breathlessly informed me, "Hey Roomie, they are going to hold a prayer meeting in your honor tonight!"

I gasped. I suddenly felt chilled and whiter than I already was. Slumping down on my bunk I argued with myself. *"Do I have to go? Yes, I have to go!"* I did not want to! It would not be simple like attending a concert with the professor. Uh-oh. Professor Patton! *That* was my trouble! I had told him my money had run out. True. I also told him I was not returning in January. Darn! I should not have talked so much. I had not been completely candid with him, as I didn't want to hurt his feelings. I had *not* told him I wanted to attend a college with more freedom. With all this confusing discussion going on in my mind, I still knew I had to show up.

The auditorium was full. The entire student body was there. So were the faculty. As they prayed, taking turns, Professor Patton seemed to pray the most fervent prayer – "Heavenly Father, Our Dear God, and Jesus, our Lord and Savior. In your kindness and generosity, we ask that you give Sharon the resources she needs — all the monetary blessings she needs, so she can return to us."

I stood there feeling huge and conspicuous, wishing to be taken up into Heaven in a golden chariot, or a rapturous trance, or a fiery flame, or among a host of angels! Just somewhere; anywhere! With my heart pounding, fearing the entire auditorium could hear it, I silently prayed, "Oh God, deliver me from this place."

Criminal Magnetism

At age fourteen, picking beans sounded far more enticing than babysitting. Rombuski, a stocky barrel-chested hired hand drove an open-backed farm truck. Each morning at 5:30 A.M. he roared down the center of Superior Street toward City Hall to collect a few of us. Bunk and I stood waiting in the chilly darkness, barely aware of each other. In the halls in Junior High Bunk had just seemed like a loud showoff. "Hubba, hubba," he'd tease, in his tight jeans with his t-shirt sleeve rolled up over his pack of cigarettes and his brown hair slicked back. "What do ya think I am, poor?" and then he'd howl at his own joke, which no one understood.

On the edge of town, we stopped at a row of temporary shacks to collect the migrant workers and continued picking up more waiting along the roadside. By the time we reached the field, the truck was so crowded we resembled a box of crayons, different colors and with no space between us. As we leapt off the back of the truck at the designated field-of-the-day, the sun rose out of the flat Michigan horizon, shining straight across the field exactly parallel with the rows, as if to say, "Pick here." We did. Endlessly.

The work was dirty and dusty. By noon it was hot. Everyone else moved down the field bent over, filling the gunny sacks on their backs, while I dragged myself, scooting along on my fanny in the furrows between the rows. It was not a quick way to stuff a sack with string beans. "*Muy loco*," the Mexican workers laughed. But I didn't care that they thought I was a little crazy. That red denim outfit in Bickert's window on Superior Street was eight dollars and I wanted it.

And college was coming.

And It's Only Monday

It was high noon on a Friday in late July. We were gathered under a giant oak in the middle of a field, eating our baloney and Wonder Bread sandwiches. Bunk was leaning against the tree, chewing Black Jack gum, his tanned chest shirtless. He was usually in constant motion, his big grin and high, quick laugh in sync with his restlessness. Now, he was still. Noticing my shoe had come untied, he walked over. As he bent down to tie the laces, he looked up without a word and smiled.

Bunk, 1952.

Bunk started to ride to my house on his bike. We sat on my front porch steps for hours and talked.

"Please Mother, I want to invite him for Thanksgiving!"

It was my first time to have a boy to dinner. "Of course, I'll wash the dishes," I promised, which I always did anyway. I felt impatient with the too-clean house but volunteered anyway to vacuum the still-spotless rug. It seemed a boring waste of time. I just wanted to have company! And fun!

My sister Linda and I carefully set the table in our tiny dining room with its organdy tieback curtains and fishbowl on the window sill. Upon the "holidays only" damask tablecloth we placed Mother's pink-flowered dishes from the Montgomery Ward catalogue. Linda, like Mother, knew where to place everything correctly.

"Linda is a perfect homemaker," Mother said. I could guess what was coming next, "She is neat, orderly, dutiful... her natural curly hair is so..."

No matter how hard I tried, I knew I was not like them. Stroking my straggly, straight locks, I moved the little divided glass relish dish to the exact center of the table. It was piled with Grandma's homemade bread and butter pickles (tart green), her tomato preserves (bitter red) and celery stalks filled with pimento creamed cheese (crunchy lime green and sticky orange). I did care about color and shapes.

41

Now there we were, our little complete family — a father, a mother, ten-year-old Linda (flirty even then, making eyes at Bunk) and kid brother Dan, age four, eating "formally" with our guest. We normally ate in the kitchen at our red-and-white enameled table. We didn't know how to be light or conversational at this seldom-used wooden table, with its uncomfortable matching chairs. Nor did we know how to have "educated" discussions, as I suspected other families on Walnut Street had. I kept peeking at Bunk. *Was he OK?* I wasn't. "Pass the rhubarb, please." Silence. "More mashed potatoes?" Silence. "Yes, thank you."

I overheard Mother say to Dad afterwards, "He is such a likable young man." Dad, sipping his buttermilk said, "Yes, but his Mother is in jail. She even wrote me a bad check at the gas station." I could imagine Mother giving him her beautiful smile, "That's OK, Everett. He can't help what his mother did."

In study hall, Connie whispered, "Did you hear? His mother tried to burn their house down once." I knew that Bunk's barely older sister was raising him and his brother in a tiny house at the end of Mechanic Street.

On school nights, Bunk and I skated on the flooded tennis court at Wright Avenue Park. The sky was navy blue, the stars crispy bright and the only sound was our skates scratching the ice as they sped us in a giant circle. I watched Bunk at my side. I liked his tall lankiness, his nose with its crook, his big happy smile.

"Last time around, OK?" he yelled. I tried to imagine what it would be like to go home to a sister; not to have your mother waiting for you. His main communication was joking around. He never mentioned her. *Was he covering?* As he sweetly knelt to pull off my skates, I wanted to say, "I am so sorry about your Mother," but I didn't. It seemed too private.

He walked me home from skating. At my house, we settled on the bottom step, the snow softly falling, the cold ignored. It was as if we were on our own private stage, with millions of sparkling diamonds covering it. Glistening icicles encircled us like a curtain.

Criminal Magnetism

Bunk slipped his hand from his glove, pulled my mitten off, and rubbed my cold fingers. I hoped Dad would not flicker the porch light to remind me to come in.

The thought occurred to me: Maybe we could freeze together, like Ruth in the Bible when she looked back and became a pillar of salt. We would be two frozen pillars, side by side.

On this sparkling night, Bunk squeezed my hand, leaned toward me and whispered in a soft voice, "Can you keep an eye out for the police, while I sneak past the station?"

I could almost taste the cold sweep through me. I looked at him intently, trying to understand. "What's it about?" I asked.

"Hubcaps," he answered quietly.

I pulled my hand away, put my mitten back on, and turning to him said, "Let's go."

We walked swiftly the four blocks toward the police station. Nearing it, he stayed back, waiting for me to motion him on, and then he quickly slipped undetected onto Superior Street and headed toward home.

* * * * *

Lorrie was in his red shiny convertible. A car was rare on campus, a brand new one even rarer. The top was down and leaves were drifting in. We had just left an initiation meeting for transferring sophomores at Michigan State University.

"Come with me to get gas!" he said, with his flirty smile and Texas tan. I got in. "Check out the glove compartment!" he demanded with a wink. I did and shuffled through a stack of black-and-white photos of a handsome guy driving the Clydesdale horses for Budweiser. "That's me!" Lorrie exclaimed. "I don't drink their beer, but I ride their horses."

I wondered why would he want to impress me with that? What I really cared about was: *did he dance?*

It was wonderfully new, my sophomore year at big, friendly squeaky-clean Michigan State. The girls wore bright pink lipstick, beige cashmere sweater sets and danced to Tommy Dorsey live. They did the jitterbug and two-step to Harry James and Benny Goodman.

Wandering around campus was Paul, singing and playing his guitar for anyone who would listen. He hadn't met Peter and Mary yet.

I never did own a cashmere sweater set like the other girls. But dancing was connected to dating and that was easy. Fourteen thousand guys and only six thousand gals.

"I am absolutely dizzy!" I wrote home on two-cent postcards. "Big classes of forty, not fifteen; nude models in life drawing; kids from as far away as California; ballet and symphonies included with tuition." And Lorrie had invited me... to a dance.

I could hear the strains of Harry James' "Stardust" as we entered the large auditorium. The high shrill of the trumpet sent chills through me.

"How much more beautiful than on a scratchy seventy-eight!" I whispered to Lorrie, not wanting to sound too impressed. The scent of the gardenia corsage he had brought and pinned to my red strapless formal mingled with my mother's Shalimar perfume. I liked the way Lorrie stood out, in his white shirt and skinny tie, wool suit and cowboy boots, unlike the conservative Michigan guys. In a crowd of four hundred it was easy to dance close to the stage with our eyes almost level with the polished shoes of famous musicians. I had hit heaven at twenty.

"'Sparkle Plenty,' you dance great," Lorrie exclaimed, brushing the glitter off his jacket that I had sprinkled in my hair. Oh, he reads Dick Tracy too, I thought, as we dipped very low. Dancing to "In the Mood," he told me his dad was president of a giant national company. I guessed it was stocks or insurance. What does a simple college girl know of that? Would it be smart to tell him my dad sold mobile homes not far from the State Penitentiary?

It was raining the night we stopped in East Lansing to get gas. Returning from the station, Lorrie slipped into the front seat and pulled out a carton of Lucky Strikes, from under his trench coat.

"Look!" he laughed. "Free!" I tried to smile but my eyes betrayed me. I turned away, staring out the window at the slowly moving windshield wipers. *Why does he have to steal? He has plenty of money!* I thought.

*****

Lorrie was getting married. It was spring of our senior year. My name was written in calligraphy and the invitation was beautiful, in heavy cream-colored paper and embossed lettering. I had never received such sophisticated mail. The boxing coach's twin daughters were the brides: a double wedding. They resembled boxers a bit themselves; sinewy, strong and attractive.

On that Saturday morning, I laid out my half-slip, garter belt, and sheerest pair of seamed hose, the basics of a well-dressed college girl going to her first grand wedding.

Then the room buzzer gave off two loud twangy rings, which meant someone was downstairs to see me. Two buzzes for me, three for my roommate. I threw on a skirt and blouse and ran down. It was Lorrie himself, the groom-to-be, freshly shaven and looking handsome in his new crewcut. He was wearing my favorite: Old Spice. *Did he remember?*

Taking my surprised hand, he led me into one of the small semi-private sitting rooms. "It's not too late," he said, putting his arms around me.

"For what?" I asked, tensing from his touch. I had not seen him up close in a year. We had dated a few more times and then floated apart.

"If you will marry me, I'll skip my wedding today."

What? I thought, pulling quickly away and remembering he was about to marry another woman. "That is crazy!" I exclaimed. Fearing I had hurt him, I added, "I'll be there watching you." *Did he have last-minute jitters? Or regrets?* We had never been serious and there was no time to analyze it now.

"I have to get ready." I laughed lightly, as though he had asked me something simple about the weather. Amazed at my coolness, as I walked away I called, "See you there!" as if we might be meeting later at the Student Union for a cup of coffee.

I watched from the back of the darkened church as twelve bridesmaids walked up the flower-festooned aisle while the twelve matching groomsmen waited at the altar. It seemed half the campus was in the wedding party, and the other half was attending.

Lorrie's bride looked hopeful and radiant. That long-ago carton of cigarettes danced in my head and faded away. It was her stolen heart that concerned me now.

* * * * *

It seemed I was a magnet for bad guys. But why? Had I been a criminal in a past life? Did I keep the keys to a prison in the sixteenth century, slipping inmates extra food or a little wine? Had we all been together as a rowdy band of thieves or a slick gang of Robin Hoods?

Whatever it was, in some unexplainable way we were drawn together. Bunk found me in a Michigan bean field and Lorrie on a college campus. Years later, Aaron flirted from a theater-box seat in New York City. He was the pastor who stole my sterling flatware. I managed to get it back, along with my heart. Elliott and I met at an ethical-society singles dance. He was a poet and writer, in and out of jail. He stole my camera, but I still save a place in my heart for him. My camera was retrieved, and it feels so good to forgive.

Paul and I met in a classy D.C. nightclub. After a few dates, I learned he was a multi-million-dollar realtor and had eighty million dollars himself (the *Washington Post* said). He also told me he'd spent time in prison as a white-collar criminal, mostly beating Watergate's Haldeman at tennis, while they served time together.

And then there was Dorie. Dorie was an attractive guy. A laborer. He had the keys to my house to do repair and painting work while I was staying in Oregon. When I returned, he had replaced my failed water heater with a new one.

"It's free to you," he said smugly, "because I stole it." He had moved himself in as well, with his clothes and tools and machinery. That very day, I threw him out. Bam! And then I took a nice hot shower to wash that man right out of my hair.

The Sailing Summers

Mother was calling! Not from across the room or on the telephone, but in my head.

It was incessant. I couldn't eat. I couldn't sleep. I just kept hearing Mother.

"I need to get to a phone," I reminded Chuck every fifty miles or so. We were on the old Pan American highway, a harrowing road without guardrails, heading north from Mexico City. There were banana trees and monkeys, men in sombreros, children wearing only undershirts, adobe houses and scrawny horses, but no telephones. Mostly, no electricity at all.

"I could have stayed forever!" I told Chuck, as I grabbed the seat to hold on while we barely missed a pothole. "Mariachi music is better than Tommy Dorsey!"

"Painting in Toluca wasn't bad," Chuck chuckled as he veered around a small boulder. We had been art students at Mexico City College. It was 1956.

"I really tried to stay, you know. My only possibility was teaching English in Pueblo at thirty dollars a month; no way to save for my next semester," I said. He had heard it all before.

Chuck, in his expensive shirt and Italian sandals, couldn't relate to my working my way through college. His Texas grandfather had oil wells. "I bought this car with my dividends," he said without bragging, slapping the dash. His new '56 MG purred back. At twenty-one he was simply used to having money.

The border at last. The road turned from dirt to pavement, and a phone appeared. Wrapped in my hot pink *rebozo*, wearing my huaraches and silver Taxco earrings, I suddenly realized I looked like a tourist.

"Thank heavens! You got my message!" Mother exclaimed on the phone, as though we used mental telepathy on a daily basis. "Don't go to Uncle Frank's in Albuquerque. Take the next bus straight home. The shipping line in Detroit called about your application days ago. If you hurry and go in person, you still might get a job."

Softy singing *"Besa me Mucho"* to tease Chuck as he kissed me on the cheek, I climbed aboard an already crowded bus. Forced to sit on the inside steps at the feet of the driver I clutched my suitcase, rolled-up watercolor paintings, a cotton sack of tiny ceramic tiles, and a ten-pound stone metate used for grinding corn for tortillas, but intended for Dad for Christmas as an ashtray.

Two days later, Mother met the bus and transferred me, along with a warm coat and a much-needed egg salad sandwich, to the Jackson train station. "All aboard for Dee-troit!" the conductor called. How chilly, gray and flat Michigan seemed after the brilliant colors and hilly tropics of Mexico. I longed for a hot cup of *cafe con leche* and a spicy tamale.

I went directly to the Georgia Bay Lines office. Mrs. Swanson, the receptionist, was an attractive, middle-aged woman in a taupe seersucker suit. Her seams were perfectly straight, a sign to me that she was very orderly and probably a perfect housekeeper. Her spectator shoes matched her purse, which sat on her nearly empty desk. In a soft and courteous manner, she inquired, "May I help you?"

"Yes," I spoke timidly but with determination, "I would like to see the President." I remembered my manners and added "Please," along with a genuine smile.

"Do you have an appointment?" she asked.

"Oh, no, but you left me a phone message." I remembered the long job application.

She looked me over. I was still wearing my now wrinkled and wilted Mexican outfit. I had slept in it in an upright position for the past three days.

"I will see," she said hesitantly and disappeared.

She returned with a quick step, wearing a smile, like she might know a secret. "Follow me," she said as she graciously led me down a hall to a formidably massive, carved door.

Mr. Lindquist was a large Swede with a stern look, who invited me to sit in a straight-backed oak chair at the side of his desk. I could see etchings of ships framed behind him and colored photos of the S.S. South American at dock in Detroit and Macinac Island. It was like seeing movie posters behind the casting director's desk when you wanted a part. Tantalizing, intensely desirable, and distracting. His stern presence surprisingly melted into kindness. In a Swedish accent reminiscent of Grandpa Roslund he asked, "So! Yah! You want to work for us?"

"With all my heart," I responded, looking into his Nordic blue eyes. "I'm working my way through college as I go, and my grandparents came from Sweden." I had heard that the college students who got hired were mainly kids from Grosse Point or were politician's kids or had wealthy fathers. Not belonging to any of these categories, and unable to think of any argument in my favor, I hoped to tap into his compassion and his love for the "old country."

"And your musical skill for participating in the ship's entertainment?" he asked, suddenly aware of my dangling earrings. "A talent is required, you know," he added.

"Baritone horn in the high-school band," I mumbled, looking at my feet. I was no award-winning tap dancer or jazz-singing beauty queen. He swallowed hard.

I sat there. He sat there. After a very long extended moment of thought, a smile spread across his strong Swedish face. He seemed to enjoy saying, "You are hired."

I looked at him, and burst into tears.

"There, there," he said kindly and reached out his massive hand to touch my shoulder.

The job gave me my seaman's papers. Good for life. You could not get them without being hired first by a shipping company. You could not

And It's Only Monday

get hired by a shipping company without them. They were as important to a seaman as a green card to an immigrant.

We sailed out of Detroit on bitterly cold May Day with a full load of First Class passengers. I carried heavy trays on tilting, rocking decks for twelve hours out of every twenty-four, for four full months. There was not one free day. Through Lake Erie to Lake Ontario and Buffalo on Saturday, Sunday in Cleveland, off to Macinac Island via Lake Huron on Monday, across Lake Superior to Duluth, Minnesota, and a quick turnaround in Chicago over Lake Michigan and back again.

*Every Thursday our sea legs did double duty. It was "Crew Night" on the S.S. South American, when the waitresses and busboys entertained. At the end of the season on Mackinac Island, we were each awarded two hundred dollars for performing on the Grand Hotel's magnificent stage. All summer we had sailed under the half-completed Bay Bridge; it opened the next year.
I am the girl on the far right, 1956.*

Thursday nights out of Duluth was the "Crew Show," presented by the greatly talented busboys and waitresses, who like me had probably played in more high-school bands than won any musical awards. At each performance, I reminded my theatrical shipmates, "Watch, I won't miss," and I never did. As a curvy "French chorus line dancer" I was adept at kicking one high-heeled shoe far out into the audience. The men roared and someone out there always caught it.

My sea legs were exhausted, but my junior year at Michigan State was financially secure.

My junior year flew and suddenly it was spring again. A new challenging bill loomed ahead. I needed one thousand, two hundred dollars for tuition, room and board by September 15, 1957... for my senior year. I had three months to find that amount. Coincidentally, at that very same time, Jane from down the hall came wandering through our dorm, searching for a passenger to share expenses to California. "Too perfect," I thought. Part of my new plan for instant wealth called for an ocean; either the Atlantic or the Pacific. I volunteered.

*****

Jane (at left) and I on June 24, 1957, leaving Michigan. 'California or Bust'

Laying on the horn as we crossed the state line, we half yelled, half sang "California here we come, right back where we started from!" Our loud off-key melody added to the headiness of the moment. We had three thousand miles ahead of us and it was a beautiful June morning. "And it's only Monday!" I shouted to the wind.

Exactly fifty dollars. That was what I had to invest. "Jane!" I tried yelling over the noise as the windows were down and we were going seventy miles an hour, her '48 Chevy beginning to shudder. No response. "Jane," I yelled again. "The amount of one thousand, two hundred dollars is haunting me! Did you know that the average income in America is four thousand, seven hundred dollars a year?" Still no answer.

That's more than Dad makes, I said to myself.

Like in the movies, going West seemed the romantic and exotic answer to any challenge. We were driving through Indiana, Jane still at the wheel, when I pulled out my money, held together with a rubber band. "One, two, three," I methodically counted out my fifty one-dollar bills. "That station ahead looks good. Twenty cents a gallon seems high though, doesn't it?" I leaned toward her and yelled in her ear. "It's my turn to pay!" She screeched from eighty down to "stop" in a minute flat. We scurried to the restroom while a wiry old gentleman in his greasy blue uniform filled the tank, checked our oil and washed every window.

"Where you pretty young things headed?" he asked with a grin.

"San Francisco," Jane answered in her deadpan way.

"By Saturday!" I added, more hopeful than convinced.

My two-cent postcards from the trip were saved by my mother.

Wednesday: *"Mountainous and barren. Saw a good movie tonite – Bernadine. Another tourist home for $2.00 a person."*

Thursday: *"Hi Pod'ners... Salt Lake City is beautiful. We went to Mormon Square to see and hear them. What Christians! It's awfully impressive. A five-hundred-and-fifty-mile day tomorrow so I'd better hang up my ten gallon hat."*

Friday: *"Reno, crazy people feeding one armed bandits. Jimmy Durante is in town but the cover charge didn't fit our pockets – so we saw a floor show at Harold's. Pretty cute but awfully off color. One nite in this town is plenty for a life time. Every woman here has 'blond' hair – wow! Even in Reno we got a $5.00 room. Great huh!"*

Jane and I had nothing in common except our destination. Although I had shared the same halls and dorm dining room with her for a year, I did not really know her. I did recall her at meals a few times saying "Please pass the salt" or calling a classmate to the single hall telephone... "Hey Judy, it's Frank!" Here on the trip we had little to

The Sailing Summers

say, except for spurts of singing and our horn-blowing signature at each state line. Iowa, honk, honk. Nebraska, honk, honk. Colorado, Utah, a movie one evening somewhere and a night in Nevada, honking into California with an exhausted sigh and one chorus of our own version of "California, here we are." We made it by Saturday.

And I still had money; exactly five dollars.

Jane's friends had mailed her a hand-drawn map to their San Francisco apartment. They were cool and indifferent. I could imagine my Grandmother calling them "a little odd." It was a kindly, country way of saying you did not care for someone.

Georgia, a coarse, husky-voiced gal of twenty-four cornered me in the kitchen, "We need to borrow some money." Two unkempt grim-faced gals stood behind her. Jane seemed to have disappeared. I did not want to admit I had only five dollars to my name, so I smiled a nervous smile. "Well, I can lend you five until tomorrow morning." Georgia snatched the bills out of my hand in a flash and said, "OK, gang, let's go." Shirley, with her greasy hair, grunted, "At least it's enough for a case of beer." With that they left, with Jane in tow, the door slamming behind them.

Sunday morning was sunny and exhilarating. The air was as fresh as a Michigan farm morning, but misted with a shimmering fog. The hills, the white-washed buildings, and the sea air sharpened my reality; I was far from home. I hummed the theme song from "Around the World in 80 Days" as I scrounged in the messy kitchen for some instant coffee. I could see by the droopy, sleeping group, sprawled on the sofas and floor, that they were not going to wake up soon and return my money. Hurriedly dressing in the tiny bathroom, helping myself to a used towel, I woke Jane and made my last request, "Please drive me around and let me off at a church. Any church." Thank goodness it was Sunday!

Eager for her to say yes, I promised, "I'll pick the closest and first one we come to." Annoyed and sleepy, Jane agreed, just as happy to see the end of me as I was of her. "Thanks, Jane. See you in the fall. Maybe." I smiled gratefully, jumping out of the car, and watching her drive away up over a steep hill and disappear into her summer.

I stood with my suitcase and radio in my best shirt-dress, hose and heels in front of a small, white, wooden Methodist church. It was the same denomination I had attended back in Alma, Michigan. The small sign read: Welcome, Sunday Service - 10:00 A.M. I was on time. We sang "God will take care of you. Be not dismayed what'er betide, God will take care of you." I didn't doubt it.

When the offering came around we sang "Praise God from whom all blessings flow." I had no money for the basket. I said an extra prayer to make up for it, "Thank you, God, for helping me get here. I'll pay you back later."

We waited in line to shake hands with the student minister, who had given the sermon on "Love thy Neighbor." He didn't look too old, probably twenty-eight. When it was my turn, I stepped up and without planning to, blurted out in one quick breath: "I'm new in town with no place to live, no job, and," I added after some hesitation, "no money." He beamed a brilliant smile and said, "Wait over there," pointing to a corner by the stairway.

He passed out more brilliant smiles and handshakes to the others in line and then led me downstairs. Can there be anything more wonderful to a hungry traveler than a potluck luncheon in a church basement? It was like having my mother's and grandmother's and my fourteen aunts' cooking all spread out on one long table. For just a second I felt homesick. The ladies cooked as well in San Francisco as in Gratiot County: fried chicken, scalloped potatoes, tomato aspic salad, and apple pie with chunks of cheddar cheese.

In line stood a pretty gal, tall with dark brown hair, beautiful kind eyes, and a soft voice.

"I want you to meet Dolores from Detroit," the minister said, nodding toward her and seemingly tickled to introduce two Michigan gals so far from home. Dolores and I clicked like we had known each other forever. She was a registered nurse and twenty-seven years old. We were together in line again for more pie when she casually said, "Why not move in with me?"

"Today?" I asked in stunned surprise, not believing my incredible luck.

"Of course, right after lunch!" she said.

We agreed on everything. She would pay the rent of sixty dollars a month; I, the groceries.

Balboa Street ran parallel with the park and all the way to the ocean. A small garden of iris, candytuft, toad flax and sweet alyssum filled her miniature front lawn. Her tiny walk-down apartment was immaculate, with a patchwork quilt on the double bed, and feather pillows with white cases edged in crocheted lace. Her family photos on the wall, especially those of her great grandparents, could have been exchanged for mine. A well-read Bible lay on the bedside table, in front of a hall tree, which held six neatly ironed white nurse's uniforms on their metal hangers. The order was offset by her cat Pansy and eight bouncing, diving, leaping kittens. I had been gone just seven days and now I was "home."

Dolores, my sweet roommate from Detroit, who lived on Balboa Street.

"Wish me luck with a job," I called through the shower door, "and thanks for the dollar loan." I slipped out and walked toward the bus stop. The bus dropped me at the bottom of Market Street on another sunny, magnificent Monday morning. *And, it's only Monday!* I thought again, remembering my cheer a week earlier. I surveyed the world, dizzy with my choices.

At the top of the hill I saw a tall, magnificent building with flags flying in front. Instantly, I knew that was where I wanted to work. I kept my eyes on it as I climbed the hill. Finally, I could read the inscription... the St. Francis Hotel. Across the street was Union Square. I had never heard of either but they looked impressive. Women were dressed in smart wool suits, hats and white gloves. Men wore white shirts, ties and three-piece suits. Some wore smart, brimmed hats. Walking into the St. Francis felt wonderful. Just being there made me feel like royalty. I forgot for a few minutes that I was seeking work as a waitress and that my black working shoes were in my bag.

A smartly uniformed doorman directed me across a wide expanse of marble floor to the *maître d'*. The high, baroque ceiling was supported by marble pillars. As I approached Mrs. Weaver, she smiled and said, "Hello. I've been waiting for you." Not allowing me to answer she continued, "Uniforms are in the dressing room, you may start immediately." I had not yet said a word. It was days later that I pondered this strange one-sided conversation. *Was it a coincidence?*

I was the new kid on the block and my station was farthest from the kitchen. The metal trays were heavy, the thick china dishes edged in gold with the St. Francis decal fired on them, heavier yet. "How on earth did you get this job?" asked Mabel, as we reset the tables following lunch. She was solidly built with fat hands and stubby fingers, her curly, gray hair caught in a hairnet, her legs encased in beige, opaque stockings. She was a portrait of efficiency in her black nylon uniform with its white starched apron and cap.

"Well," I answered, "I just walked in and got it."

"Ridiculous!" Mabel retorted. "For me, six months on a waiting list! This is a coveted job for a *professional* waitress." She pierced me with an unkind look.

I did not know what to say. I didn't understand it myself.

When the shift was over, I hurried out onto Union Square. "Which way is the shipping yard?" I needed the seafarer's hall. I asked several bench sitters who were reading the San Francisco Chronicle or feeding the pigeons. They didn't have any better idea than I, so I headed downhill toward the ocean.

The Merchant Marine shipping hall was chilly and damp, high ceilinged and vault-like. There were backless benches facing a huge blackboard. As a ship entered port, available positions were written out, with the departure date, time and pier number. I desperately looked for "food handler". Nothing. I sat down to watch and wait. The long, cold bench gave little comfort. Looking around, I realized I was the only female in the entire, vast hall except for one woman. She sat in a far corner in a small cage-like booth.

Seamen were everywhere: leaning, lounging, sleeping, chewing and smoking. Some were scruffy, smelly and tattooed. A few looked like they could play the meanest man in a gangster movie. I was thankful my parents couldn't see where I was. I was not sure I was safe.

My legs ached and my calf muscles burned. There was nothing tougher than waitressing on marble. It didn't give; it punished. But, sitting there watching the board, I knew that ship floors were wood. Wood gives. They would be a welcome relief.

The summer before, when I had worked on the S.S. South American, I had learned all about shipboard life: the swaying and heaving and the giant swells that could send an entire place setting for five hundred crashing to the floor in a million pieces in a second. I had also heard the rumor that big money was to be made if you could land a job on a first-class ocean liner. Here in the hiring hall, pinned in the lining of my purse, were my seaman's papers. They were my ticket. Now all I needed was a ship.

S.S. Matsonia, 1957.

As I sat on the bench, knowing I had to be back at the St. Francis for tomorrow's breakfast shift, I could only bear to sit five hours. I had already worked a long split-shift day. I had not realized I would have to camp out day after day in this sordid place, watching the board, fighting for the position once it was announced and then be ready to board at a moment's notice. Finally, I went to the far corner to speak with the lady in the cage. Rosie O'Kane (her real name) was all business. Her face was so deeply wrinkled that when she spoke you could see the crevices deepen, then open and close, like an earthquake in action. "Girl, if you can't sit here, you can't sit here!" she snapped, her face moving like expanding lines on a graph. No encouragement.

I had my eye on the S.S. Mariposa or the S.S. Monterey because they went to the Fiji Islands and Tahiti. But they were not scheduled to be in port for two more weeks. In desperation, I walked back to the cage. "Here is my number. If something happens, could you call me?" I asked timidly. Rosie yanked my paper away, her facial lines freezing for a minute, and replied in her grating voice, "Don't count on it."

I took the trolley and bus home. I decided to tell Dolores my dream and show her my invaluable papers. "I'm really discouraged," I confessed. "I'm sorry. I know the only way to make my goal is to go to sea. I cannot make enough on land in time for college in the fall." I realized that even more, when I counted the day's tips.

"I understand," she said. We popped corn, found big-band music on my radio, and dodged the crazy kittens. I loved having a good friend.

We planned to take a picnic down to the ocean on Saturday, our first day off since we met. Early Saturday morning, buried under the covers and attempting to sleep in, the kittens were racing all across the top of the patchwork quilt. They would hide in a valley and leap over the mountains of knees and feet. We just wanted to sleep. When the phone rang, Dolores answered and with raised eyebrows handed it to me. The cord could barely reach but I sleepily leaned in. "You have a job, girl," Rosie's scratchy voice came through loudly. "Brenda got drunk and can't stand up." My fear became panic. This was too sudden. I was scared to ask if it was going to Tahiti and Fiji but I had to.

"Where is it sailing?"

"Hawaii. It's the S.S. Matsonia. Now make up your mind. You have one minute!" she barked.

I felt ill. "Hawaii?" I said aloud. My heart sank. I wanted Tahiti. And Fiji. I couldn't think. I looked at Dolores, who was looking puzzled, unable to help.

I remembered my goal. "Yes," I said and thought I would be sick.

"Dolores, I'm leaving! Will you call a cab please? O'Kane said one hour; that's sixty minutes! I'll quit the hotel and get my paycheck on my way... pay you first time in port. Keep my radio." My nervousness made my mind race, my words run.

"You can bring me a seashell!" Dolores laughed to comfort my fear.

"I'll miss you, my friend of one week," I called as I climbed into the cab, almost in tears. *I will find her something wonderful in Hawaii*, I promised myself.

The ship's horns were blasting and the passengers, all First Class, were hanging over the railings waving to their friends. The gangplank was about to be rolled up. At the steward's office, I was handed a uniform and shown the women's quarters where I was to bunk. In minutes, I was being jostled by forty-nine other women in line in the galley to pick up baskets of hot breads and relishes. Passengers had boarded and half of them were already arriving in the dining room for the first seating.

Forty separate languages were being spoken in the galley. Everyone was yelling, dishing out, flirting, pouring, ladling, swearing, shouting, stacking, and bumping rudely into each other and into me. The ship was tossing heavily because San Francisco Bay was much rougher than the open sea, due to the cross currents. My station of three tables was one of the farthest from the galley... a very long walk on a rolling floor, carrying a tray of food stacked three tiers high. I balanced it like a tightrope walker. Thank goodness, I had not forgotten how to use my Swedish sea legs, educated on the Great Lakes. I was a natural.

This would be my first of eleven round-trips to Hawaii that summer. Each round-trip voyage lasted eleven days.

And It's Only Monday

Everyone dressed up for "Captain's Night." Note the orchids on the table. Hawaii overflowed with exotic blooms, which were still a rarity in the United States. It became a state two years later, in 1959, and orchids gradually made their way to the mainland.

Four days later, as everyone excitedly cried, "We can see it" and "It's in sight!" it seemed that every single passenger, all five hundred of them, were on the decks peering and cheering and kissing and posing for pictures. It is a wonder the ship didn't tip over. As one of the few new crew members who had never seen the Hawaiian Islands and was not yet jaded, I rushed up to the crew's aft deck. The breeze was a soothing seventy-two degrees. So pleasant, you could not even feel it against your skin. The sun was warm, not hot. This was the kind of weather they say is perpetual on the astral plane. Hawaiian boys, golden brown with glistening black hair, swam more than a mile out from shore to greet the ship. Dugout canoes, guided by beautifully

The Sailing Summers

toned men rowed out beside them. I may not have been a first-class passenger but I felt first class! "Oh thank you, God," I murmured to myself. "God is in His heaven and all is well."

Once the gangplank was secured, the passengers streamed out. I was one of the first crew to follow. On the dock stood several exquisite barefooted women wearing orchids in their hair and native *muumuus*. "Please miss... Aloha!" said one girl, who stepped forward and put a freshly woven *lei* of orchids around my neck. I was surprised, as I was only the help. It felt like magic. The ship's live band had moved onto shore and was playing Hawaiian music.

"Oh, they are beautiful. Thank you!" I gushed. They smelled divine, a little like Mother's perfume but fresher, as I lifted them and brushed them against my cheek. "Are you Hawaiian?" I asked. What a complicated question, I realized too late. It was just an island, not a state.

"Oh yes, I'm a Kanaka," said the girl with black, silky hair that almost swept the ground. And pointing to her friend at her side, "She is, too!"

"I am Chinese," said another. "But, may we ask you a question? What is snow like?"

I loved snow as much as I loved ice cream. How could I explain it? "Do you like ice cream?" I asked.

"Yes," they said in unison.

"Well, snow is like vanilla ice cream, only broken into a million tiny droplets and sprinkled from the sky. But it doesn't have a taste."

They giggled and smiled and one elbowed another. The Chinese girl stepped forward and pinned an orchid in my hair. It made me want to own a *muumuu* and wear flowers in my hair forever.

"Where is the telegraph office?" I inquired from a Japanese man selling monkey-pod wooden bowls on the corner. It was time to let my parents know where I was. They had not heard from me, except for my three postcards, since Jane and I had driven off almost three weeks earlier. Telephones were not used for long distance except for a death, and often not even then. "Write your message here, Ma'am." I returned the paper to the clerk, along with three dollars. It read "safe in Hawaii love sharon." I would explain it all in a letter.

And It's Only Monday

My next errand was a florist shop set up for foreign tourists. Hawaii was two years away from becoming a state. I selected a pink and yellow *lei* that I was certain Mother would adore. The *lei* and shipping came to twelve dollars, a big splurge, as that would pay for two used textbooks. Later Mother wrote, "I even wear it to the laundromat!" I bought another *lei* for Dolores. I knew Tony "the Italian" would keep it cool for me in his salad refrigerator on the ship.

The women crew members, exactly fifty of us, lived behind twenty-inch-thick steel doors, far below the water level. We had no portholes. Any time the alarm rang for a fire drill or emergency — and each night for our "safe keeping" — we were sealed in, the watertight massive doors clanging shut with a horrific clash of steel meeting steel. It was unnerving. Partly, it was for the safety of us women to keep at bay the four hundred and fifty male crew members. Secondly, it was to seal in air instantly, to help keep the ship afloat in case of trouble. In an emergency, we had to race like crazy to slip out before the doors crashed shut. Once in a while, in the middle of the night, I had the uneasy thought that the ship could sink and seal me in.

July 11 - Leaving Hawaii for the first time in my "tea timer" dress. (I must have gone shopping.)

My roommates Rita, Pearly, and Bobbie were over thirty years of age — as were all the other forty-six women. I was at least nine years younger than every female aboard. We four shared a tiny space and two sets of bunkbeds.

62

The Sailing Summers

Rita was in love with peroxide. She used it straight. The result was a head of white, dry and very brittle straw. Tan as could be, Rita looked like a chocolate popsicle topped with white sugar spikes. Our first time in port, I asked her if we could go to shore together. "Honey, there's not room for three in a bed," she tossed at me as she hurried away. I couldn't believe it.

Pearly was in love with Pierre from Paris. I could see why. He was six-foot-three, slender, blond and sinfully handsome. As the head baker, he was in charge of making fresh rolls and bread for a thousand persons every day. Every eleven days, back in port, the flour room was shoveled full of white flour, all the way to the ceiling. Halfway through the voyage the flour was down to eye level. Pierre spoke only French, but although I did not understand a word (I had flunked French), I never tired of listening to his deep voice, speaking unintelligible words. In port, Pearly and Pierre always rushed off together.

One afternoon, while we were resting on our bunks, Pearly bounced in.

"What on earth!" Rita cried out, sitting bolt upright.

"A snowman in July!" squealed Bobbie.

Pearly laughed and more flour dropped to the floor. Completely covered, head to toe, she spun around and showered all of us. "Pierre and I had a little date," she said. And winked.

Bobbie, with her brown, short-cropped hair and deep, almost ebony, tan, was the most sensitive and thoughtful one. She used fewer swear words than the others. She started bringing me breakfast in bed when we were in port and didn't have to serve the guests. She also liked to brush my hair. I was starting to enjoy the attention when she suddenly stopped. She did not become unfriendly, just preoccupied.

"What has happened to Bobbie?" I asked Pearly one day, showing a little disappointment. "She's not around much anymore."

"Dummy! Don't you know? She's a fairy!"

"A fairy? I've heard men are… but girls, too?"

"You weren't interested. She found Nancy." Pearly was impatient with me at times. I was trying. There was so much to learn.

At least I could do something: lose weight. I had nowhere to go, there was an afternoon break with free time for my high school gym calisthenics, and a private aft deck on the ship for the crew. I decided to lose twenty pounds because fresh papayas and mangos and filet mignon were always free and available... and I had the help of my roommates. "Tie me down if you have to!" I demanded. "Don't let me eat." They were a strong force.

Tom and Jerry boarded in late July as busboys. Pre-med students from UCLA, they were my age! I had been like a kid on a street of grown-ups, yearning to have a playmate, and suddenly two appeared. The strain of living and working with everyone over age thirty — a crew of four hundred and ninety-nine old people — had thankfully come to an end.

"You will just have to *double date* us," teased Jerry. Red headed and freckled, my height and slender, he was a fun new pal.

Tom and Jerry, docked in Hilo, Hawaii: my "double dates."

"Will you go out with us?" asked Tom, in a more serious tone. He had wavy brown hair with a strong jaw and masculine build, which made him physically appealing. They thought it funny; I felt it was awkward. But they had no choice. I was it. I had absolutely no competition, unless one could imagine mermaids circling the ship on a moonlit night.

"How can you two be such good friends, really?" I asked them.

"No competition with us," laughed Jerry as he held my right hand.

"That's true," said Tom, as he took my left hand.

The Sailing Summers

We swam at Waikiki beach, all white sand and a few lonely surfers. Sand and surf and the three of us. Oh, and the charming pink Royal Hawaiian Hotel. It was the only structure there. Nothing else existed on the beach. Yet.

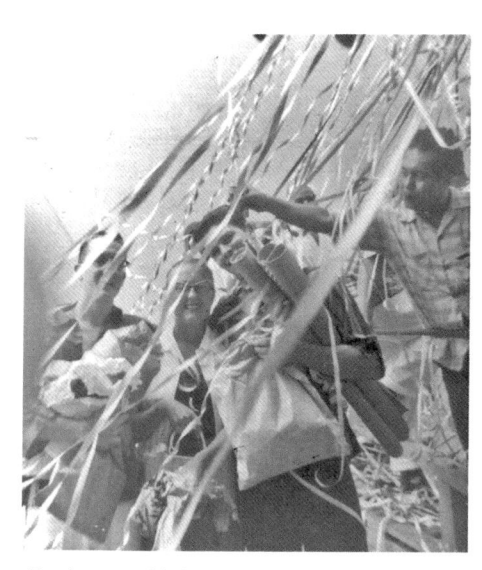

On one voyage, we skipped San Francisco and sailed to San Diego instead. We were in port just after Disneyland first opened. A new thrill for the still innocent world. We did the Ferris wheel, roller coaster, and the merry-go-round. We were always connected, hand-in-hand, the three of us.

Back at the ship, standing in front of the ominous steel doors, ready to swallow me up at a moment's notice of disaster, we kissed goodnight. Jerry gave me a long, sweet, romantic kiss, taking his time, while Tom turned his back and patiently tapped his foot. Then Tom took me in his arms to receive his good night kiss... even longer and sweeter.

Back to work! Jerry, me and Tom returning to the ship with our woven beach mats from Waikiki Beach. The ship docked for only seven daylight hours. In all eleven round trips, I never once saw the islands after dark.

* * * * *

By the end of that summer I loved the West Coast with a passion and toyed with the idea of going to Berkeley for my senior year... and not returning to Michigan State. I knew that Dolores wanted the best for me and used her religious fervor to pray that I could arrange it. One morning I was alone on the ship while all the other female crew were on shore. I had been assigned to stay on board to serve the Captain his meals, a job we took turns doing.

As I was sitting up in my bunk, contemplating my life choices, Jesus appeared at the foot of my bed. He said nothing. I felt more fear

65

than awe and I thought I was imagining it. I blinked my eyes to make Him go away. *This must be my imagination.* Each time I blinked He remained. I believed: *Dolores must have sent Him to convince me to stay in California.* After a few minutes, He vanished.

Despite this sudden appearance of Jesus, I could not manage the switch and I had to return to Michigan... and to the regrettable karmic adventures that followed. Many decades later, I now look back. Perhaps Jesus appeared with overflowing compassion to strengthen me by His presence. He knew what was coming and He was letting me know I was not alone.

Instead of returning to Michigan by bus, it made sense financially for me to make one last Hawaiian voyage and then fly home.

My money for tuition, room and board was laid aside. If there was any leftover, I could treat myself. The ship photographer became my friend and at the end of the last voyage, he met me at a San Francisco camera shop. "This will serve you well," he said, and selected a small black camera for one hundred, thirty-eight dollars. I had my plane fare paid for and, best of all, like topping on a cake, one hundred dollars still remained for a California wardrobe.

Aunt Gladys, married to my Uncle Art, Dad's brother, lived in L.A., where we conveniently docked for two days in early September. She was sweetness personified and oozed with patience. For an entire day, she took me shopping around "Hollywood." Aunt Gladys sat in the little dressing rooms with me, nodding and smiling, while I selected five outfits, each one twenty dollars, and far more beautiful and original than clothes back home. Back then, there were no shopping centers or nationwide department stores. What I bought in the West was not to be found in the East. I was fashionably unique back on the cold Michigan State University campus, with new clothes, long brown hair with a white streak made from Rita's peroxide, a Hawaiian tan, and a slender figure.

"Stand up! Is that you?" said my professor, pointing me out to my last year's classmates.

My senior year was here. I had no spending money, but I was very rich.

Short Skirts – High Manners

This can't be, I whispered to myself, peering closely at my sleeping husband. *He looks Chinese!* I leaned forward. His features looked Asian and his robe now appeared to be smooth cotton. I was awake and clear-headed and yet this was true.

The bedroom was dusky on that late wintry afternoon in Fairfax, Virginia. Derek lay on the bed with his head on a feather pillow, its case edged in crocheted lace. He was wrapped in his terrycloth robe on grandmother's Michigan quilt — a typical thirty-year-old Caucasian man taking a nap. Without waking him, I looked down at myself and realized I appeared Asian also. It seemed so natural and quietly reasonable. *I will tell him later*, I thought and fell asleep.

The next morning, the Washington Post slammed against our orange-painted front door.

"Perfect aim again," I muttered, but it only made me want to call up this bulls-eye paper boy and stop delivery. The travel and society pages were tiring and tedious. "I don't want to read about *other* people's lives. I want to do something about ours!"

We had married and moved to Washington, D.C., where Derek took a job with the Department of Agriculture... and I dutifully decided to finish what I had started... a Master's degree in social work. My undergraduate degree was useless. I had chosen this career with about as much enthusiasm as I had entered my marriage.

Art had always been my passion. I crammed in as much of it as I could and took twenty-one credits a semester to do so. The Art Department head at Michigan State University asked, "Why don't you major in art?" Little did he know that at night, I did the sketches and assignments for my classmates and saw my work hanging on the art department walls with their names signed in the lower right-hand corner. I guess that was cheating. I got them A's at times when my own work was "uptight" and I only earned a B on my own creations. So, I got both A's and B's. I think that was a distorted way of pleasing others.

The migraine headaches stopped at the same time my social work thesis was completed. Fresh out of grad school I thought, "It's time to save the world!" I was not unlike most social workers I knew. Rescuing others seemed easier than trying to understand myself. I went looking for work and soon found employment.

There was no pill yet in 1962, so homes for "unwed mothers" dotted the country. I was hired to use my new skills as a group worker at such a home in D.C. The girls huddled in secret shame on the top of a hill in the Florence Crittenton Home off posh Foxhall Road, just two miles from the White House. Few women kept and raised a child out of wedlock. To do so meant scorn, judgment and ostracism.

"My parents can never know this happened," Sarah sighed.

"He's married. I'll never tell him," Debra said.

We were all about the same age, mid-twenties; the girls with their secret burdens, and I, the sincere but helpless helper. I drove to work each day in our little black Triumph TR-3 with an ache in my heart for a child of my own. At age twenty-six I had started to feel a yearning. Our desire for a baby had increased and we experienced month after month disappointment. The girls were driven up that long winding driveway and dropped off, hiding under scarves and dark glasses, about to part with their own flesh and blood. It was a miserable place!

The girls were there for their last six weeks of pregnancy and I was the group worker who led their initiation meeting. I smiled. "Good morning!" I said.

Silence.

"Welcome to your temporary home." I tried again with a better smile.

Silence.

The semi-circle of watermelon sized girls wore sullen, depressed, or blank faces. Take your pick. This circle of fruit was ready to burst with a burden that should have been a celebration.

"I have decided not to even peek at my baby," Irene said somberly. "If I were to hold it, I would die."

"Not me," said Jennifer, in a voice a little too gay. "I'll care for it for my allotted time, and then say farewell. Forever." She rushed from the room.

Sylvia vowed, "I'll burn a candle on his birthday for the rest of my life, if I can bear to stay alive."

Many girls thought they knew exactly how and when it happened. Perhaps I could learn from them. I listened and collected ideas. But not from Esther.

She said day after day, "It's impossible! How could I have gotten this way? I've never been *near* a man!" She was no help.

On our way to Ocean City for a weekend camping trip, I asked my husband, "A girl at the home got pregnant standing on her head in a tent. Do you believe it could work?" I felt ridiculous considering such a feat. What was I thinking? I must have been feeling desperate. Not a romantic, Derek gave a short, dismissive laugh.

I, who wanted a baby but had no luck conceiving, was immersed with dozens of gals who didn't... or if they did, could not keep them. They were like a bushel of apples, all plump and red and juicy. I was like a piece of shriveled fruit set off to the side.

Their sorrow pressed upon me from all directions. Some Friday nights I dove into bed and stayed there until Monday morning. I even had the envious thought that *Everyone is going to the prom but poor me. Even if they don't like their dates, they at least have one.* Guilt rushed in: *How selfish of me!* All I could think of was Grandma's dreadful cliché, "Water, water, everywhere and not a drop to drink."

"Can't you adopt my baby?" June pleaded, at twenty-nine an old maid.

"No, take mine, it'll be smart like me!" coaxed Sue, a thirteen-year-old blonde with pigtails. She let out a rare laugh.

*****

One winter day, Carla showed up at the initiation meeting. *Why does she look so familiar?* I wondered, embarrassed at possibly recognizing someone I knew.

"It's you!" she said angrily. "You're always in my life when something bad happens!"

Oh yes, the ship. Her boyfriend. I remembered. We were college students, working the Great Lakes on the S.S. South American. Carla and I were Michigan waitresses in starched uniforms by day, and French chorus-line dancers by night. On the last big weekend of the season, Lucky, my boyfriend, and I were out on the deck off the galley where he worked. He could peel a bushel of potatoes at lightning speed while listening, his brown eyes compassionate, to my stories. It was the only place we could safely meet, out of sight of guests and crew, he being black and forbidden, although he was allowed to sing and play drums on stage with "us." Lucky also represented the black men in the Seafarer's Union in Detroit. Segregation was in full force. If we were seen together we would both lose our jobs... or worse.

We were hanging on the railing watching the engines churn the dark cold water of Lake Michigan as we pulled away from Mackinac Island. Two hundred guests were having cocktails above while the orchestra played "Love Letters in the Sand." Suddenly, along the deck raced a figure. Tommy, a busboy and Carla's boyfriend, rushed past us, leapt to the rail and dove overboard. His dive was far, clean, and deep.

"Is he coming up? Where is he?" Lucky cried out.

I didn't wait but ran to the Captain's bridge, yelling, "Tommy's tried to swim to shore! Stop the engines." I screamed again, "Stop the ship!" The captain shook his head at me and continued to back the ship away from shore out into the black waters.

The next morning Carla heard that her summer love, Tommy, had washed up dead on shore, right where we had docked.

"Now I'm losing another one I love. My baby!" Carla whispered hoarsely, glaring at me, dry eyed. She wasn't angry now. She was mourning, curled up on the main lounge sofa. I too felt helpless. For the second time, I could not help Carla.

Tangelene arrived just ahead of her mother Marguerite.

"I've come to volunteer," Marguerite announced bravely, knowing she was helping her daughter give up a baby and also parting with her own grandchild.

"Let's have lunch," she suggested to me a week later. I wanted to. My friendship would mean she had someone she didn't have to hide the secret from. She could safely talk to me. I liked her. However, we could not be friends and I could not tell her why. As my mother often said, "Honey, this hurts me more than it does you." Marguerite's husband was my husband's boss's boss on the top rung of the Department and no one could ever know I knew. I felt as though I was working as a double agent for the CIA. "I'm busy," I said with forced nonchalance, hating myself.

*****

"Let's sew some draperies, girls!"

The place was dreary, downright dismal. "Color will help!" We painted. We stitched. Our working together made a difference. The place began to look and feel lighter. It was superior to the dull group meetings. But, it did not lessen my paperwork. The hours spent writing required reports far exceeded any contact with the women. I could spend a day in the little brown office at the little beige desk filling little tan files with: "She shared with me… She projected onto me… She indicated to me…" reports no one in the whole world would ever read.

In the busy-ness of cheering up the outer environment with the girls, I wondered, *When is the next staff meeting? Hmmm, it's been a long time.* I dropped my paintbrush and walked to the executive director's door, knocked, and heard a pleasant "Come in." The opened door revealed the entire surprised staff — all of the women, all older and more experienced than I, all unmarried — in the midst of a staff meeting. Somehow they had forgotten to notify me.

"I believe you would rather be an interior designer than a social worker," the director said to me later that day.

"What a wonderful idea!" I replied. "I agree." I had been thinking along that line, myself.

Before I packed up and left the unwed world, I had a chance as an insider to get my own baby.

Mrs. Burgess, from the Peirce-Warwick Adoption Service of the Washington Home for Foundlings (Linda Cannon Burgess, 1911-2000, author of "The Art of Adoption" in 1976, placed nine hundred babies in her career, but not mine), had the "best babies in town," the *crème de la crème*. That fact was taken for granted in the inner circles of adoption in Washington. She took me aside one day at work in the borrowed office she used to interview the girls. In her friendly way, dressed in a smart navy blue suit, she had my admiration and attention.

"I can get you a special baby," she smiled. I hesitated and she continued, perhaps aware of my salary, but more I sensed because she liked me and enjoyed playing the role of matchmaker. It was February. With twinkling eyes, she asked, "How about a George Washington's Birthday Sale baby?" She mentioned eight hundred dollars. That was half what her agency charged at the time.

It wasn't about money. I saw the girls, and which agencies they were assigned to. Although all "facts" were sealed forever by rewriting nationality, education, profession and place, there was an orderly system to it all. The Catholic girls' babies were easy; they went to the Catholic agencies and were passed out to the Catholic "Thank-you-Mother-Mary" homes. The Lutheran babies went to the Lutherans. The Congressmen's daughters, State Department officials' girls, and private school young women's babies were selected by Peirce-Warwick. The "regular" girls' babies who were left over were taken from the remaining pool and included in the placements for the nearby government county agencies.

In the end, I just didn't like the idea of choosing "a better baby." It seemed prejudiced and holier-than-thou. Perhaps my place in society was to be proud to have come from common stock. I was second generation Swedish/German. In God's eyes, I knew everyone was equal and I felt exactly as God did. The county agency was perfectly fine.

I packed. I left. As though a color wheel was turning, my career spun from caring for sad girls to designing cheerful settings. I was already decorating homes for free for couples at church and when the satisfied recipients wanted more, my missionary zeal for free hand-outs waned. I observed how the professionals presented their bids using tiny two-by-two-inch samples of paint and fabrics. I thought, *How can those CEOs and office managers choose from such small pieces?*

I gave my presentations using large swatches of fabrics for upholstery and window treatments and eight-by-ten-inch paint samples. I won bids. Our contract required that ten percent of their budget would be spent on art. I was heady with purchasing and delegating. My artist friends were in heaven… Gwendolyn's metal wall sculpture, Muriel's weaving, and Sally's oil painting were installed. I was able to squeeze in Fred's bronze. I did not take a cut.

It was a large right-angle corner in a reception area in an office building on K Street Northwest that stumped me. I had to have *something* in a specific size and color. It was quite a trek to several artists' studios in Alexandria and Georgetown. Nothing was right and all were above budget. There was only one solution. I had a giant canvas stretched (six-by-eight feet), set it up in my dining room, mixed paint to the exact color of the fabrics and carpeting, and painted a scene of modern sharp-edged hills.

"How on earth did you find such a perfect painting?" the boss asked. "Amazing! it matches the room! In fact, it matches everything!"

It was a joy to be where I felt I belonged. I stopped sleeping my weekends away.

This work I could carry on and still adopt a child.

Amy arrived at the same time my three girlfriends at church gave birth. While they were wearing maternity clothes and feeling heavy, I painted a Noah's Ark mural on our baby's room wall. We four gals had babies together. And baby showers.

The check was solemnly written. The sound of pen on paper, echoing into the future, made the commitment: "Pay to the order of Fairfax County in the amount of Ten Dollars."

Ten dollars for a baby even in 1964 was an unforgettable price. At the county animal shelter a cat cost five dollars and a dog seven.

Two years later we adopted Adam. Another ten dollars well spent. Joy!

*****

And now the newspaper kept slamming against our door each morning, broadcasting the exciting lives of others. It was soon after that I saw our Asian-figure-selves in the bedroom. The ether was stirred. I was feeling restless; I had made some money decorating and I wanted to splurge.

My darling ten-dollar baby... Adam at my father's mobile home sales in Jackson, Michigan, Christmas 1968.

In my expansive enthusiasm, I purchased Arthur Frommer's "Europe on Five Dollars a Day" and booked us on a cruise ship to France, the S.S. Holland American.

"Honey, I'm treating us to Europe!" I said, hugging Derek. "And if we're very careful, the money can last us a month." I was hoping he would be elated because I was paying for the entire trip, and taking a ship over, especially to please him, so he could read a week of paperbacks in a rolling deck chair. I had had enough of ships at sea but he had not. Derek had paddled a rowboat as a kid and only rented a sailboat in college, so it was his turn.

I was spending the entire amount I'd earned doing an interior design job in Bethesda, Maryland. My Dad said, "You're spending two thousand dollars on a vacation? You should save it. You've always been so careful before." And my quick defense was, "My life is getting squashed. I want to do this."

Life does not wait to measure out our blessings and our tests; they come unbeckoned. Good or bad things can pile up instead of being spread out evenly and peacefully.

* * * * *

There was a shift. The universe had heard my desire for a more involving life. Within a month Derek, who was a speech writer at the Agriculture Department, was offered an assignment in Tokyo to help set up and promote an American grocery store. The Japanese could now experience the thrill of buying peanut butter and standing in a check-out line. It was 1967.

My dream of doing *something* was fast coming true. We'd be connected to the State Department via the American Embassy. That sounded absolutely exotic! But, before his job offer, a mere week earlier, I had already booked that cruise ship. I had no idea the Tokyo assignment was going to happen, of course, so off we sailed. We would do it all. We would see Paris, Rome, and Pompeii, return home to pick up the children, who would stay with the two sets of Michigan grandparents while we were away, and then fly all four of us on to Tokyo.

* * * * *

To add to the fun, I was designing my own outfits to wear to Europe. My dreamed-up wardrobe would now get to do double service! I would wear my creations in Paris and then in Tokyo! To my artistic soul, fashion was art! Fashion was theater! Paris and Tokyo! Goodbye, reading-about-other-people's lives.

I stopped the paper, watched the food bill, and carefully shopped. "I love you, dear K-Mart!" There were high, white shiny boots in one aisle and a white vinyl hat in another. Perfect. Fifteen dollars total. Just as I had drawn cut-out clothes for my homemade paper dolls, I was now making sketches for real dresses I could wear on the sidewalks of *foreign cities*. Shivers of delight! I was coming alive! No smudged-ink piping or brown-crayoned stitches. No faded construction paper and gray cardboard. They would be my designs in fabric. Simple and short. I had heard that in Paris the hemlines were worn shockingly far above the knee.

My seamstress neighborhood friend studied the dress sketches of my two simple and extremely short dresses. "I can do that," she mused, "for five dollars each."

"Do I look cosmopolitan and Paris-y?" I asked, turning as she checked a hem.

Mumbling through the straight pins in her mouth, "Don't know. Not been there. But, you sure don't look like Annandale."

— Paris —

The flirting French waiter in the warm September sun increased the *café au lait*'s flavor from delicious to superb. Having said goodbye to Derek until dinner, I could do my own Paris thing. But what? September issues of Vogue were stacked on the sidewalk at the newsstand. Most of the words from college French class were eluding me, so a magazine with more photos than copy was appealing. Yves Saint Laurent's ad on page twenty-seven featured a thin and haughty model in an outlandishly extravagant outfit. *Oh, Mr. Laurent*, I noted, *We're both thirty-one years old and look what you are doing with your life! Am I getting anywhere at all with mine?* I wondered. At the bottom of the page I noted an address. *Maybe I can find his place!*

I stopped a lady with a hesitant, "Pardon me, er, *moi*," and pantomimed my question by pointing at the address and then giving her my blankest look. She understood and graciously pointed with her gloved hand to the north. At the end of a long block I repeated my pantomimed question, stopping a gentleman dressed like a model himself. He quietly read the address and gestured ahead, keeping his look noncommittal as he took in my shiny white vinyl boots and matching hat.

My plastic boots were getting more and more scuffed the further I walked, but the closer I got, the more refined became my enthusiasm. I slowed down when I approached the daunting entrance, with no idea what I planned to do. All I was sure of was the correct words to say should be *merci beaucoup*.

I gingerly stepped inside and a tall, dark beauty, in flawless make-up, quickly looked me over, and then her beautiful lips, outlined in brilliant fuchsia, formed the words, "The press?" I smiled awkwardly, much too off-guard to say my *merci*, and followed her. I found myself seated in a tiny gold chair in the front row of a long runway surrounded by stunning women, dressed like the society ladies in the wrinkled magazine I clutched.

It was the height of the fall fashion shows.

Oh, Mother! was my first thought. I had read that dying soldiers called for their mothers on the battlefield. I longed to cry out to mine because I too was dying: of shock and excitement. I wanted to shout to the woman who adored fashion more than I and had taught me to love clothes, now back in Michigan in a mobile home with Dad, babysitting my children so I could be here, of all places. *I cannot believe this is happening! Mother, you should be here, not me!*

It was as though I had received a personal, embossed invitation and knew exactly what time to arrive. I was on time. I was spinning! I was like a French tourist who had decided to walk by the White House out of curiosity and suddenly was ushered inside to sit in the Blue Room and attend a coveted press conference at the exact moment the President took the mike.

Each day that week I donned my K-Mart Special and visited the Paris fashion houses for the Fall Showings: Emanuel Ungaro, Hubert de Givenchy and Christian Dior. When Derek heard the shocking fact that the models did not wear bras, unheard of yet in the rest of the civilized world, he decided to join me on the last day. I mumbled quietly, "The Press" and this time added, *"Mon assistant,"* nodding toward Derek.

— Tokyo —

The twenty-hour flight to Japan went on as one very long, dark evening. We went from night into night. When Amy and Adam weren't chasing each other up and down the aisle, they were sitting on laps and being cute for the other passengers. At ages one and three, our adopted towheads didn't look a drop like us. We could enjoy their adorability, too, without conceit. They stayed awake and played all the way. I kept wondering if the vision on the bed of Derek and me looking Chinese had been about Japan? Was it an omen? I believed I would know as soon as I stepped off the plane. I stood at the top of the metal steps and my intuition told me instantly the vision had not been of Japan. Disappointed, I picked up Adam, smoothing my sticky yellow vinyl skirt (what a mess!) and started down the steep steps to the tarmac below. Derek carried Amy, who had finally fallen asleep.

On the far side of the runway stood a formally dressed couple, waving. "You aren't the Browns, are you?" they asked cautiously, as they looked hopefully past us at the few passengers still descending.

"Yes, we are," said Derek, quickly deploying his professional smile and shooting out a hand.

"We're here, sent by the attaché, and we will take you to your temporary quarters," Mr. Casey announced, looking a bit wary. He reached for one of our bags.

Carolyn, his wife, was a prettily coifed study in detail, with her eyebrows and rouge applied like you might paint a doll's face. Her voice was the surprise, not unlike a wind-up toy, but with a mechanical difference: she spoke with the sweetest Southern accent you could ever stand to hear. "Now, Sharon, y'all goin' to come with me *right now*. We'll pick up the attache's wife, Mrs. Rupert, and Mary Sell from our agriculture group, and have a little lunch." She saw my dismay and I saw her hesitation, "You look just fine the way you are," she said, eyeing my skirt.

"And Mr. Brown will watch the children, won't you... is it Derek?" She smiled more primly and did a stiff curtsy, the movement resembling a rigid iron gate, coated with sugar instead of rust.

"It's just a little thing we do with someone new, take them to lunch. We want to learn all about you," Carolyn continued, her voice winding down.

From movies I had seen, this invitation to lunch looked to be more like an arrest, followed by questioning.

Sleep deprivation under bright lights. It was noon. *Isn't it last night or is it tomorrow night?* I was a captured zombie after twenty hours of travel, too dazed to be cautious.

"No, I've never played bridge. I'm sorry. I'm afraid I don't have the desire."

"Do I give formal dinner parties? How formal? Did I ship over my best china and sterling? What sterling!"

"Prejudiced? Me? Well, I certainly try not to be. I went to Howard University partly to experience being in a minority. Where? Oh, in D.C., a Negro school you know."

"A maid? I've never had one. Really! I have to get a live-in maid?"

I wasn't feeling the warmth of my new circle of girlfriends. Maybe I was chilly from no sleep. Mrs. Rupert's eyes were half closed, her mouth set in a firm horizontal in her oval face. It got quiet. Somehow, I don't think I should have skipped that "Preparation for Embassy Duty" invitation sent from the State Department. I had been in Europe.

"Tomorrow there will be a women's tea at the Embassy. Two o'clock sharp," Carolyn chirped as she dropped me off. "Goodbye, y'all." She waved.

"Fine." I staggered away, wanting sleep and a clear head. A clean head. A shower and a brain.

* * * * *

"Derek, do you think this will look good for the tea?" I asked my distracted husband, who was tensing his neck as he straightened his tie. No answer. Of course, why should he pay attention to fashion? That was my territory, the look and length of things. The mirror reflected a black-and-white herringbone dress, four inches above the knee, and opaque white hose with my black leather pumps. Perfect and smart and quite French-y, I thought. I still felt uneasy about yesterday's lunch with Carolyn and the ladies, but dressing for this tea was a cinch. Especially after my fashion success in Paris.

The large drawing room of the American Embassy was filled with conservatively dressed women. If I had had my camera, snapped a photo, and later showed it to a friend, she would have said, "Oh, when was this? 1957?" I had stepped back in time as far as fashion went. Their skirts were mid-calf, a good decade behind the times. Amazed but confident, I got into the receiving line to meet the Ambassador's wife, Mrs. Johnson.

The line was long. As each woman shook her hand ahead of me, I heard Mrs. Johnson say, again and again, "Welcome! So nice to have you in Tokyo." "Welcome, so nice to have you in Tokyo." There was the same soft and even-toned message for each woman. When I finally came and stood before her, Mrs. Johnson looked me in the eye, not looking down nor to either side, and without a smile said, "Lengthen that skirt." I walked on in dismay, while she continued her steady drone to the ladies behind me. "Welcome! So nice to have you in Tokyo." "Welcome, so nice to have you in Tokyo."

There was no tea and cookies for me. I was swiftly ushered to the door. I made a solitary exit from the refined gathering.

The next day, Derek came home considerably annoyed. "I was told by the Ag attaché himself," he stressed. "You are to lower your dress hems. Cover yourself up! Ankle length."

Ankle length! Didn't the men have better business to attend to, such as diplomatic affairs between the Japanese and the United States? They were busy attending to affairs all right, I learned later: geisha ones. The Embassy itself arranged all-night evenings for the American men. Some participated.

I scoured the Ginza for dresses in my size. There were thousands of smart dresses in "one size fits all." "All" meant a size five or smaller.

* * * * * *

"Do you sell sewing machines?" I asked the sergeant at the Yokohama P.X. "And easy-to-sew patterns? Yes, a simple maternity pattern will

Short Skirts – High Manners

fit the occasion just fine. Am I pregnant? No! Just expecting trouble if I don't get some new dresses, quick!"

My new machine whirred. I fumed. Not only did I have to dress down, but also I was not allowed to work. I had left behind interior design jobs back in Washington, D.C., to be here. Why won't they let us Embassy wives be productive? They will only allow little busy things: flower arranging and *sumi* painting, which are wonderful as a side dish but not a main course. *Do they think we're dumb?* Everyone is acting like the ugly Americans that the world seems to think we are. My thoughts rattled along with the sewing machine.

After the war, in our occupation of Japan, they agreed as penalty for their part in WWII, to give us the Sanno Hotel in a prize location in Tokyo. We have never given it back. I understand that was an agreement but it seemed sad, knowing Japanese friends later, as I did, and it all seemed so unfair. That is war. *What if the Japanese had won the war, had taken over the Shoreham Hotel in D.C. in 1946 and twenty years later still kept it?* It is crazy! *And this dress is going to be ugly!* There are five hundred American families still "occupying" Tokyo right now as I sit here sewing! But, it is true, I am pretty new at this and not fully informed. Just frustrated.

One week, the wives were asked to go out to Atsugi Naval Air Base and visit the boys flown in from Vietnam, fresh off the battlefield. I asked, "Why?"

I was uncomfortable; fearful. *What could I possibly do or say to men my age with no arms or legs? Or eyes!* I was told, "They miss seeing American women. Just go. Sit by their beds, hold their hands. Speak English. Just be there."

I expected to meet many wives at the train station for the day's trip to the base. Two of us showed up for that cold, unheated train ride. *Where were the four hundred and ninety-eight others? The wives of State Department career men must be numb… or have become jaded. Perhaps they acquiesced after some time, and settled into their role. Was I just a rebel? If this was Derek's career and not just one assignment, I could very possibly become like the women I am seeing here. They entertain themselves with hairdresser visits, lunches, shopping, flower arranging, beauty treatments and massages, jaunts to Hong Kong or spas across Japan and, of course, the dinners they are required to attend, enduring their husbands slipping off with geishas.*

This is not an easy assignment, I observed.

Derek and I were ordered to attend State Department dinners or cocktail parties a minimum of five nights a week. Since part-time or evening baby sitters didn't exist in Japan, all couples with children had no choice but to hire a maid. We went through live-in maids like flour goes through a sieve. Number Two taught Amy how to eat Cheerios with chopsticks. Number Three taught Adam his first words: *domo* and *dozo*, as he bowed dutifully from his high chair.

Number Six quit in the middle of our first real dinner party for Carolyn and the Agriculture gang. We had attended five dinners in ten days, each one the same: ham and scalloped potatoes, a Jell-O fruit salad, and pound cake with strawberries, all from the Yokohama P.X., served on fine china, with white linen napkins, cut-glass serving dishes, and heavy sterling flatware. Each couple in the group served this same monotonous menu with the same monotonous smiles and seemingly with no memory of us having all eaten it together just the night before last! Were they competing to see who could bake the best canned ham, purchased from the same P.X. freezer? Or were they actually testing for memory loss?

It came our turn to have the group to our place. I planned the menu in my new brown sack-dress with the attitude of "Do as the Romans Do When Cornered." I hoped my guests would have as much fun as I was having in preparing for the dinner. The tiny unheated shop down the street sold simple wooden chopsticks, exquisite blue and white rice bowls, and heavy hand-thrown sake cups. Another tiny stall-shop sold cotton fabric for yukatas in delightful Japanese designs. I sent Number Six to shop for sukiyaki ingredients. She cooked and I sewed dinner napkins and a tablecloth and set the buffet table with flowers in a vase... but not an exquisite flower arrangement like some of the women were learning. I never did manage that. It was all quite refreshing! For a reason I could not decipher, Number Six quit in the middle of preparing dinner. I grabbed her mama-san apron, tossed down an extra shot of hot sake, and served our guests myself. *"Watashitachi no ie ni yōkoso,"* I said and bowed.

Amy-chan visits Kyoto! Japan, Spring 1968.

The group was very quiet. Perhaps they did not know what to say. A few asked for a fork and as the evening meandered, the sake helped a lot. They kindly invited us to their next ham dinner.

Good fortune came our way when we were asked to meet "a fellow from some puppet show" at the airport. Derek and I greeted

Bob McGrath, a handsome man our age who played with puppets. *Why not?* I thought, *Whoever he is.* I took the opportunity to ask him if I could throw a small dinner party for him. He graciously agreed. It was Japanese style: the chopsticks, the same rice bowls and sake cups, and with the help of Number Seven, another sumptuous *sukiyaki* dinner. Sesame Street was about to premier on television that fall of 1969 back in the States. None of us had heard of it. During his stay I saw Bob with a beautiful Japanese movie star out and about in Tokyo. Later on, I saw him for years on television.

I have to admit, life was cheering up. At one Embassy breakfast, I was in the presence of our latest astronaut and knew I should go and shake his hand. But he was surrounded by men and I was not enthusiastic about cars, machines and space in those days. Regrettably, I stayed at my place and missed shaking his hand. He was nice looking is all I recall.

One evening at the grandest hotel in Tokyo, after we had dined with a generous diplomat, I passed through the lobby seeking the ladies' room. Twiggy was the fashion news all over the world and there she was — I recognized her. She stood, giggling with her girlfriends, skinny as paper, making me feel fat. She was friendly, so I asked her for her autograph.

At a luncheon a month later, I noticed Mrs. Johnson, the Ambassador's wife, was wearing opaque white hose, just like the ones I had introduced everyone to at that disastrous first reception. It was whispered that she had found nurses' hosiery at the P.X. Maybe the ice was melting. *Weren't her hems slightly shorter?*

Then I got the call. The Embassy was giving a fashion show for all of the Japanese princesses and for the women of the other Tokyo embassies from around the world. "Would you like to be in charge?" the Deputy Chief of Mission asked me. She was extremely nice and I was flattered.

I recalled Paris. "Oh yes, I would love that!" I couldn't wait to begin. "We'll need giant revolving spotlights." Yves Saint Laurent had flooded his models in colored lights. A ramp was built in the main room of the Embassy. And did I dare? "We must have a special kimono sewn. Short, above the knee."

The press came. There was a photo in a Japanese fashion magazine. Some young American woman had modeled a mini-kimono, it was reported.

*****

We were moved to the fast lane. The special invitation of the Ambassador to the horse races produced new friends from the Swedish and English business world. To woo Ingrid I said, "I am Swedish, too." To Eleanor, I bragged, "I have a pen pal in England." We had a grand time mixing our lives.

One memory of triumph was the intimate little lunch I enjoyed with Mrs. Johnson and her best friend, the Deputy of Missions, at the close of Derek's assignment. We three laughed at our saga, and how serious we had been. War had been avoided, due to fashionable diplomatic events.

Derek and I packed up our chopsticks and rice bowls, our wood block prints and *yukatas*, and returned home with a love for *tonkatsu* (pork chops) and shrimp *tempura*. We left behind Number Nine, waving us goodbye.

Sayōnara shin'ainaru yūjin. (Farewell, my dear friends).

Development

Once something becomes important to you, you can think back and recall exactly the moment you laid eyes on it. That wild monkey-fur cape at the flea market in Rome, the antique French clock at the old man's farmhouse in Michigan, the poor imitation of a famous felt doll in Mexico City; and my Japanese camera.

The camera rests on the scale, weighing in at three and a half pounds, nearing its fortieth birthday.

It stayed with me when everyone else left. It's been lost and found, broken and fixed, stolen and retrieved, fought over and won. But always my faithful friend. We can't part now. It's taken us decades together to find our focus.

There is hardly a person I have met, known or unknown, whose image hasn't appeared through its lens. "Stop! Smile! Hold still!"

I was living in Tokyo with my husband and two children. Derek's embassy job was to help set up an American grocery store, so the Japanese could experience standing in a checkout line, unknown in Japan in the sixties. I waited until the end of our year there before buying what I most wanted to take back: a camera. It was as though I had eaten nearly all of the cake without frosting and decided to let myself have an extra dollop of whipped cream with the last piece. A typical cab driver, usually silent and expressionless, let me out at my memorized destination... *koko de tomatte kudasai*. A gentleman with gleaming black hair, dressed in black perhaps to match his cameras, bowed as I entered his Ginza camera shop. I returned the bow and smiled, hoping my friendliness would make up for the fact that I was another American who couldn't speak Japanese. In addition to a camera, I especially wanted a telephoto lens, to bring distant subjects into close range. I pointed into a glass case of neatly lined up lenses and then demonstrated my wish by walking to the front of the shop and motioning across to the far side of the street. He nodded so many times I felt sure he understood.

Just as I had made myself wait until Derek's assignment was nearly over before getting a new camera, I also decided I didn't really need to have what I thought was the best, a Nikon. Depression-consciousness clung to me like a silk under-slip. A Nikormat would do because the lenses were almost the same, I convinced myself. Time later proved they were the same, but not after believing for countless years that I didn't own the best.

Returning to Meguro Eki, the closest train station to our house, I realized my communication skills through pantomime had failed. By mistake, I had been sold a short telephoto lens, mainly suited for tight portraits or perhaps sleuthing. But none of this dented my joy at owning a new camera.

The next morning, I left Adam, aged one, and Amy, three, in the care of our live-in maid and went down the street with a fresh roll of film. Here was a chance to create something I was in charge of. The maid cleaned the clothes, the house, and the children. The maid or a restaurant or an embassy prepared the food. A taxi driver did the driving. I was as useless as every other Embassy wife who wasn't allowed to work. "Going bananas" is a good term for rinsing out your own hosiery, cleaning contact lenses, doing a little *sumi* painting and a bit of flower arranging as one's purpose in life. Standing on the sidelines, smiling dutifully, saying nothing of any significance, and showing up for little teas and endless on-demand dinners added to the condition. At the same time, we kept busy looking the other way while the late-night geishas entertained our missing husbands.

So, my camera was about to perform a mental health act. At least I had been adamant about living "on the economy," which meant we were out in a Japanese neighborhood and not in the enclosed American compound.

Like most early spring days this one was cold, gray and damp. No matter the weather, my camera was already elevating my spirit.

I was off to photograph life around me, where I couldn't understand a word anyone said. Many homes had shoji-screened walls and tiny raked stone gardens behind bamboo fences. I poked my new lens through a gap and was surprised to see an honorable gentleman sitting peacefully on a mat, teacup poised, while incense curled lazily toward the gray Tokyo sky. I memorized the scene and decided not to take the picture. It seemed unfair to invade his privacy.

A week later I took a cab alone into the countryside, camera in hand, but not to shoot scenery. Derek and I had been to a handsome couple's home for dinner the night before. They fit perfectly into their setting in their stylish dress and elegant furnishings. They had filled their home with treasures from their State Department tours and already, in their mid-thirties, seemed prepared to open their own Museum of Asian Art. I most admired the centuries-old tombstones that lined one edge of an antique Korean carpet spread below a breathtaking Chinese tapestry. They had removed the tombstones from a nearby cemetery. When we took our after-dinner wine, petits fours and demitasse coffee in their formal living room, I was convinced I was lounging in the Metropolitan Museum of Art and coveted a little of that atmosphere for my own living room back in the States. As impeccably polite hosts, they graciously drew me a map, along with directions in Japanese, so I might find one or two tombstones for myself.

The very long and expensive cab ride into the country was worth it. I traveled through a *sumi* painting; the taxi and I on the winding road were the black brush strokes, the mist the white rice paper. But the beauty of the trip did not compare to the eerie sacredness of the centuries-old cemetery. I was alone in a hushed outdoor cathedral. A teahouse sat on the edge of a stream nearby, empty but warmly inviting, as though waiting for ghosts to come and take tea. One withered old man appeared out of the fog and wandered up and down the dirt paths with his walking stick, paying no attention to me. It would have been easy to carry off a free treasure.

The cab driver had agreed to wait an hour. I took my time to study the stones with their weathered indentations, some covered in moss and many too ancient to decipher any markings at all. I realized these grave sites were tended far more carefully than my grandparents' plots in Michigan. As I walked along the path, I noticed each stone was exquisite in its own way. It was hard to decide. I finally selected a tall narrow one with perfect proportions, seemingly hundreds of years old, and stood before it.

Suddenly, grief engulfed me, surprised me. Not for the cremated soul, but for myself who would dare do this. I knew I could not remove even a pebble. What if they were my family? They felt like my family. Flowers were growing, more flowers were placed in jars, sticks of incense were burning. Someone must have just lit them. A soft breeze blew that seemed to permeate the place with centuries of love and the air was heavy with the vibrations of prayer. I opened my camera case and after a few reverent shots I walked quietly back to the waiting cab.

*****

Wherever I went, I took both camera and purse. Derek and I and our favorite couple, the Rosenblums, had just left a dining hot spot in the Ginza and all of us were guessing at the cause of the commotion in the middle of an intersection.

"Let me try something," I said. "This worked once on my windowsill on a rainy night when I was twelve." Without a tripod, I had to depend on steady footing and no breath. I pointed into the dark and pushed the shutter release button, keeping it open to the count of ten. Would the camera offer an answer? We were all surprised a few days later to see the resulting snapshot of a ceremony with candles and incense and kneeling Buddhist monks blessing the street-repair project.

Just before we returned to the States, our social obligations intensified. Two embassy girlfriends invited me to join them. "Come shopping!" they said. "It will be a wild Hong Kong weekend!" It was my only chance to see that exotic city, and for the bargain price of sixty dollars in airfare. But my smiling daughter Amy looked at me and held up four fingers. "How can I leave her on her birthday?" I thought. I

Development

considered the gifts I could buy her. I imagined a breeze off the South China Sea ruffling a new red quilted jacket. And snakeskin shoes with rhinestones kicked up their heels in my mind.

I have a photo I took from that weekend in1968. It shows Amy-chan with her blonde hair and pink cake, little embassy Jane with her red curls and flowered dress, petite Yoko and her sister Ayano from the neighborhood playground with their straight black hair and tiny slippers. All cautiously smiling. Happy Birthday, Dear Amy, ahh so, *Otanjōbiomedetōgozaimasu*. (Happy Birthday).

* * * * *

Home from Japan, I went beyond birthday and holiday shots. I shot the golden in-between days. Within the year I had a biological surprise; baby Zandy arrived to join our adopted Amy and Adam, so I posed the three together, laid myself flat on the carpet, and tried for floor-level angles. I wanted to shoot movement so I coached gently, "See if you can jump higher!" I liked dirty faces, windblown hair, even mud and grime and tears. Nothing was headier than the darkroom magic at Montgomery College, watching the children's eyes appear out of the developing solution, making them darker or softer. I would literally jump with joy myself.

The photo instructor emphasized, "Keep your film in the refrigerator." If that was good, why not store the entire camera there? I did that and it stopped working. "It's like sitting it out in the rain," was the repairman's scowling report. It appears I tried too hard, but how can one always know? Well-meant intentions are not necessarily wise ones. A well-meaning plan to marry the right person did not make it right, either.

* * * * *

At the same time I was practicing photography, I was developing my skill as a builder-contractor on our own house in Fairfax. I hired and then photographed every carpenter, roofer, plumber and drywall man. I shot Derek hammering endlessly on the seventy-foot deck through every step of the nine-month project. Sixty-eight pilings were driven into the flood plain to place the house up and out of the, well…

mud. It seems land is cheaper if it unexpectedly goes under water every once in a while.

We transplanted bamboo. On wet days, we could almost grow rice. The scene was set for peace and tranquility. But as soon as we moved our collection of stuff, the kids, cat, dog, old farm trailer, and cars to the new house we started on a slow descent toward a divorce. I'd heard that often building a house is a last-ditch effort to save a marriage, the final sign before a split. In the meantime, we built shelves, painted rooms and went to parties.

* * * * *

"Would I be gauche," I asked, "If I took my camera?"

"Oh, please don't," sighed Derek. We were headed out to Middleburg to Senator John Warner's farm, where he and his new wife Elizabeth Taylor lived. More than once, my next-door neighbor, an avid political volunteer, said, "Oh, Elizabeth was here for dinner last night. I meant to invite you." She always told me the morning after. But, when she gave me the tip that we could go to a fundraiser for only thirty-five dollars a couple, I was delighted and instantly overflowed with forgiveness. I didn't even care that they were all Republicans. The first movie I recall seeing was Lassie Come Home starring Ms. Taylor in 1943. I cried for the dog. I cried for her. She was so beautiful and just a few years older than I. I felt we had almost grown up together, and now I was going to her home for a picnic. Over the years, the press made her younger and younger. In time, she got younger than me! You can do that when you are a movie star.

A small group dressed for a barbecue was milling around that humid summer evening, waiting for Elizabeth to come out on the porch to give a little speech for John. I cared much more about seeing her than hearing the political talk and wondered if the others, in all their studied casualness, weren't really there for the same reason.

In such a small group, I felt conspicuous with my large camera in its brown leather case, almost the size of my purse, until I spied two men in sport shirts and Bermuda shorts close up by the back deck. They had brought cameras, too! So, it seemed like a natural thing to go up and join them; to be one of the boys. We three clicked a few clicks at the Warners and then headed for the hot dogs. Published a few days later were photos remarkably similar to mine. One in Time. One in Newsweek. The men hadn't looked like reporters to me. In the pictures, Elizabeth's beauty and violet eyes sang out like the movie star she was. In person, she had seemed as regular looking as any other attractive woman. So that's what photogenic means, I realized.

A year later, 1978, Derek and I were deeply immersed in bitter chaos. Like most family splits, it was awful. I gave up rights to his retirement benefits. To keep the house, I had to buy him out, which took forever. But when it came down to the very last little thing I was to fork over, my camera, I felt pure rage. *What?! He's never taken a picture in his life!* All I really wanted was my children, number one. And my camera, for Heaven's sake. This was one of the (too few) times I was adamant with my lawyer. "Absolutely not!" I said and I meant it. She proved to be far better at protecting cameras than protecting children.

I naturally stopped taking photos of Derek. He took the boys against my will when they each turned twelve. That was also the age when Amy was diagnosed with schizophrenia and needed hospital care. I missed most of their birthdays and holidays from then on. I might have snapped their closed doors, empty beds and silent rooms. I didn't. I began to photograph strangers.

From a safe distance, I shot a bony couple walking hand-and-hand past my house, the black man with a huge limp who trekked back and forth endlessly on the edge of Route 236 to the Seven-Eleven, the flagmen on the road, children in the doctor's waiting room, and new immigrants waiting at the bus stop.

A few years after the divorce, a summer night in Fairfax in 1984, I was heart-broken to realize that my camera was missing. It wasn't on its shelf. But, the trail was still hot. Elliott, my former lover, who had become simply my crazy artist, poet, writer and drugged friend, had just been over for dinner to give me feedback on my latest sculpture and discuss, as usual, the end of mankind and his money-making scheme to send other people's cremated remains to the moon.

It was late and I didn't have time to waste. A lot of his 'work' seemed to happen in the middle of very dark nights.

I flew out the door to my pickup and sped around the Capital Beltway to Silver Spring, knowing every minute counted if I was to save my camera. Up around the side of his father's house ran the driveway and in the back were all the family cars. I parked and barged in without knocking. Elliot lay in his narrow cot in the basement with his dog and stacks of poetry notebooks. Beside him, on the floor, was my camera and even my three precious lenses.

"How could you?" I hissed. He looked sweet, guilty, and very drunk. He rolled over and groaned, "Goodnight." I grabbed my camera and lenses and scrambled up the wooden stairs.

A day later Elliott was regretting his personal theft. "I'm sorry, Honey." He joked, "I told you I was bad for you." He had built shelves for my clay studio, held hands with me in the movies, read me his poetry, made me his guest at a soup kitchen, and was kind to Zandy. I remembered all of that and more. Yet, my camera and I had to move on, winding the film forward.

* * * * *

With my camera in its twenty-fifth year and me in my fifties, I made a new friend from D.C. Doraleen made a concerted effort to be elegant and sophisticated. She was a fellow artist, a painter, who played the role of an aristocrat. Her past was humble, but she fought hard to rise above it. As we planned a trip together to Santa Fe, N.M., she pointed to my camera and said, "You should leave that old thing at home. When you need to take a picture, you can use mine." Her camera was new, shiny, expensive and lightweight — just like her. I considered it. I wanted to keep her friendship, and I knew that depended on agreeing with her.

Doraleen made her wishes known with a refined and genteel smile: "Don't carry coffee on the plane; don't joke with strangers; it's embarrassing to be seen with you in those garish cowboy boots." And now I was supposed to leave at home the one thing that added so much joy to my travels? By then I was taking pictures of waitresses and shop girls and the crafts persons selling their wares to tourists. I was even snapping pictures of the tourists! I would return home, get the film developed, and mail the photos back to them. What my friend was asking me to do didn't make sense.

I was torn. But not for long. I decided to keep my camera and give up my friend.

*****

Losing my camera was unthinkable. I once left it on the floor of a Los Angeles Starbucks. When I realized my mistake, I raced back, retracing the blocks with my heart pounding, as though I had forgotten and left my child in the bathtub and gone off to the grocery. "Did you see a camera?" I nearly yelled at the pudgy cheerful teenager behind the espresso machine. "Is this it?" He reached under the counter and came up swinging it nonchalantly as though it were weightless and unbreakable. "It looked like a worthless old Polaroid to me," he added. Thank you, God, for clueless youth.

*****

With time — and experiences with men like Elliott — I grew single. Singleness overrode the old married me, and eventually my divorced self. It was as though I had always been alone.

I never saw the same person twice in a natural run-into way. I bought my groceries at the Giant three miles from my house for twenty years and only once saw a person I knew. The only people I ever saw twice were the gals at the bank, the gas station men, the grocery store clerks and the 7-11 cashiers.

I saw Fairfax County go from dull lily-white to a marvelous mixture of people from all over the world. I always carried my camera. "May I? Smile! May I have your address? I'll mail you your photo." Like the pizza guy, sometimes I delivered. If they lived near my neighborhood or where I shopped, I had the fun of giving them their pictures in person. I wasn't aware of what made me do this at first. I just knew it made me happy. I was practicing an art and I didn't have to worry about promoting or selling it. I just gave it away and everyone was happy. There would be no chance later to crop or to improve the lighting. I had one quick chance to get it right. Art on the run.

Secretly, I wanted my pictures to journey around the world. It was the idea of expansion — left over from my yearnings to be a missionary when I was in high school. A Methodist missionary in a foreign land. It was always those deep, mysterious jungles of Africa that the visiting missionaries spoke of in the side lounge in the First Methodist Church in Alma. But now, right in my backyard, I could photograph exotic strangers and make them a part of my life. Some loved it. It pleased them, and made me happy. Strangers would smile and take home this silent gift to be tacked to a wall, or on their refrigerator, or slipped in a book. Here or, even better, in distant lands.

Over the years, I have shot and then mailed hundreds of photos. I have heard back from three of these strangers: a couple I met on Mount Hood, who were hiking three thousand miles from South America to Alaska; an elegant woman with her elderly mother, having cocktails in the Algonquin hotel; and a couple from Brazil who were also tourists in Times Square and invited me to get pizza with them before the theater. This would seem to show that New Yorkers, Brazilians and hikers are grateful people.

But, I realize I don't do it for thanks or I would have stopped years ago. Sometimes it is confusing to keep track of who is who, with a roll of film filled with strangers and addresses scribbled down in all sorts of places so I could match them up when I returned home.

One time in New York City I had some spiffy photos of a bus driver and a door man. One man was black, the other white. My notes were so poor I couldn't tell whose address was whose. I was so obsessed that I sent them both one of each, so at least one of their photos was of them and they could always wonder who the other fellow was.

* * * * *

I did have a couple of shots in the dark, or false hopes, that were exposed but not developed. A subject changes slowly and, like life, its light brightens and dims, dims and brightens. In 1987 there was an exquisite stolen hour when I got my children together at Olan Mills

Development

Studio. Adam, twenty-one, looked vacant-eyed like he may have had no sleep or a little pot; Amy, twenty-three, was bursting with joy from seeing her brothers on her visit home from the mental hospital. Zandy was in high school and growing bushy eyebrows. I am grinning like a mama bear who had finally found her lost cubs wandering in the woods.

After three decades with family photo shoots diminishing, I turned closer and closer to those around me. And a strange thing started to happen. I began to love the people in the photos. I feared I began to love them too much for the casual connection. One afternoon I drove by a young boy from El Salvador holding up a "Slow" sign for the road crew on Prosperity Avenue. He must have a mother somewhere, I thought. Like many of the young Latino men I had talked to, I suspected that he had also left home much too young, came to work in the United States and faithfully made his weekly trip to the 7-11 or Shopper's Food Warehouse to buy a money order and mail it back to his family. I felt I knew exactly what his mother might love to have. I pulled over to the side of the road, took his photo, got her address, and told him in my poor Spanish, "Por favor... I will send photo home. *Enviaré su foto a casa de su madre en El Salvadore.*"

* * * * *

I loved Mr. Mindrimi, so shy and sad, standing behind the glass partition to take my bank deposit. He was right out of a disastrously glum Russian novel. He agreed reluctantly to my "just one picture" as he stood at the copy machine. Neither he nor I was aware until it was processed that there was a poster of a Russian toy on the wall of Riggs bank behind him. Weeks later, he said, with a now warmer but still reticent smile, "Thank you. My parents in Russia loved my photo." It wasn't From Russia with Love, it was To Russia with Love. I couldn't have been happier if my Grandma Roslund, with her Swedish accent, had come down from Heaven and said, "Oh, ya did such a nice ting for the old country." At age nineteen she had emigrated from Sweden and never saw her mother again. She often sent back letters with a photo tucked in to warm her mother's broken heart.

Some photos I made doubles of to keep as mementos:

"Look! This one could be used in a detective story," I coaxed the entire bank staff to stand outside for a group picture, realizing later the bank was totally empty and while they all straightened up and posed, and I yelled "Smile," a robber could have slipped past us and gotten away with millions.

Another. The skies are so generous. A United Airlines pilot cheerfully stepped outside in front of his jumbo jet on the runway to pose with Amy when I treated her to California.

I see the photo of the road crew who came onto the street one fall day, climbing high on the yellow county truck to pose, and remember sending their photos back to El Salvador and Guatemala and Mexico. I have a zinger of a trash-man photo so beautiful he could be the center fold of Playgirl. After he gave his photo to his girlfriend, he came back and asked for one for his mother. From then on, for years in fact, he would lay on that huge foghorn of his mammoth truck as a friendly signal to let me know he was driving by. "Did you hear me last week?" he would ask. I heard him all right. I wonder now what happened to him. I know his mother has his photo and that makes me happy. It might be how Johnny Apple Seed felt, planting little seeds of joy!

The hair stylists at Vidal Sassoon, the Shoppers Food Warehouse clerks representing at least twenty countries, the Trader Joe's staff from California, the Iranian gas station owner, the Vietnamese mailman, the Culpeper gutter guy couldn't look better.

They are all in my life. They are my large and colorful make-believe family.

The Tree on Gallows Road

From the bottom of the hill I could hear the trash truck descending, its rusty brakes bringing it to a screeching stop at each house. Junk and garbage flew, metal cans dropped with a clang. Hoots and shouting.

I was ready. I grabbed his gift, a tiny ceramic replica of a trash can, with "E.J. Trash" printed on the side, and ran out to the road. "E.J, stop!" I shouted. He grinned from behind the wheel and leaned out the window.

"Yes ma'am?" he said, his gleaming white teeth centering his smile, the "ma'am" spoken in a slow Culpeper drawl. His hired help, Junior, scrawny but muscled, swung down from his back perch to get a look.

"Here, I made this for you," I said, as pleased as if I had baked my first perfect soufflé.

It was the early 1980's. Newly divorced and determined to make my living in ceramics, I spent long hours struggling to sculpt serious works of art and relieved the pressure by making silly presents. My brother got a coffee mug with bulbous breasts for a handle, a girlfriend got a sculpted feline urn for her late cat's ashes, and Uncle Bud got a hollow male figure, open at the neck where the head should attach, an original Uncle "Bud Vase".

A week later, E.J. stood at my front door, his clothes rumpled, cap greasy, enveloped in a profound odor of garbage. I looked at him up close for the first time. He seemed to be about my age, mid-forties, and smiled with an open friendliness. He was pleasant looking, nice nose and good teeth. "Would you go out with me?" he asked. Until I had offered my little trash can gift, E.J. and I had had a casual relationship of waving and my yelling "Thank you," if I happened to be out at the road.

Of course not, shot through my mind, but I caught it like a mean ball in midair and said instead, "Oh, no thank you. I can't."

Another week passed and E.J. was back at my door. I wanted to prove to him that I was not prejudiced — not against black men, not against trash men. He didn't try and hide his condition. He was unapologetically grubby. He didn't clean up for his pitch but concentrated on persuasiveness. I concentrated on a politely delicate and careful "no." Had he been a white guy, I might have said "no is no" or even "get lost."

When the iris sprouted in my muddy yard, spring must have given E.J. a creative push, too. The past three months had not daunted his quest. "Ma'am" — He was still calling me this and I was still squirming. You didn't call Michigan women that unless you wanted to make them feel old. This day he was unusually intense. "Please, just once? Saturday is my birthday."

The birthday got to me. "OK," I said. Earlier, I had reaped a lot of dinner dates from my singles ad in the Washingtonian. I'd found food, not love. But, I knew good restaurants, so I made dinner reservations as E.J. requested.

The chrome, the fins, the white walls! The old Cadillac was polished so that E.J. himself shone in its reflection. It contrasted to all the Mercedes that lived on the street. I was aware of six, all beige, the correct color in 1981.

"Do you like French?" I asked. "La Guinguette is four miles from here on Gallows Road."

As we drove up the hill and away from my neighborhood, I thought of a 1951 automobile drive in another old Cadillac when I was invited to ride with Uncle Bud from Michigan to North Carolina and got my introduction to racial prejudice. I also experienced my first reporter frenzy. I couldn't wait to get back to my high school paper, The Student Voice, with my shocking editorial:

"There is a great barrier between Negroes and Whites in North Carolina.

I attended the movies with my Cousin Frieda to find the balcony sadly set aside for the Negroes only. Drinking fountains in city hall wore a sign, "For Whites Only" or vice versa. It was very disheartening to find such a wall between races — especially when they didn't speak or walk near each other on the streets.

E.J. and I took the back route to get onto Gallows Road. I had lived a block off the same road twenty years before — two of my children were adopted there and another was born to me at Fairfax Hospital. Gallows Road then was a narrow country lane with woods on each side, so close that in summer the trees grew over and intermixed their branches, creating a dark canopy.

Now, as E.J. and I drove, I noted the trees were being cut to widen the road, the hospital was expanding, and there was one stop light on the way to La Guinguette. The popular restaurant was tucked unpretentiously in a corner of Merrifield, where Gallows Road and Lee Highway met.

When my husband and I first moved to Virginia in 1959 the state was more South than North. "What are those kids doing on opposite corners, separated, waiting for different buses?" I asked my husband. "This is 1963!" It was two more years before Luther Jackson High School, situated on Gallows Road, was integrated.

The restaurant was dimly candlelit and thick carpeting gave it an air of opulence. As we got used to the light, we realized all of the waiters were black, wearing white jackets, and all the male clientele were white, wearing dark jackets. As we walked in together, the *maître d'* disguised his curiosity by casually looking at us sideways.

E.J. took the weighty leather-bound menu our staring waiter gave him and handled it gingerly. He hid. Would he ever come out from behind it and give me a suggestion of what we might order? I watched the back of it, waiting. Finally, he slowly let the menu down. I first saw his eyes, brown and desperate like a shy woman peering over the top of her fan. He looked squarely at me with a hopeless look, "Order for me, please," he whispered. It took me a minute to catch on. He couldn't read. I wanted to put him at ease.

"Oh, let me give you some ideas, since you've not eaten here before," I said a little too dramatically. I wanted to introduce him to every exotic food in the world in one short meal... like he was a baby who had been fed oatmeal and strained carrots and now was going to get a sudden rush of syrups, sauces and sweets. Oh, let me save this man! Let me share my knowledge, that I hadn't learned that long ago myself.

"*Vichyssoise*, please, to start. We'll have the *champignons farcis*, *pommes duchesse*, seafood with *mornay* sauce and chocolate mousse. Perhaps liqueured coffee at the end," I added with a dash.

"And how did you get into the trash business?" I asked.

E.J. didn't seem thrilled with the cold soup, stirring more than eating, but he was warm with his story. "Grew up south of Culpeper, in the real country. My aunt and uncle, they raised me. I quit school when I was fourteen and started right in at the gravel pit. I hated it. I made up my mind to save every penny and start my own business. Took nine years to get the best used trash truck I could find. Now, I have seven!"

"How smart you were," I said sincerely.

I really wanted to say "courageous." From where I was sitting, I could look across from the restaurant to the opposite corner of the crossroads, where the hanging tree had stood. I realized we were sitting a few hundred yards from its location. Now gone, cut down. I remembered the gnarled old black man, his own limbs knotted like a twisted tree trunk, telling me about it, as we stood at the side of Gallows Road, in my old neighborhood. I was twenty-six. When I first moved to Fairfax I used to drive by the mammoth tree. I could still picture it: at least one hundred feet high, with giant spreading branches.

"They used to march us colored folks down this road to that tree and hang us — those who were criminals, that is," said the old man. "All the way up from Alexandria."

So, that's where they got the name, I thought.

The entrée arrived. Here we were, a black man and a white woman having dinner almost in the shadow of that tree.

"E.J., did you read in the paper recently about the high-school principal?"

He looked puzzled. What was I saying? I stopped myself. If he couldn't read the menu, he couldn't read the paper. I had wanted to discuss the write-up in the Post about the assistant principal in Manassas, Virginia, who had been asked to display on his work desk a photo of a white woman as his wife. He was white, but his wife was black. He refused and lost his job. Would E.J. care about that?

E.J. did not respond. It seemed he didn't need any complicated situations to discuss. He kept things simple. I decided to follow suit.

As we headed back to my house, he was a fine diplomat. "Well, at least those little mashed potatoes tasted good," he said.

We laughed.

Two months later, now midsummer, I was wedging clay on the back deck, the humidity kept at bay by all the bamboo and tall trees. I heard heavy footsteps coming around on the side walkway. "Oh, hello, E.J." I was surprised to see him. He was dirty and disheveled, as usual, and more serious than I remembered.

"Well," he said, taking a sip of the iced tea I offered and then getting down to business. "I've been thinking a lot. You're a hard-working woman. I believe you'd make a good wife."

I stopped to listen. How kind. What a nice compliment... the hard-working part!

"If you'd marry me, I'd give you two of my trash trucks," he offered hesitantly.

That was probably the kindest marriage proposal I could ever get.

Both knowing the answer, we smiled at each other in silence.

The Bandidos

When I search my atlas, I cannot even find it on the map, that tiny, dusty, seemingly innocent village. But I wasn't innocent; not after my visit.

What a great relief to step out of my brother's yellow jeep and head toward the ticket counter. I did not mind that the bus station was dirty, the line long, and the heat heavy. I had to get away. Leaving my brother's home in Phoenix, where my parents were visiting from Oregon and I from the East, seemed the sanest thing to do. The apartment was tiny, I was sleeping on an air mattress, and I felt "visited out." We had hashed out old family events enough, and I was licking my wounds. More importantly, Mexico was so close! I opted to escape. Mexico was like a tantalizing magnet, beckoning me. I love that country.

"Dan, just drop me off at the bus station," I told my brother. "I'll be back on Sunday night in time to catch my plane."

I felt smartly dressed in my white linen pants suit, straw hat, red heeled sandals and carry-all bag. My dyed blonde hair was pulled back to show my favorite sterling earrings, and my red lipstick exactly matched my shoes.

Armed with my driver's license and a little money, I bought a one-way ticket and climbed aboard the creaky, rusty third-class bus. At the back by the window was an empty seat, seemingly quiet and alone. By the time we pulled away we sat four and five abreast and the aisle was jammed. It seemed the whole country of Mexico was going home.

Almost in exact proportion to the miles slipping by, my resentments melted. By noon I had forgiven all. I love you, Mother, I thought to myself. The bumping and jostling didn't bother me at all. The closeness just made me want to be able to respond to their beaming friendliness with some intelligent Spanish of my own. As I had done often in the past, I vowed to learn more Spanish words as soon as I returned home.

I remembered thirty years earlier, in Mexico City, when I was an art student dating a Mexican pilot. He flew between Cuba and Los Angeles in a small two-seater open-cockpit plane. Although I was charmed by him, with his goggles and leather jacket, I turned down his invitations to go flying. I was not brave enough to play Amelia Earhart.

I did accept car dates. He picked me up close to midnight and we would go to a cabaret to watch the flamenco dancers and listen to the mesmerizing bands... screaming trumpets to fill your heart. He could cha-cha far better than I could do the Michigan jitterbug.

One crisp, starlit evening we went to Mexico City's one drive-in movie theater. "East of Eden" was playing; an American film with Spanish subtitles. I understood the spoken word; he the written. Ne'er the twain did meet.

He was very enthusiastic about something. "*Por favor, más despacio,*" I pleaded over and over. I had him repeat slowly several times about his *bambino,* until I finally understood that his *esposa* (wife) had just had a baby that morning. I cried for days and refused to see him ever again. Knowing more Spanish could have saved my broken heart.

Returning to Mexico, my old desire was being rekindled. Fluent Spanish could have added flavor and wisdom to this trip, but I had procrastinated. In the past thirty years, I had not extended my vocabulary. Even so, I planned to get off at the first charming town, where I anticipated shops, cafes, and a colorful square (*zocalo*) with a small church. Perhaps I would find a quaint hotel. But each village looked bare and disappointing and I remained on the bus, stop after stop. "*Donde, Señora?*" asked the driver, looking at me for a sign. I kept shaking my head and smiling, "Not yet."

The Bandidos

Suddenly it seemed late and I knew I must get off. It was getting dark. At the very next village I disembarked and saw an empty, long, dusty road ahead. All of the adobe houses were shuttered to the street; their wooden doors closed.

As I walked, I felt uneasy and out of place and much too conspicuous. One door was ajar and I got a quick peek into a dirt-floored home with a small courtyard in the back where several children were playing and chickens were scratching. The wonderful smell of tortillas cooking in oil made me realize I was hungry. Far ahead and up a hill a neon sign glowed "Carta Blanca".

At a small metal table, I was served a chilled bottle of *cervesa* with lime slices. Women and children in the background appeared curious about me, but shy. Several young men approached me with enthusiasm to show off their English to the *gringa*. "Where from, lady?" "Oh, Washington!" "Eat with President?" This last question was almost the exact one my farming uncles in Michigan asked.

Gratefully, I took directions from them to the only motel in town, a good distance further in the dark. Was I crazy?

In the eerie yellow bug light outside *La Casa Grande*, I could make out a few horses and some dilapidated cars, rusty pickups, and a Jeep. They smelled of low octane gasoline. So much for a charming hotel. I was just grateful to find lodging.

After paying the short, portly clerk and getting my room key, I walked into the noisy bar-restaurant. It was smoky and dim, but as my eyes adjusted, I was startled to see the type of men I had only seen in movies. Grade B movies. Bad men.

On every bar stool sat a cowboy in a ten-gallon hat, high-heeled and very pointed-toe boots with polished, sharp, silver spurs, tight jeans and glistening guns in the holsters on their hips. Several had large black mustaches; all wore grim faces. They did not smile. Although an Augustine Laura love song was coming from the old jukebox, the scene was not romantic; it was tense.

I felt their eyes on me.

I sat down at a small oil-clothed table. This was no boy-girl interest that I enjoyed in the old college library. Danger flashed in my mind. My realization and fear mixed to create a sickening feeling in my stomach; I heard and understood one cowboy to ask the clerk, while nodding toward me, "What's her room number?"

Fear catapulted me into action. As I desperately searched the room, I saw two men about my age at a table nearby, who possibly might be American or speak English. Within a split second, I was at their table and without being invited to, I pulled out the third chair and quickly dropped into it. They were very surprised. And amazingly polite. In a hoarse whisper, I asked, "Do you speak English? I'm in trouble!"

James and Eduardo agreed it was not a good situation. They didn't like it much themselves, they confided. I thought it seemed strange that two rugged men with calloused hands and authentic "stone washed" jeans, deeply suntanned and unshaven, were almost as wary as I was. "Don't you know?" they asked. "We are in the heart of drug country."

I ordered tamales but couldn't swallow them. They ate heartily; hefty steaks with stacks of tortillas, chilies and refried beans. They were men of few words, but James did explain he was originally from Texas and Eduardo from Guadalajara. They had hooked up as gold mining partners and were back in town from the hills for the night. I was cordially invited to sleep in their room. Actually, what James said, with a touch of shyness but with great forcefulness, was: "You cannot go anywhere near your room."

Their room had a bare tiled floor, twin beds that sagged like hammocks, a wooden nightstand, a small hammered-tin cross above the door and a dull yellow bulb in the center of the ceiling. A thin cotton spread on each bed did not begin to take care of the chill.

James, pointed out one bed for me and one for Eduardo. Then he took the floor on the far side of the room, away from the door. He ordered us not to even walk near it.

All three of us slept in our clothes. Lying there in the dark, even with my now dirty white suit on and a sweater from my bag, I was not warm enough. Whenever I heard footsteps on the gravel outside our

The Bandidos

room, I tensed and listened. I realized no one on this earth knew where I was. Maybe I had been too hasty. It was embarrassing, sleeping in a motel room with two strange men. But they seemed a little shy and ill at ease themselves, and we were all about the same age. Thinking in the dark, my relief and gratefulness began to outweigh my discomfort. I was safe.

Finally, I could hear my roommates breathing heavily; asleep, I assumed. So, just at dawn, I let myself sleep too.

In the morning, in the now-safe restaurant with no sign of any bandidos, we ordered *huevos rancheros* and thick black coffee boiled with sugar. The walls, tiled in a million tiny multicolored pieces, reflected the brilliance of the sun. I did not want to leave. I now felt safe. The danger had passed like nothing had happened and I had two new friends.

"I wonder what our take will be today?" Eduardo said. "Perhaps we'll be rich men!" he chuckled for the first time since we met. "So, let's get out of here and check it out," added James.

We three piled into their Jeep. I got a quick peek at the town square as we drove to their work shack, where they stored their equipment and supplies and washed their concentrates. Overnight they had been rinsing their concentrates with cyanide to leach out the smaller bits of gold. From James' quiet grin I guessed they probably had reaped a golden harvest.

I was a little sad to say goodbye and step out of their Jeep… this time to join a crowd gathered to catch a bus heading *norte* (north).

One bus arrived fully loaded. Passengers were hanging off both sides and swinging from the back. Luggage was piled on top almost as high as the bus itself. One boy from our group managed to jump onto the tail end and he was still hanging there when the bus passed out of sight.

Another bus came, totally full. Now it was late. A third bus just sped by.

I learned a taxi was my only hope. I searched my bag for enough *dinero* and hired a cab for the four-hour race to the border. "Come along!" I shouted to some hopeful travelers standing beside me, inviting along as many guests as there was room for. Seven of us squished in. I endured the most kamikaze ride of my life.

* * * * *

"Thanks, Dan. Yes, off to the airport! We're late for the plane, but no matter how fast you want to drive, you can't scare me, not after the ride I just had!" I said to my brother.

How could I tell him that Mexico had given me a grand time... taken me on a dangerous roller-coaster ride but landed me safely, given me two new friends, and taught me that, just like looking for love, you have to take your chances?

An Angel in August

"My main desire," I told Jean, "is to go to Mexico and buy my dear friend Elaine an angel for her meditation room." It seemed simple to me. It was August in Escondido, California, and I was on vacation.

Elaine had been one of the first devotees to welcome me to our Washington, D.C., Self Realization Center. She had smiled patiently and lovingly at my endless enthusiasm over "my luck" at finding Master. She also held Thursday evening meditations in her ocher-walled upper room, a holy place where an angel might reside.

Jean and I picked a day. Early in the morning of our adventure we stopped at a bank for a stack of one dollar bills ("American money is best to use," Jean said, "quicker for bargaining.") and drove south to the border at Tijuana. She had a clear plan as she often takes friends shopping in Mexico. We would leave the car at a shopping mall and walk three miles to cross the border to save time and for the car's safety. Easy enough. Locking our purses in the trunk, light handed, off we hiked.

We ate our way along, buying from the street vendors offering fried *churros*, jicama with fresh lime juice, and a brown sugar caramelized confection so sweet our teeth ached. We ended the feast in downtown Tijuana, with a lunch of *tamales* and *flan* in a café overlooking the crowded street below.

I soaked up the language, sounds and smells, feeling overwhelmed, almost jolted by it all. I had just spent a week at Convocation in Los Angeles in silent meditation, chanting and attending classes. Five thousand other devotees and I had heard the monks and sisters speak on using our power of thought and the divine gift given us of the power of our will. I wanted to practice it. Today!

Now! Of course, you are supposed to keep God in the background of your mind at all times while doing it. A giant order.

Stuffed and happy, we set off to pick out the perfect angel statue from the hundreds I visualized in the "statue-stores." From my earlier visits to Mexico City I imagined there were wonderful stalls full of sculptures of Mary and Jesus and saints and angels. We memorized our line perfectly: *"Necesito una estatua de un angel."*

Asking directions, we went where told. No one knew exactly but they thought those types of shops would be ten blocks to the right. Zero. The people "ten blocks right" believed there was a store fifteen blocks north. The "fifteen blocks north" folks (anyone in the street who knew any English at all) felt for sure there was a place by taxi outside of the city. We did not go there.

One eager Mexican gentleman said he would lead us to "exactamento" where we wanted to be. He ran ahead, Jean behind him. I ran after Jean, as we went down one block, up another, in between narrow stalls of baskets and serapes and pottery, winding our way into a hidden back-street market. I just knew the statue would be there.

At last, I spotted a little tucked-away shop of church memorabilia. Looking excitedly, I found Virgin Marys, Josephs and saints of every size. And millions of Jesuses.

"Donde esta los angeles?" I asked. "Only in December, *Señora*. Only at Christmas. There are no angels in this city in August." They knew little English. My Spanish was very poor. How could I explain? Jean dropped some money in our guide's waiting palm and we went back out into the sunny street.

Undaunted, we learned from a silversmith that perhaps the lady on the sidewalk in the shadow of the cathedral might sell statues. We found a very wrinkled lady with a few small children and other assorted relatives and friends sitting behind a table of Catholic rosary beads and colorful photo cards of the Virgin of Guadalupe. We asked our much-repeated question and she looked puzzled; but an even older man, knowing English a "leetle" said *"Si,* come back in thirty minutes." Jean and I imagined he was going to a warehouse of angels in the wholesale district.

An hour later we hesitantly went back to the church, our feet a little weary, our minds a little doubtful. But half a block away, over the crowds of people, I could see a pink angel. She stood over two feet tall, her hands held in prayer, her wings pointing toward heaven. My heartbeat sped up in sync with my footsteps. But up close she looked rather shabby, with a crudely molded face. She was not pretty.

The lady gave her price and I was shocked. First of all, I presume Americans seem rich compared to Mexican sidewalk vendors. (In truth, we are.) Secondly, once I think in Mexican pesos and money changes in my head, the American dollar unfairly seems more valuable. A trick of my mind. Lastly, I had bought a shiny new angel in Mexico City a few years earlier for less. However, deep down, I would have paid anything to get Elaine an angel.

I pointed out the broken wing. What I thought they said was: "No problem, we'll fix it. Come back in an hour."

We trudged back to the center of town and shopped for a red leather purse and a painted ceramic parrot. We had not gone back in one hour and I had not thought of God even once. What!? It was 7 P.M. — past supper time. Our feet said "midnight." Jean put it to me. She looked me straight in the eye, as a very diplomatic hostess, who had just happily given a day of her life might do when the guest had overstayed, possibly hoping and praying I would say no. "OK, Sharon. Last chance. Do we walk seven blocks back to that cathedral and hope the lady hasn't gone home? Or do we call it quits and start the trek back over the border now?"

I remembered the lessons from Convocation: perseverance, determination, concentration, and — is it worth it?

I sat there numbly and heard myself say, "We'll get the angel."

Back at the church, the lady smiled. As I peered closer I saw the angel's wing was now broken in a new place as well. In their enthusiasm to repair her wing they had broken it again. I now suspected she came from their private home. My heart was melting. Although she was quite homely, she seemed to be no ordinary angel.

This was a much "prayed to" angel. And although a little dirty, she was pink; the color of love.

As I opened my money belt, there was Yogananda's picture smiling at me. I laughed. Master had been with me the entire time. His photo was there with the money; reminding me it wasn't easy to think of God every minute, but, I was loved anyway.

"*Si, muchas gracias,*" I repeated several times to the delighted lady and her now expanded family and even more smiling friends.

Jean cheerfully said, "I'll sneak you back into the country — don't worry." And we made our way. With my arms aching from carrying this two-and-a-half-foot treasure, we trekked back to the border bridge, through inspection, and on to the car.

Driving into the California sunset, we felt in our hearts — and feet — that we had discovered the only available angel in August.

As carry-on luggage for flying home it was far too big and fragile for the upper bins or under my seat. I told the stewardess I had a very valuable statue for a "church," so she respectfully and gently took the angel from me. "I'll put her up in first class with the wine," she said.

The wine will certainly be blessed, I thought and thanked her.

I had left this winged celestial being wrapped in cardboard and rope, just as it had been prepared in Escondido for the trip back to Washington. A few days before Christmas, I added red and green paper and a hot pink bow and drove to Elaine's home. She slowly and lovingly unwrapped the mystery package. With honest awe, she exclaimed, "Oh, how beautiful!"

I looked at Elaine, who was looking at her angel. Then I looked at the pink angel myself, not believing what I was seeing. She had become extraordinarily beautiful. Since I had wrapped her up, she had been somehow transformed. Her face was exquisite, like a Dresden doll's face. Her coarse features had been replaced with silky smooth skin and a lovely feminine mouth... and a delicate nose.

Later, to double check my shock, memory and mental state, I phoned Jean... careful not to coach her. I asked how she remembered the angel. She hesitated before she spoke and tactfully said, "She was not very attractive, but she did have charm."

It was then that I realized, even with our power of thought and our power of will, God is the Doer.

Om   Peace   Amen

Dad's Gift

"Dad is dying, but you don't need to come," my brother Dan said on the phone.

"I'm on my way," I responded, as I dragged my suitcase from the attic. Packing was like making lasagna: a layer of lingerie, a layer of tears, a layer of sweaters and another layer of salty memories. "Dad, wait for me," I said softly.

Being curled in the window seat on the plane was comforting. The five-hour flight from Dulles, Virginia, to San Diego gave me time to remember odd little pieces of our life together. I thought about Dad telling me that I was born "wide awake." He was amazed at how I opened my eyes immediately and looked straight at him, and then around the room at the nurse, doctor, Aunt Billie and Aunt Hulda — all squeezed around the sagging bed with the rusty springs. Mother always added, "And I could smell the hot dogs!" Far below my parents' tiny walk-up apartment, the Detroit State Fair was in full swing. It was Sunday and "Free Day." Crowded, sunny, in the mid 70's, a riot of noise and excitement rose up from below. If I had been able to look farther, past the room and out the window, I might have seen a small child waving from the top of the Ferris wheel.

Now, I was going to be with Dad. He had lovingly greeted me when I was born, I would now bid him farewell.

* * * * *

Gardening was Dad's second love. Mother was his first. She appreciated every flower he ever grew, so it gave him double satisfaction.

I gave him a large, bare twig once when I was out West visiting. "Here's a pretty stick I found near my exhibition booth!" I said. "It was thrown out with some wilting flowers in the alley." He knew I had driven to San Francisco and from my look could tell I had had few sales at the Art Show in the shadow of Golden Gate Bridge.

"Sorry," he said and smiled gently. Dad could show empathy with a simple word. And I had pleased him. He liked the strange, curly stick. A few weeks in his dirt and with his tender nursing, it grew leaves, and then a flower.

*****

"Number One Kid, I can't go on," he would phone. The "Number One" was not because I was the favorite: I was the oldest. I was born five years before my sister Linda and eleven years before my brother Dan.

At age eighty, Dad was the sole caretaker for my Mother. Bedridden with arthritis, she rang her little bell. "Orange juice, please," she would call and he would run to her within minutes; around-the-clock service. He phoned me at home in Virginia each time he felt he could not take it any longer and I would fly out to Oregon on a day's notice. I was the available one, the artist who did not make much money anyway. I don't care; I'm needed, I thought. It makes me happy. Who else would help? My brother Dan was a successful loan officer, devoted to business. My sister Linda was a doctor's wife, busy with her youngest child Molly, still at home, and gardening, dinner parties, decorating, and keeping both her in-town estate and ranch house in exquisite order.

That same spring, I called Dad one morning at six, Oregon time, knowing he would be up with his coffee and paper. "Your Number One Kid is coming out for a few months! I'll help you." I could hear his silence and then his muffled crying. *I'm saving his life*, I hoped.

The next week, I was in Oregon, riding in the back seat on our Sunday drive, just like we had all done together fifty years earlier. I could almost hear Tommy Dorsey's orchestra playing "Star Dust" on the old car radio... booming its deep base from the only clear station, WJR, Detroit. Dad's voice was just as strong in my memory: "We can

Dad's Gift

only get single-dip cones, remember." Yes, I recalled; five cents a dip. The 1931 Chevy kicked up dust on the gravel road as we headed out to Crystal Lake. Driving slowly around the lake, coveting every little cottage, laughing at the names — "Dew Drop Inn," "Hide-a-Way Heaven" and "Bide-a-Wee" — was our favorite Sunday entertainment. Dad was able to save enough money once to get us a week's rental there. Our week at the one-room cabin, with its rickety dock and row boat, was our only vacation in eleven years. It rained all seven days.

* * * * *

The Bush Barn in Salem, Oregon, rented out studio space. I applied and was accepted. The studio barn sat in a lovely park with a rose garden, just a few miles away from Mother and Dad's small bungalow. A ceramic artist by day, I came "home" in the evening to make a tray of snacks and take over Dad's watch for the night.

"Still sleeping?" I called. "Wake up! Herrreeee's Johnny!" They'd gone to bed with the birds and were rested enough for a midnight party and the daily report. "First, you should know, on my way home, there was a traffic jam. Three cars at a light!" Like a stand-up comedian, at the foot of their bed, I tried to lend a little humor. Any laugh I earned was simply parental appreciation. I had been a lousy actress in our high-school play and age had not improved my ability. Lucy, their Russian next-door neighbor, furnished the comic material. Lucy's extra-large nose nearly hid the rest of her face, which bothered none of us.

Nearing ninety, Lucy spoke with a melodious accent and had a sweet, if conspiratorial, personality. "The CIA has bugged my house," Lucy reported from her back yard, with at least a dozen adopted cats trailing behind. On a different day; "Everett, will you check for hidden wiring again?" Another time, "They're listening to all my conversations!" Dad was exasperated. Mother was entertained. We all loved Lucy. My nightly silly jokes about her aliens or the CIA brought chuckles. And, I was getting the attention I hadn't realized I had always yearned for.

The bad times were fading. The gruff scoldings from Dad were being washed away. "Don't you know when to come in out of the rain?" or, "You're dating a *spic*?" or, "You're trying to be a jack-of-all-trades, why not do one thing right!" or, "You want to be a missionary? Try doing some good at home!"

*****

Mother and Dad rarely got a visit from Linda. Both of them missed her but Mother suffered the most. Linda was Mother's favorite ever since the day she was born, with her darling, chubby face and naturally curly hair. In fact, she was the reason Mother dragged Dad away from Michigan out to Oregon — to settle near Linda. They were already in their sixties at that point.

Linda called her surgeon husband "Bill," but the rest of us were asked to call him "Dr. Bill." I skipped diplomacy. "My children *have* a doctor. They need an *uncle!*"

Linda and Bill were busy traveling between their home on a golf course in Portland and their 2,000-acre ranch near Dalles, in Oregon. After they had lived a few years in Oregon, Mother and Dad seemed no longer convenient to Linda and Bill's "commute" path, missing it by living fifty miles too far south.

Mother was weak, frail, her energy seeping away, and deeply lonesome for Linda. What could we do? I plotted with Mother, "We'll give a dinner party! How can they resist a formal invitation and a great meal?" The three of us could hardly believe we had to do this to get them to visit. We were gleefully satisfied, however: co-conspirators with a mission. Our family thrived on projects.

"Use the best tablecloth!" Mother ordered from her upholstered pink chair, colorful pillows tucked in around her. "Please touch it up with the iron again."

"Yes, and I'll make lots of flower arrangements, too," I said. Dad's garden was bountiful, a kaleidoscope of color, and wafted a heavenly aroma. *Even a bouquet for the back of the toilet,* I mused. Dad carefully swept the entire driveway and along the curbs.

They came, the doctor and his wife. Linda was thin, tanned and elegant in a flowing silk dress. Her prematurely white hair was smartly cut. Her wedding ring, which they recently had reset with a much larger diamond, sparkled brilliantly. Bill, tall and good-looking, carried himself with confident charm, looking perfectly the part of

Chief of Staff of two Portland hospitals. They nibbled on Mother's salmon paté, ate Dad's trout, sipped the best wine we knew to buy, ate my "from-scratch" Wacky cake, and laughed a lot. Everyone acted happy.

"Bill, another glass of wine?" Dad asked with a smile. "Thanks," Bill nodded, graciously.

Dad showed no outward sign that a few years earlier he had lent Linda and Bill his entire life savings to help with land investments and expansion, trusting they would pay it back. Dad had been forced to hire a lawyer to retrieve his loan.

No one would have guessed it by watching them. Like re-frozen ice, everything was smoothed over so cool and hard. But Dad had shown his steely-ness before. He gave up smoking, cold turkey. After forty years of two-packs-of-Camels-a-day, he stopped overnight. When Dad had his teeth pulled for false ones, he did not complain. Perhaps being stoic explained his many nights on bread and milk to soothe his ulcers.

But wasn't this case different? I wondered if he was grappling with the same indecisions I lived with. Did I take after him? I never could find an easy balance between demanding self-respect and being forgiving and loving.

Secretly, I watched the strain; Mother's yearning for her favorite child. Mother took Linda's hand, patted her arm, pulled her down for a kiss. I knew in my heart that if Linda were available to her, I would not be there. I would not be needed. Did Linda realize what a backhanded favor she was doing for me? It was the only time we all got together during my five-month stay.

* * * * *

It was not yet seven A.M. and my bedroom door banged open. The paper shot through the air so fast it hit my pillow with a thud. "Paperboy!" Dad laughed, excited and grinning. I had been deep asleep. "Dad! Can't you see...?" but I reached to look. There was a front page photo of me, the middle-aged divorcée, sitting on her father's fishing stool at the Bush Barn Art Fair, in her booth of ceramic jewelry and masks. *Dad is proud of me,* I thought, hardly believing it. I was not used to this.

"I guess I'll take a hot cup of coffee!" I laughed, settling back into my pillow.

Lucy "baby-sat" Mother so Dad and I could get away a few times to fish. We bought chocolate malts and bait on the way up the mountain. The icy-cold trout stream near Detroit Dam was so deserted and beautiful that we dubbed it our private "resort." We stood beside the loud rushing water, tossing the slippery trout into the blue cooler. Except for a rare bouncing raft full of shouting vacationers shooting by, we saw no one. "You've turned out to be a pretty good fisherman, Kid," Dad said, as he patiently baited my hooks and removed my catches. I kept our thermos cups full.

One warm, sunny day we piled Mother, her aluminum deck chair, tackle box, poles, and braunschweiger sandwiches into the van. In the late 1980's I was into "creative visualization" and decided we should use it to catch fish. "New Age thinking is practical," I informed them. I could have been a teenager again, by the look they gave each other.

Dad's surprisingly large trout was fighting him, taking out his line, and he had calculated wrong by putting on too weak a filament. "This line may not hold," he called.

"Don't worry," I yelled above the sound of the rushing current, as though he wasn't an authority on fishing. "We'll tie a rope around my waist so I'm not swept away and put Mom on the shore with the other end around her as my anchor!" Mother smiled in agreement. She had her hearing aids in, but still had no idea what we were saying.

With a long-handled net, I walked gingerly into the frigid stream, while Dad steadied his pole, fighting the fish for a long, draining hour. He gave the fish slack and then gently pulled it in, over and over again.

"Who's going to wear out first?" Dad called happily. At the same time, I tried to clearly visualize our glistening catch swimming straight into the net. I coaxed and called, "Here little fish, come here," exactly like I called my cat. Mother cheered, "Don't give up! Don't give up!" The fish finally came, heading straight into the net like a predatory

Dad's Gift

shark streaming toward his prey. That night Dad pan fried him and he was split three ways.

* * * * *

That winter, Mother moved into a nursing home. She died the next April, during the week I arrived back in Salem, Oregon. The day before her death, near her seventy-seventh birthday, at her request, she had had Daphne, her young hairdresser, come to the nursing home and do her hair. Always fashionable, she hinted to me what suit, shirt and tie Dad looked best in. As though she knew. She looked so pretty, almost without a wrinkle. The most beautiful girl in Gratiot County, so voted in 1928, was leaving.

I sat beside her as she lay daintily on a clean white sheet in that sterile room, holding her hand, saying prayers. That last night, I wanted to stay with her overnight but she shooed me out, saying, "Go to dinner with your girlfriend and get some sleep." I could not eat. The next morning Dad called me from home to her bedside, and I rushed over to give Dad a short break. Running in breathlessly and pointing to my wet hair, I said, "Sorry about this mess, Mom." She looked up at me sweetly and said, with an approving smile, "It's OK, Honey." For the very first time in my life, my hair had been all right with my mother.

Dad was barely out the door, when Mother lifted her hand to motion me closer, and said in a faint whisper, "Sharon, I'm dying." She was so weak she could barely smile. I took her hand, closed my eyes and prayed: "Babaji, please come." On the train ride out to Oregon I had just reread "Autobiography of a Yogi." After Lahiri was initiated by Babaji in the sacred cave and Lahiri said goodbye, Babaji consoled Lahiri with these words: "Wherever you are, whenever you call me, I shall be with you instantly." So, I asked Babaji to come and be with Mother.

I was new to the path. This seemed right. Mother loved that book, and said upon finishing it, "What is there after this?"

Dad had gone home for a short break and returned in a rush. Taking a look at Mother, he gasped, "She's gone!" I had my eyes closed, praying, and she had left so quietly that I was not aware of her final breath. Dad was distraught that he had gone home and was not present when she passed. We hugged in silence.

*****

The year after Mother died, Dad sold his Oregon home and gave up his glorious garden. Linda and I helped him pack and hold his final garage sale, so he could move near my brother Dan, in California. Linda had Dad's green thumb and should have been the recipient, but she needed to leave early.

"Here, take these," Dad said, pushing two paper bags of daffodil bulbs into my arms. He knew that I had no sunlight in my woods and that I was not a gardener. I had never grown anything in my life except bamboo, which grows itself.

"Dig little holes, drop them in. It's easy!" he said. It was October and the perfect month back home in Virginia to put bulbs in the ground.

The following March I called him to confess, "I never had time to plant them." I didn't want to tell him they looked shrunken and dried out, resembling empty onion skins. It was still winter with a cold and nasty wind. Utterly patient, knowing I was much more an artist than a gardener, he laughed. "Put them in anyway. Anywhere you feel like!" he said. I did. Nothing happened. Not even shoots.

*****

Now it was five years since Mother died and that garage sale and the failed planting of the bulbs. Dan, meeting me at the airport, sped me at lightning speed in his white Mercedes, north to Escondido. Dad needed me for the last time. There he was, in the bed by the door. We had two hours alone, while Dan raced back to the airport to pick up Linda. They stopped for lunch.

At first I wondered, *What is keeping them so long?* Then I understood. I had been given more time alone with Dad. "I love you," I whispered to him, grateful he had waited for me. Dad could not open his eyes or speak. For two precious hours, I never let go of his hand and managed, without letting go, to strip off my long johns and the

Dad's Gift

wool sweater that I had worn on the plane. "I love you, Dad," I whispered, "And I forgot how darn hot it is out here."

After the peace and stillness, Linda and Dan burst in, loudly proclaiming their love. "We're here, Dad," Linda called out. She knew what to do. Trained as a nurse, she smoothed his face with her hands and tenderly gave him a sip of water. (Water had never entered my mind.) Dad made an extreme effort to sit up to reach her. Even though he could not speak, I could see he was overwhelmingly happy.

Dan, with compassion on his tanned face, said, "You can go now, we're all here," feeling that Dad had waited until we were all by his side. Linda added, "Dad, we love you. It's OK." A few minutes later, Dad took his last breath. Peace settled on the room. I stayed with him, still holding his hand, until a dreadful man wheeled in a body bag. I knew Dad was no longer in his body and his soul was free, but I didn't want to leave him.

I took possession of Dad's ashes after the funeral in California. They were in a small cardboard box, wrapped in plain brown paper. There was to be another funeral, the one in Michigan where most of his eight brothers, spouses, nieces and nephews, at least seventy strong, lived, and where Mother's ashes were buried. "I'm not going out for that one," Dan said, turning to me. "Nor I," said Linda. "You take care of it."

* * * * *

Following the funeral in Michigan, I drove home with his ashes. "Well, Dad, here we go," I whispered, as I merged onto the Ohio Turnpike to drive the seven hundred and fifty miles back to Virginia.

It gradually dawned on me that I could no longer call Dad for our weekly chat. It was hard to realize he was gone. I was missing him already. I drove slowly down the long hill on my street and turned the corner.

The scene before me looked like a pale green painting with splashes of bright yellow dotting the canvas. Sprouting everywhere, blooming gorgeously beside my mailbox, along the roadside, by my walkway and all through the woods, were Dad's daffodils.

Apartment for Rent

What?! It's 3 A.M. and he's cutting her in half again! When will I learn? Oh, yes, and now the samba-mambo routine. Click, slide, bam. I knew when Mandrake the Magician and his girlfriend rented my apartment that he wanted a smooth floor with a big open space for practicing dance routines. I didn't expect that to happen in the middle of the night. They returned from their gigs on college campuses in the wee hours with their huge metal cases swaying side to side behind them, rattling along my wooden walkway, hard enough to knock out the slats. His combination of magic tricks and salsa dancing practice at any time, day or night, was his normal. The middle of the night, of course, was the time of day when he used his magic to skip out for good. You might imagine he left behind his last rent check written in disappearing ink. No, just a normal check — that bounced.

I might have known. I should be more cautious, but it is the hostess in me. I don't rent out half of my house to be entertained or to entertain. I should remember that. I need the income. But each time a new tenant pulls into the driveway with a moving van or loaded pickup or a car bulging with boxes, I feel a visitor has arrived. My new house guests will enjoy life here. It is almost secondary that they pay on the first of the month. But I expect it, of course. A landlady's vision of happiness.

"Does he like chocolate cake? Will she enjoy the Mexican tiles in the kitchenette? Will he be pleased in the winter to see the deer that prance by each morning to eat the bamboo?" I am happy when a nature lover moves in who says he'll like living beside the fox trail and hearing the raccoons rummaging around at night to eat my leftovers.

The possibility of becoming a landlady came up when I was thirty-nine. As my husband and I had our house built, I laid out the floor plan for the children's quarters: three small bedrooms, a large playroom with a sink in the corner, bath and separate entrance which could, with one closed door, cleverly be transformed into a rental apartment. "For my income in my old age," I joked. Within four years, divorce papers in hand, I needed it. I had not foreseen the necessity would come so soon, but was grateful for my unintended foresight.

I need to find a replacement quickly when a renter moves away. Missing a month of income hurts. My nagging but concerned friends warn, "They are not! your! friend! It is strictly business." My own commonsense says that I should not be hasty, should run a credit check, and never accept their mother's name as a reference, or an uncle's phone number as their pastor's.

"Hello, Ma'am." Is Jerry honest? "Yes, Ma'am." Doesn't drink? "No, Ma'am. Ah-men." Doesn't smoke? "Ah-men, No." Never misses church? I thought I might as well ask. "Never, Ma'am. Ah-men," backed up by a long chuckle. Jerry was applying for a space and had given me his pastor's number as a reference. I met Jerry's uncle later and realized that he was the make-believe "Ah-men" preacher.

My list of what to watch out for the next time is getting longer. "No smoking" does not mean standing in the doorway while the heat escapes and the smoke swirls back inside. It does not mean a girlfriend hidden in the closet to sneak food to and keep as his guest for a week, until a feminine squeal in the night gives her away. Nor does it mean a cat neglected for days so it climbs the blinds, attacks the draperies, and is so confused, it can't locate the kitty box. And definitely no more renter's guests, who take such long, hot baths that the fifty-gallon water heater is emptied.

"My buddy was cold so he spent the night in the tub," said Randy.

In time, I added even more warnings to myself: no more violent stalkers who murdered a gal in the back woods, and no menagerie of loose, flying birds. The "beware of" list is to protect me from another mistake. You think you are ready for the next test in life and will be able to identify it, when suddenly something you never dreamed of appears. Life is like the weighted duck you try to knock down at the carnival. It flips back up. My ducks keep flipping back up. That's the pattern. Maybe everyone's life is like that. Whatever I do, even renting out an apartment, is a microcosm of my life. Each little part mimics the large part. If I could learn to "rent out" more wisely, might it indicate I'm living a life better? Being business-like is difficult. It feels so unspontaneous.

That is exactly why running my art business is awkward for me. I love the creative part, but pricing and collecting money seems secondary. Deep down, it makes me happy to make others happy… so if I create something they like, that is what feels most important. The money hardly matters in my mind. It's not a virtue to brag about, it's just me. That makes for a poor business person. One has to be tough and firm… neither of which is a strong characteristic of mine.

* * * * *

The stalker happened in my earliest days of renting. I don't recall checking any references. Perry looked fine to me and had his first month's rent in single bills pressed between his long, bony fingers. He was skinny all over, with thin, hairy arms and long, dark, stringy hair parted in the middle. Army fatigues, combat boots, and a loose belt with a knife sheath made up his wardrobe. He pulled the shiny knife out constantly and flashed it around.

Every day he walked into the woods behind the house, choosing a different path each time, like a pioneer might do in undeveloped territory, in order to seek a better trail. I would notice him disappearing into the woods for hours.

One day there was a news report: "Girl bludgeoned near Eakin Park," specifically, just off the bike path by the frog pond. *That's right behind my property*, I realized with a jolt. The offender was described as a man with long hair, wearing army fatigues and a knife sheath on his belt.

My phone was in the kitchen and I grabbed it…. 911! Fairfax police! I was trembling, hardly able to dial, but feeling Sherlock Holmes pounding in my blood. "I have your man!" I hissed, trying not to yell. "Send someone quick! The culprit's here in my house, a few feet away in the other room, with only a locked door between us."

I felt *so* brilliant and knowing. And impatient. I continued, fast, "My renter wears fatigues, walks in that same woods every day, carries a knife, and came home hours after the crime. I saw he'd cut his hair off and he'd turned up the heat. It's ninety degrees in there!" I could feel the whole house steaming, even from my side. I knew from the Perry Mason shows that a drastic change of behavior was a strong sign of guilt.

Too many hours later, a detective came. Perry the renter was still locked in the apartment with his hot heat and short hair.

"I suggest you leave town, until we get him out of your place and lock him up," warned the detective. My bags were already packed. I stayed in Florida a week and returned to find Perry. He was still living in my house, heat turned back down to normal, unbothered by the police. "We don't have enough evidence," the detective said matter-of-factly.

Incompetents! I thought. More fury than fear set in. I cannot stay here! My true-blue friend Cleo raced to the rescue. In the meantime, Perry had thankfully gone out. Perry the Murderous Renter meets Sherlock Holmes, the Landlady… with her sidekick Watson. Cleo and I hurriedly packed up his few possessions and drove them to his father's home in Arlington, his in-case-of-emergency reference. His almost comatose, mild-mannered father could not have cared less about our explanation and suspicions about his son. "He is a fine boy," he said, without a trace of emotion. Cleo and I raced back to change the locks. Perry never appeared at my place again. It remains a cold case to this day.

*****

Vincent was one of my renters whom I came to love. Maybe it was because on Mother's Day he slipped an ornate card into my kitchen and I found it on the counter. That was the only one I got that year.

He came to answer the ad on a Sunday after church. I opened the door to a handsome man in his mid-twenties, with a quiet regal manner, wearing a dark suit, impeccable white shirt and lavender tie.

"I have come to take the apartment," he said, looking down on me from his six-foot-seven-inch height. Vincent didn't ask, just stated it in a simple, trusting way. He was never more complicated than that.

In those days, the apartment was furnished with the leftovers of my married life. In the corner of the large living area beside the small sink, I had added a counter stove top and a refrigerator. The red lacquered table and benches from the kids "playroom," along with a 1900 delicate wicker sofa and an old coffee table, made up the seating area.

Vincent chose the bedroom with bunk beds, providentially seven feet long, giving him just enough room to wiggle his toes. Chen, the other renter already living there, had the center bedroom.

I ran ads that said "Roommate to Share," which were far less expensive than ads that said "Apartment for Rent." Therefore, I saved money by introducing and matching up roommates. They didn't always move in in sync and they didn't always click.

"You will like Chen," I promised Vincent. "He's quiet."

He was too quiet. Chen, from Shanghai, got a 4.0 at NOVA, a local community college, and could read and write English perfectly. However, he could not speak it. When Chen moved on to Harvard, Vincent politely suggested, "Find someone I can talk to, please."

Finding a renter was easy in the early 1980's. There were more renters than apartments, so immediately I found two men in succession who answered my ad, liked the place, and took Vincent's number at work so they could arrange to meet him before moving in. Each fellow in turn went to meet Vincent and then backed out.

One called back, said "I've changed my mind," and hung up without an explanation. The second one called me, "I was tricked. Who do you think I am?" he yelled.

"What's going on?" I asked my girlfriend Cleo. "Why so rude?"

"They're obviously prejudiced. You should warn whoever calls that they'll room with a black guy. Tell them up front," Cleo recommended.

"Are you sure? I can't do that," I said, and considered temporarily crossing her off my girlfriend list.

It was late December and I felt the pressure of a new month looming. Someone had to move in within two days. Ralph Waldo Emerson said, "All men are always praying and all prayers are always answered." Maybe.

I said a fervent prayer that night. I didn't like the pressure, but I believe desperation adds sincerity to praying. *Dear God, please send a nice roommate for Vincent.* And I added a bit wistfully, *Please let the new roommate have a sofa. The wicker one is fragile and not very comfortable.*

The next morning, I got a phone call from a James. "I'll stop by on my lunch hour and check it out." When I saw his polished car speed into the driveway, I walked out to meet him. Out stepped a swashbuckling man, mid-twenties, hair slicked back, wearing a brown leather ankle-length trench coat.

He grabbed my hand to shake it, "I'm a pizza salesman," he said. I could have fainted and not because he was charming and promised me a chance for free pizzas. He was black.

Is God doing this? Buoyed by the thought that Vincent might finally get a roommate, I was oozing with gratitude and nearly hugged him. I was overly cheerful. Everything went perfectly. James loved the place, noted Vincent's tape collection matched his own taste in music, and was impressed that the brass name plate Vincent displayed on his bookcase was the last name of a famous basketball player (a North Carolina cousin of Vincent's, to be exact). James enthusiastically took Vincent's work number. This time it will work, I thought. I would bet on it.

"I'll get back with you early evening," James said, laughing as he sped away, sending a spray of snow my way.

There was no call that evening. I watched the clock. I felt let down. I finally ignored all protocol and called James at ten-thirty that night. His demeanor had changed. He sounded distant.

"Please come back and take another look at the place," I urged. "Vincent must be working a double shift, so he isn't here. Who cares if it's midnight?"

James arrived, paced around the apartment, looking at everything all over again; the cassette tape titles, the plaque... then he took a longer look at the delicate wicker settee. He finally stopped to look straight at me.

"I have a problem. I like Vincent fine, he's a cool guy. We'd get along. But you see, I've got this…"

"What is it?" I said. "Tell me."

"Would I be allowed to… well, I have a very massive, overstuffed sofa."

Oh, JOY! Dear God, I thought. "Of course! Move it in!" I said out loud, not telling him how he had answered a double-edged prayer.

Vincent and James became such good friends that when they moved away, they moved on together.

*****

Chico and Lawrence were a handsome couple. Chico was short and muscular, with a thin black mustache and a Latin accent. Lawrence was a sexy hunk from Texas with red hair, a strong chin and chiseled cheekbones, who wore loafers without socks.

They made the apartment look like the Taj Mahal. I would often stand outside their windows and look in, wishing I could move into their half of the house. The draperies were tied back with silk tassels; the white brocade rugs were impeccable… even their tortoise-shell brushes and combs were laid out on their dresser in a design pattern. Their elegant fur-dripping cat, Jezebel, added to the ambiance. They were ready at all times for "House Beautiful" photographers to show up to do a center spread. Being florists, they stored hundreds of pots of flowering trees and palms along the outside deck.

That was the beauty side, the appealing surface. There were also the spats. They argued and stole each other's clothes, and I felt I had to take sides. Both sides.

"Here, hide this at your place. He wants my favorite leather jacket!" Chico whispered at the door, thrusting it at me.

"Quick, keep these silk shirts for me," said Lawrence. My attic became an exotic boutique of men's wear.

They said they hated the notes I wrote and pushed under their door. Perhaps I would not like renting from me either: "Flash! Your AC is running icy cold, and your windows are open." "You blocked the driveway again." "Please help drag the cans to the street. It's your trash, too." It felt like I was scolding my sons. Deep down, was I trying to build a surrogate family? I do not think so in this case, but one's true motives can be devious.

Chico was a devout Catholic and insisted on burning candles to the Virgin of Guadalupe twenty-four hours a day. "I respect your reverence, but it's too dangerous when you aren't home," I said.

"I must," he said and turned his back on me. I knew he was making a nasty face.

It was either the Virgin Mary, full of compassion — or me, full of desire to save my house.

The men moved out, but not before their cat Jezebel died, and we three held a burial service in the back woods where my cat, Tonkatsu, also rests in peace. I said a prayer. Chico cried.

* * * * *

Although the Russians were not family, I might have come to think of them as such in time. I regret not allowing Irina's father to move in and live with them. Tall, strong Irina from Russia hid the poor man on Vincent's old top bunk. I could have let her father live there for free, and it would not have hurt me. Instead, I chased him away.

When I noticed one day that they did not have a wedding photo, I asked Irina and Viktor to pose and surprised them with a framed "wedding portrait." Irina cried softy to me and whispered, "We are not really married." "You're not?" I said, remembering their misleading application. "That's OK," I replied comfortingly. She worked so hard.

One night, they had a big Russian party and moved the giant-sized picnic table from the deck into their main room. The room filled up to the brim with food, friends and laughter. It was just like my Swedish grandparents' parties. Viktor invited me to join them.

I wish now that I'd ignored those "heat" fights. "Turn the heat down!" I said. I wish that I hadn't felt that money mattered so much. Life often has its regrets. When they moved away, she was pregnant. I could have been more understanding, and perhaps had a tiny renter to spoil.

*****

I am happy I agreed to move out to a friend's house for a night in the Fall and again in the Spring so that Jim and Hank could throw their all-night bashes. My neighbors cared about the loud music and called the police, but I wasn't home so it didn't bother me. Jim was a great host to his friends, but only up to a point. He was a diplomatic rascal. If a hungover friend crashed and Jim wanted him to leave, he turned off the heat. As soon as it got so cold that the hungover guy hurried away, Jim immediately jacked the heat back up to warm and cozy.

Jim and Hank might have been substitutes for my sons, who were seldom around. I may have attempted to mother them a bit with my advice. I always dried my clothes out on the deck railings. "Don't you guys like hanging your clothes out to dry? Your sheets would smell so nice," I suggested. They shrugged me off and surprised me with a clothes dryer for the place.

My first try at building a torii gate happened under their watch. "Would you help me tie the bamboo up once I have painted it red?" I asked. They were game, and they risked their necks, twelve feet up on my shaky step ladder, tying the poles together. The First Edition Torii Gate lasted one season.

Jim moved out to marry his adorable girlfriend, who spent her entire visits sitting on his lap. I never saw her use a chair. I certainly should not have been disappointed when I was not invited to their wedding, but I was. Oh-oh, caring too much and feeling attachment. But strangely, neither was his faithful roommate, Hank, invited. However, Hank was cool about it.

*****

Lindsay, a pretty blonde with a sultry voice, knocked on my door one night at midnight. She needed a place, quick. So did her lizard, parakeets and African gray parrot. But Lindsay had a habit of disappearing for days. When she didn't come home, I went in, like an actor from Hitchcock's "The Birds," ducking, covering my head with newspapers, to put water out for them. The entire apartment was their cage and they swished by, zooming back and forth, their colored wings brushing against me. I was on safari in my own home. I missed the strange squawks when she left.

*****

A few years back, Gwendolyn moved in with her guitars, books on psychology, and Olivia the cat. Her credit was perfect. All four of her references said she was their "best friend." I liked her. Maybe my ducks are in a row, I thought. At last! I was at a point in my own aging when renting to only one person seemed more civilized, and I envisioned an unattached human being with quiet hobbies; no knives, banging, squealing, or loud music. No comings and goings in the night, no non-married couples. "Oh no, I do not date men," Gwendolyn said, making intent eye contact during our interview. I gave a contented, secret sigh. That will simplify everything... until I passed her living room one night, curtains open to the walkway, and saw Gwendolyn in the arms of a woman. They were kissing. They fell so in love that most nights, from then on, there were two again in the apartment. They posed for my camera at breakfast on the deck and I acclimated myself to their world. When Gwendolyn was later dumped and left alone again, I found myself worrying about her. A heartbreak is a heartbreak.

*****

For thirty-five years, I have had visitors. I am becoming a woman who remembers fondly the old guests she has lost contact with. The memories are not jarring anymore; they are more like family that have moved away and moved on, which is what my real family did.

I'm still trying to remember that the tenants and I are not related. Renting is all business. But, the truth is I just put some cookies on top of the washing machine for Michael, my newest renter.

How I Almost Got New Nipples

Who wants even to think about losing such a delicate and embarrassing body part?

I grew up in the 1940's, when the word "nipple" was barely whispered. Movie stars and housewives wore thick, pointed bras and a mother nursed her baby in the back bedroom.

We high-school girls in the early 1950's wore our breasts like a badge... at least I did. Although they were held proud and high in a tight sweater, there was nary a hint of a nipple. The informal contest for the most "stacked" co-ed in my college dorm took place in sweaters. No skin, no nakedness. In fact, no drugs, no alcohol on campus, no co-ed dorms, no men past the lobby, no males inside the locked front door past midnight. We were covered.

Paris and its haute couture fashion houses changed all that in the fall of 1968. My husband and I were on vacation. He chose the Eiffel Tower and I chose apparel. I bought from the sidewalk newsstand a French Vogue Magazine and thumbed through the pages. Below the ads were addresses of Givenchy, Yves Saint Laurent, Balmain, Dior and Chanel. I was on my way. As I walked, I asked directions by pointing at the address, and the friendly French directed me. Block after block, I strode in my new white, shiny, vinyl boots and hat purchased from the Annandale, Virginia, K-Mart. They eventually got me to Yves Saint Laurent. I really had no idea what I would do when I got there.

I have believed my entire life that there are no coincidences. How could I have unknowingly gotten a date right and a time exact? Out of the blue, I was exactly on time.

I knocked on a massive, elaborately carved door and the most astonishingly beautiful woman opened it. She smiled down at me. Her coal-black hair was twisted into a knot at the nape of her neck and her eyes were shadowed in shades of cream and nutmeg to match her skin-tight sheath.

"The Press?" she asked.

That was the only word I understood from her rapidly spoken greeting. I flunked French in college, so I dared not say a thing. I returned her smile and she ushered me to a front-row seat in a line of golden chairs, filled with golden women. It was as though I had accidentally stumbled into a dream world of fabric and color and foreign sounds so exotically whipped together that my artistic being leapt a little closer to heaven. I looked around and realized I was sitting among international buyers, checking out next spring's collection, that would influence women all over the *entire* world. I had no time to savor the power of this momentous occasion because the show was just starting. The hauntingly slender models swept past in organdy and voile, and they were not... wearing... bras. Their nipples showed through their clothes! I could have fallen off that golden chair in my fabulously tacky outfit and ruined America's reputation for Wild West bravery.

Before continuing, there is a small bit of personal mammary-gland history I must address. You see, I do not feel comfortable even writing other words that could describe them... so embarrassed am I, even writing alone in my own home. It feels exactly like the weird warmth and slowed-down breathing I get when I watch those couples in Viagra ads grin into each other's eyes and I believe I know what they are thinking. I am home alone, but not only am I embarrassed for me, but I am also embarrassed for *them*. Are they married and in love or just actors paid to look lustful? Do they meet up after the photo shoot and climb into the same bathtub?

Once, my very conservative father, who I never heard swear, said "titties." I was as horrified as though that word was a curse word. I wanted to believe he was speaking of the cows he milked, growing up.

Secretly, I wanted to nurse my adopted daughter in 1964. I heard that a breast pump had just been invented that could force a woman to lactate, even though she had never been pregnant. A subject like this wasn't discussed among woman friends, so my fear of being laughed at, and the lack of knowing how to research it, drove me to silence. Two years later, Adam joined our family: another darling baby who "grew under my heart, and not in my stomach," using a well-worn cliché. Then I got pregnant, which researchers said happened to eight percent of women who adopted. I could now nurse a baby! At Fairfax Hospital, I explained my plan to the nurses. For six months, I had enthusiastically told my doctor, so he clearly knew my intentions. After the miraculous event, I lay awake all night, staring out the window into the dark June sky, too happy to sleep, thanking God for another child. I also waited to nurse. Where was he? As the hours passed, my breasts began to ache, engorged with milk. Twenty-four hours later I was still without my supposedly hungry baby.

"They are feeding him a bottle in the back," whispered a kindly nurse. Bottle feeding was the new rule and my doctor had not been candid with me. Nor fair. I did not understand the power of "current medical scientific beliefs." It happened to be a very bad year in America for breastfeeding babies (and their mothers). Sick and impatient, I said to my husband, "Please take us home."

I fed Zandy on demand: at the Michigan family reunion, sitting on street curbs and in Maryland restaurants. I felt like a rebel with a cause, joining my Grandma Roslund with her eleven babies, and my Grandma Sandy with her five. The Milkmaid Brigade.

All too soon, Zandy rebelled. It was a cheerful morning when I was nursing my cuddly nine-month-old, and sipping a cup of coffee. To my surprise, he suddenly slipped down off my lap and toddled off. I chased him through the house. He giggled and ran faster. (Yes,

Grandpa Sandy. You were right when you let me tag along as you led your horse to the horse trough and told me, "You can lead a horse to water but you can't...").

I phoned as many neighbors with new babies in New Mark Commons as I could reach and begged to be their "wet nurse." No one accepted my offer. It was 1970 and I was a century too late.

*****

Breast cancer is a round-about way to replace old nipples with new ones. It all started in 1992 when I was fifty-six and my left breast was removed to stop the spread of cancer. At that time, if you could survive five years, you had licked it. For the next seventeen years, I was lopsided, with a flat left chest. There was just bare skin, with no fat, stretched across my ribs. That side was cold in winter and clammy in summer. From the left side, I had the silhouette of a boy. From my right side, you saw a curvaceous woman. I covered the flat side with a one-pound polyurethane facsimile that I tucked into my bra. At times, it fell out. Once, when walking out of church, it plopped to the ground in front of me and other startled devotees.

My removable breast did come in handy, though, when I attended my Weight Watcher "weigh-in" and needed to lose a quick pound. Into my purse it went, helping me stay within my lifetime goal and later, with a twinkle in my eye, I inserted it back into my bra like a lady of the night might tuck away a fifty.

Two decades ago, I spent a cozy evening with an old high-school love. I had taken a trip up to my Michigan hometown to visit relatives and to see Bunk. I traveled from my contemporary home outside of Washington, D.C., to a tiny farmhouse ten country miles from Alma. Bunk, also divorced, was proud of his matching sofa tables, made from two farmhouse hand pumps (wired for a bulb and a lamp shade) that he had painted barn red. I was innocently watching his black-and-white television, which sat solo in the corner with a single cream-colored doily on it, reminiscing about our high-school days. Then he surprised me and grabbed my fake left mound. He leaned in to kiss my neck and whispered, "It feels just like old times." Little did he know.

In 2008, the Cancer Statistics Bureau upped the five-year survival rate of breast cancer to seventeen years. In that seventeenth year, mine came back.

When I learned that my cancer was back and my right breast would also be removed, I opted for two implants. In my imagination, a totally flat front seemed like driving a car with no front engine (and front hood for protection). I would now have the body of a red-carpet movie starlet.

While I waited for the healing of my new scar, which had to take place before I could have implants, I embroidered a square for the Arlington Hospital's cancer quilt. I dug out my mother's embroidery hoops and passed some fabric tautly between them. I designed two cotton stuffed breasts and each was crowned with a nipple surrounded with antique Austrian rhinestones. At the bottom of the square, I stitched the message, "I am not the body. I am the soul." I wanted to believe that deeply.

Life follows art! Dr. Rhim, my plastic surgeon at Kaiser, used "embroidery hoops" (medical equipment that looked similar) a month later in his own artwork on my chest. As he explained to me, Dr. Rhim cut across both breast areas, from armpit to armpit, and laid inside each space, a medical hoop that was encased in a deflated rubber balloon. Then he sewed me up. Once these incisions were healed, and the chemotherapy was completed, my body was ready for the next procedure.

I called them "expansion" parties. At each event, the surgeon, his nurse, and my girlfriend Vicky, who squeezed my hand and smiled, took part in inserting a needle through my skin and into the balloon, gradually inflating it with liquid. I could bear about four ounces a session. My willingness to suffer was in direct proportion to what size bra I would wear in the future.

"Make it a B. No, stop! An A cup will do fine!"

The left side was the most painful, as that skin had been a small patch for seventeen years and now needed to stretch to enclose an implant. It looked impossible. It felt worse. Even with two weeks between liquid additions, it hurt. "You will be glad later," my girlfriends promised, as they bounced around with their lovely natural boobs.

I was finally "pumped up" to a nice size B, but the embroidery hoops started to scream. What did a World War II soldier do when metal parts were shot deep into his body and they could not be removed? Thank goodness, I could have the darn things out. Seven months had passed and the breast area raged like a searing fever. All I could feel were the hoops, in my imagination, hard against my ribs. It felt like my blood vessels and inside tissue might be growing around them. Later I learned they were. The body will always try to assimilate.

With a quick three hours in the operating room, the hoops were removed and I was sent home within two hours... wearing an old lady's training bra, clutching a bottle of Percocet, and feeling no pain.

Sadly, back in 1993, I had been forced to hang away a favorite silk dress that showed a touch of cleavage. I tried to wear it using my foam prosthesis, but the concave hole behind it looked dumb. Now with my two new implants, I would have lovely cleavage and could finally wear that dress again. I might even have another chance at looking sexy.

Still minus nipples, but now with two breasts, my body felt normal again and naturally balanced. And, I didn't need nipples to try on bras. I spied the lingerie department while out shopping and headed for the magical Wonderbra. Making its debut in 1994, this was the new push-up underwire brassiere — and I had missed it by two years. Finally, here was my first chance to try one on. I carried several sizes and shapes into the dressing room.

Now, as an artist, I had many years of experience sculpting female figures, so I knew the gentle slope of a nicely shaped breast. Reflected in the mirror I saw the bare and misshapen naked truth. If I were a skier, I would say there was a steep plunge from my neck down and then a sudden ledge jutting out at a right angle... making it possible for me to fly right off a cliff. And the snow (skin) changed color in mid-plunge! No magic brassiere could soften these edges. The implants were nicely placed and the stitches done with perfect skill, but my dear surgeon couldn't shoot in "filler fat" like an insulation man shoots foam into your attic. In normal breast enlargements, there is body fat to work with. It can be taken from the stomach. But not in the case of implants. My "fat" was gone and so was my dream of a bare-skinned shimmering bosom.

My lovely oncologist, Dr. Pandellapalli from India, announced the inevitable one day: "You are now ready for nipples and what luck for you, as Dr. Rhim creates beautiful ones. They look better than many women's originals."

Later that day, I sat on a stool before this handsome, smiling man to discuss the details of what he would do for my finishing touch. I was already grateful for his gentle manner and the surgery he had completed.

"I will make your aureolas from your groin skin. It is darker, so it looks more natural," he said.

"You mean from *down there*?" I asked, making a face.

"Yes. The operation lasts about two hours. Like any operation there is a slight risk... especially as one gets older. And of course, it will take a few months for you to regain your strength again. You have already gone through two surgeries."

Sometimes women die during a facelift, I thought. I had always judged skin stretching and cutting to be unnecessary and a bit egotistical. Perhaps nipples are in the same category. *Was I taking myself out of the running for becoming a finished product?*

Jane, my Montana girlfriend wrote, "Why not consider tattoos?" They can be done very artfully, with dyes... in pinks and lavenders and touches of yellow ochre. They appear almost three-dimensional. A trick to the eye," she said, adding, "in the dark, of course!" She laughed.

Oh, no! Needles again. I had just done that. And dye? *Who would see them anyway?*

Who would *want* to see them anyway?

After a long, discriminating analysis, it came to me.

I am not the body. I am the soul.

I Frame My Friends

On display were eighty-four photos of her family. Just them. Judy and I were college best friends and now it was three decades later. She lived with a charming architect husband and four stunningly photogenic children in an austerely gorgeous "House Beautiful" home in Cleveland, Ohio. The six of them were posed in four-by-five-foot photographs, which hung overhead, looking down on a clean arrangement of Charles Ames chairs and Mies van der Rohe sofas. Small framed photos sat on Eero Saarinen side tables.

When Judy was reading by the pool, I walked through the maze of elegant rooms and counted the photos. It was always just the six of them, in twos, or just the men, or just the girls, all together or separate, a gallery of blond, smiling faces.

I had stopped as always on my yearly drive up to Michigan. In contrast to Judy, I was newly divorced and my children were scattered. Judy's family scene shouted "We," "Us"; and occasionally "Me." I felt naked, stripped. I no longer had a group to gather together for a family portrait. My loss pushed up from my unconscious mind a stinging awareness, and I saw the possibility of a bigger picture.

Where were Judy's friends? Photographs of them, I mean. She had a slew of girlfriends, and Tom had tennis buddies and men at his firm. Why were none of them on display?

Based on observing this situation for years, I have come to believe that people mainly put themselves on exhibit, along with relatives, and romantic partners. Perhaps they are proclaiming a sign of belonging.

You can't make a family. Getting a framed picture on the wall of a home where you are considered special cannot be bought. Presidents earn space in federal buildings and school lobbies, criminals have their grim faces pinned up in post offices, and saints' images are hung in churches, temples, and meditation rooms. That serenity prayer about accepting the things you cannot change? It comes in handy more and more for me.

I put pictures of my friends right out front, so when they walk into my home they can gasp, rub their eyes, pat their warming heart, and shyly think... "Is that *me?*"

I've loved to photograph people since I was ten. In my purse, my camera is as equal in importance as a tube of lipstick. This passion has produced my photo gallery which is the centerpiece of my living room.

*****

My fireplace wall was empty for years. Then I stumbled upon a warped two-by-ten pine plank left over from building my house, lying in the mud underneath. After many coats of white paint, I hung it as the fireplace mantle. The mantle first held a blaze of candles, and then gradually became a photo gallery.

My friends are lined up.

At the far left on the mantle is Momi in a simple Plexiglas frame. With a multi-colored pashmina thrown over her shoulder and her dark hair pulled back, she looks serenely into the camera. As always, she is lovely and poised. Her countenance is the same when cooking for, and serving, a party of seventy. I can almost hear her say my name. Her lovely accent makes it sound deliciously foreign.

We met twenty years ago. I was living in the house my former husband and I built, high and dry on sixty-eight pilings, twelve feet above the ground (like a beach house) but in a Fairfax County flood plain in Virginia. Already divorced, I was there when Momi and her husband Harry wanted to build their home across the street. For some mysterious reason, there was neighborhood resistance and a hearing was called. They were strangers to me; we had not met, but I was out to defend righteousness. I donned my war suit, black and tailored, and

I Frame My Friends

added a smart black hat and very high heels to intensify my image as a serious speaker. There the neighbors sat, row upon row, before the Hearing Commission Board. I waited nervously, alone, but stood my ground when I was called to testify. "I do not understand. Why can't they build? Their land is not in the flood zone. I built in worse conditions. As a matter of fact, my land is completely submerged at times! Why should anyone disapprove?"

Momi Sekhon and her husband Harkewal (Harry) in his pink turban. 'An arranged marriage that clicked!'

Momi and I never talked, that I recall, until Halloween a year or two after their house was built. I was following a group of costumed children down the street from house to house, photographing them as they trick-or-treated so I could give their parents a photo of their little monsters later. I followed them up to Momi's front door and to my surprise, Momi and Harry stepped outside with a *treat for me*: "Come in and join us for dinner!" I was hungry, not as much for food as for a meal with friends: with a complete family, to be exact.

"Do you *all* live here?" I asked, once seated at their table. I was introduced to their darling teenaged daughters, Momi's mother, Harry's sister Kuldip, and several cousins, all living together and now including me around their lazy susan of food loaded with marvelous curries, rice and vegetables. I was squeezed in between Puneet and Ka Ka, savoring new names and spiced pakoras. It was my introduction to India. Little did I know there was much more to come.

In time, they invited me to a festive dinner party, held on their pink living room carpet. We had color in common; my rusty truck had recently been painted a hot pink. Harry's favorite turban was pink. I was welcomed into a new world of women in sumptuous silk saris and men in smartly wrapped turbans and shoes that curled at the toes. I longed to understand Punjabi (or Hindi?) and ask the ladies about the villages they had left behind. But of even more interest to me were their arranged marriages.

Today, Momi and I are theater and book club pals and like her, I now wear pashminas.

*****

You cannot look for love. Nor for friends. They happen... and then end up on the fireplace mantle.

Meg's photo, in a brushed aluminum frame, stands next to Momi's.

Meg is tall, curvaceous and her shimmering blonde hair swings. Her smile is resoundingly genuine, and her rosebud lips, in the right era, would win her a silent-screen starring role.

Meg is beautiful. I call her Meg-O-My-Heart. She is not a nurse but a person heading up marketing efforts for a newspaper that serves the U.S. military throughout the world, The Stars and Stripes. I count her as a friend, because soon after we met I got cancer and she dropped her high-pressure demanding work to come and cut out two hundred and eighty paper hearts at my dining-room table. She helped bald headed, shaky, weak me make valentines. A comrade in art!

I had to have regular shots after surgery and friends took turns. In a heavy snow storm my anesthesiologist neighbor Jim up the street trudged down through two feet of snow to give me my crucial injections. "I didn't even feel that," I praised. "Let's hope not. I've done a million," he said.

When the weather worsened, Meg was called into service. I sat in total trust, watching her fill the syringe and test for bubbles. She concentrated with professional confidence. Suddenly, her needle slammed into my arm. My chair sailed across the dining room floor with me on it. She had not practiced on an orange. She practiced on me.

Thanksgiving is a rough holiday without family. Memories can swirl up and knock you down. I was pretty well knocked down when

I Frame My Friends

Meg took me with her to a feast with her amazingly entertaining brothers and their equally extraordinary offspring up in Pennsylvania. Most precious of all, was her wisdom. "You are thinking of moving four thousand miles away to Sweden to marry a man who took you to tea in a castle? Where is your mind, girlfriend? He's married!"

I am alive and well and Meg's photo will be there, as long as this house stands. No, as long as *I* stand!

* * * * *

I call her "Angel Janice." She is refined, self-contained and at peace with herself. When cancer struck, I was older, with less energy, and pushing a vacuum cleaner was unthinkable.

Janice had regular house-cleaning and yard help, so was free to be a lady of leisure in that category — although she did service projects non-stop: delivering food to the sick, and serving as office receptionist for her husband (finances) and daughter (doctor). A friend indeed, Janice came over weekly and vacuumed my house. I wanted to do double duty; surprise her with a thank-you gift and also have a photo of her for the mantle. What a good sport she was, posing as I requested. I wrapped her surprise in shiny paper with a silver bow and presented it to her. "Oh, I'm not a Democrat," she said, in her sweet and polite manner, seeing herself with the life-size cutout of the President. I didn't know that. Too late. She and cardboard

149

Obama are smiling, side by side. You might have thought she had voted for him.

*****

A special space is reserved for Marabelle. She is sending a photo from her new home in New England, where she lives near her twins. It's been too many years. The world might say that we have grown old since we last saw each other. Yes, but only in years. Under her tussle of cascading red curls, I recall a sweet smile and kind face. Those attributes do not age.

You cannot look for friends. Sometimes they are sent. I am certain God sent Marabelle, Special Delivery, as a giant bandage for my heart. She phoned me the summer my son Zandy turned twelve. "I have your son here. He broke his arm and the doctor cannot set it without parental permission. It's taken over an hour to persuade him to give us your number. He fears his father will find out. You *are* his mother?"

Zandy had been left "home alone" to care for the skunks, cats and dogs. He had recently been taken against my will by my ex-husband and was living with him. He and his live-in girlfriend had gone on a two-week vacation out West to meet her parents without leaving Marabelle, their down-the-street neighbor, (nor anyone else), any contact information. My other son, Adam, fifteen, and the girlfriend's son who also lived there, had gone off on their own independent vacations to stay with their teenaged friends.

While on his own, Zandy wandered into Marabelle's kitchen from time to time. Sometimes to play ping-pong with her twins, and sometimes just for company. "I guess I am staying with you, sort of," he told her. He was honing his skateboard skills in the street when one of the dogs tripped him and he broke his arm.

"Yes, yes. I am his mother! I will be right there," I cried out to this stranger on the phone. My heart was like a discordant orchestra with each instrument playing its own tune. Compassion for his broken arm, fear of being "caught" by my ex, and the loudest feeling — *Joy!* I cried as I drove the five miles. *I am going to see my son! Take care of him! Bring him home!*

I Frame My Friends

It was the last time I ever got to pamper Zandy. I gave him breakfast in bed and for two nights and three days we laughed and remembered. "Oh, you were so small! You hid inside the coffee table cube!" "Oh, and remember when you were only six and stopped me from accepting a ride with a strange Chinaman in San Francisco? You probably saved our lives!" As we talked, we felt our deep bond of love returning. "Momma, I love you *so much*... and your Wacky cakes!" He softened. "I miss you." Time stood still. We both knew we were stealing it.

He finally begged, "You *have got to take me back before they get home.* They can't find out I was here with you. Ever." They didn't.

But Marabelle was still there. She became the watchtower, the lighthouse, my one connection with my sons. My secret eyes. My sanity.

"I drove them to school today." "Adam has a cold and missed classes." "They are out in the street playing touch football." "Zandy rode with me to school this morning. He did not say much but seems fine."

Nearly forty years later we still exchange cards. Marabelle's worth to me is jewel-like. I really should put her picture in a solid gold frame... with sparkling lights.

* * * * *

An act of nature can bring in friends who, unbeknownst to them, end up getting framed themselves. This next photo shows Walter standing proudly in front of the fireplace, handsome even in his paint clothes, showing off his new beard with one of his Jose cousins. If he picked up a guitar he might be a stand-in for a *muy seductor* (very alluring) mariachi.

A giant tree branch crashed into my living room a few storms ago and I can say that Walter followed on a warm breeze. He came to help, brought in by Mansour.

My insurance company had sent Mansour (from Iran) to be the contractor and under his watch were Walter and his four El Salvadoran cousins, Jose's One, Two, Three, and Four. As Walter brought his cousins one by one to the job, it was I who added the numerals after their names. They permanently adopted their assigned numbers and use them to this day. "*Hola, Señora. Este es Jose Dos.* I can do everything, remember? I clean carpets today!"

Walter's job was to paint. He worked wonders with a roller and a huge brush.

Mansour rented scaffolding in order to work on the twenty-seven-foot ceiling and to repair the gaping hole in the roof.

"While you are up there, why not add a ceiling fan?" I asked. It seemed fair to take advantage of this tree-crashing event. There are no coincidences, I thought. It still amazed me that my tree-hugging "I love you's" to that giant tree for thirty-five years had resulted in this magnificent gift. I was not expecting a return for my affection.

A week later I brought out my antique mirrored ball to be installed. "Hey, guys, *por favor*. Can we hang this, too? Imagine magical colored lights swirling at night, circling over everything in the room, over the walls, the ceilings, as well as outside over the trees, and streaking across the bamboo." The men were listening. "It's something I have dreamed of owning since I danced under one, on my sixteenth birthday." Guy Lombardo and his orchestra were playing, "Enjoy Yourself, It's Later Than You Think." It did not seem late then.

"Who?" they asked in unison, but agreed to wire the ball so it would turn on with the flick of a switch.

A week after that I suggested, "Mansour, could you please leave the scaffolding up for an extra month?" I was never satisfied. I asked Mansour, my new Iranian friend who was earning his place in the sun. (My mantle of photos is in direct sunlight half of the day). "We could paint a mural!" I said, glancing up at the twenty-seven-foot peak and at Walter, working across the room. My lifelong dream of painting a three-story mural on the side of a skyscraper was fading but I could visualize one above the fireplace.

"Walter?"

"Walter! *Por favor!* Where are you? *Donde?*" I practiced my broken Spanish with a smile that I hoped was beguiling.

"Walter. Help!" Walter had never held an artist's brush and did not know a flat from a pointed tip. I gingerly climbed to the first level of the scaffolding, peering fearfully down as though I was on a ten-story roof. Nine feet was plenty high for me. He fearlessly went to the top.

I was gaining a grandson. Walter, twenty-six, sweet and thoughtful, began calling me *Abuela*, (grandmother). His simple English was far better than my Spanish but we were both novices with each other's language and it was *muy difficile* to communicate. He had the job of painting the bamboo stalks at the very top, which were supposed to exactly match the lower part of each stalk, done by a skilled professional painter (me).

I stood below near the sofa and yelled up, "Walter! No... no... turn the brush. *Si. Muy malo. Si demasiado, si*. Eeks! No. No, no no... noooo! Too *bajo*, too low. It is *not* enough paint."

We did this for three days. His patience was supreme. I was still tired and recovering from cancer. All I wanted to do was lie down. Walter laughed as he clambered up and down, as though his shoes had springs in them, and the bamboo grew beautifully. A green stalk, a brown, one almost pink. It was Art 101 for him.

"I think I will paint a mural in my village in El Salvador," he said, grinning. "Maybe you can visit with me. My grandmother there is exactly your age. You are alike," Walter said.

"How?" I asked.

"She loves to work hard like you do. She makes tortillas every morning.

"You make coffee," he added.

Martin, Carlos holding Midnite the cat, and Walter.

And It's Only Monday

Walter, mi amigo.

*****

Everyone has their own way of displaying their possessions, and choosing what to share.

When my Hollywood-handsome Uncle Jim died, he left my forever-youthful Aunt Hulda sad and single. Except for her nose that could not be smoothed out and manipulated, her face was taut and lovely following her facelift. I wrote a strongly suggestive letter to Ed, an old family friend, whose dear wife Mary Ellen had recently passed away.

Uncle Ed Frost and Aunt Hulda, 1988.

"Please, Ed, could you take my Aunt Hulda out to dinner? You're both out there in Los Angeles." He did, and then married her.

On my next trip out West I visited them. Aunt Hulda had moved into Ed's house. In his nicely furnished dining room with his crystal and his china, under his chandelier, sat an ornate 14 x 17-inch sterling silver frame, holding a photo of his recently deceased but still smiling wife. Mary Ellen sat on the sleek sideboard just five feet away and gazed at us while we ate dinner.

"He won't take her down," Aunt Hulda whispered to me as we did up the dishes. "He won't even put her in a back room."

After two years of being stared at, Aunt Hulda got indigestion. That was probably the cause of their divorce. Ed was left alone again with Mary Ellen, smiling coyly in the dining room.

*****

I have been observing this subject for years and I have come to believe that people mainly frame and pin up themselves... their relatives... or those they romantically love. Perhaps it is a sign of belonging. (Long ago African head-hunter tribes displayed their conquests by hanging them up, but I do not believe this falls in the same category.)

Deitz was an exception. He made his picturesque way into a small compact family via the discreet heart strings of my friend Rin's mother. Rin, an only child, and a computer scientist with a Harley and a Dungeons and Dragons zest, displays his parent's 1946 wedding portrait on the bed backboard of the guest room. Evelyn and Paul look appropriately content. Next to their portrait is an action shot of Paul's rival Deitz. Deitz smiles broadly, seemingly proud to be protecting an African boy who is seated in a chair, holding a scorpion on his lap.

Deitz was Paul's understudy to marry Evelyn if Paul didn't survive the Army Air Force in World War II. After the war and Evelyn's wedding, Deitz collected a wife of his own, as well as gorillas for American zoos. He was an old-fashioned naturalist. He phoned Rin's mother collect over the next forty years, hanging up when Evelyn answered and waiting for her to call him back. She secretly mailed him packages with unsuspicious postmarks when she traveled, to keep Deitz's jealous wife off guard.

After Paul died, Evelyn was free to place a photo of Deitz out in the open. Now, how could Rin ever remove Mother's old flame from the roster? It is like having a missing rascally uncle, who was endlessly up to a little monkey business, now sitting in with the family. He finally belongs.

*****

I Frame My Friends

I have not yet walked into a friend's home and seen my photo or any of their other friends smiling from a fireplace mantle, or even hanging in a hallway leading out to the garage. A survey could be interesting. But of course, I am not Mr. George Gallup and don't know how to conduct a real "Gallup Poll." I met him once on a train to New York and should have asked him how to do it. Instead, I grabbed his empty beer can when he laid it down to save for my son Adam's beer-can collection.

People display, over and over, loved ones and family. I would guess that a few thoughtful souls might exhibit out of duty. "We'll keep his picture out in case he unexpectedly drops in."

* * * * *

I still can envision the rooms I spent time in during my childhood. My Catholic friend Sharon Ann's living room held a hard-as-stone sofa mated with a Sears Roebuck end table that her mother soaked with furniture polish every Saturday. On the wall, hung high near the ceiling, was a picture of Jesus in tin foil with a palm frond from Palm Sunday drooping forlornly over it. Sharon Ann's grandparents' photo was in a standup frame on the table, although they lived just two miles away and saw them every day.

* * * * *

I made a stab at making my own family wall display. Not long after the divorce, Amy was living far away in the state mental hospital and the boys I seldom saw. I had paid for a photo special from Olan Mills Studio... a set of four family sittings a few months apart. I got my sons from their Dad's place and put a doll on my lap to represent Amy (the hospital was a hundred and fifty miles away). That was photo number one.

When Amy came home for a visit, we all posed again, but this time with Amy's gigantic smile showing her joy at being home. My grin nearly outshines Amy's, as I had all my children together. I had not yet begun to learn about non-attachment.

My boyfriend Elliott agreed to pose as "my husband" for appointment number three. It was an impromptu affair so he grabbed an old T-shirt and faded Army jacket from my attic. (What could he have been wearing that was worse?) I decided to display one of my not-so-popular "lips" necklaces that were selling at Bloomingdales. Afterwards he laughed. "We look like an old married couple who are going bowling." When Elliott died young, at age fifty, that was the only formal photo of any kind that existed of him, so his father accepted my gift graciously. His brother Ted groaned.

I skipped the fourth sitting.

* * * * *

Photos can be used to fight a war. Family wars at least. They can be used to cut out, to isolate, to show someone they do not matter. They can also embrace, encourage, exhibit love, include and show belonging. *Oh, the possibilities.*

* * * * *

I fell into the trap of looking for love in all the wrong venues... and that does make me ponder the power of photos and the messages they send.

My son Zandy lives a three-hour drive away. I looked yearningly for a sign of acceptance on my last visit, nearly two years ago now.

Did I think that a photo could help me read between the lines or more clearly understand the situation? Even though Zandy and his wife spend all holidays with her family — and most of the times in between — I wished for my grandsons to consider me one of their grandmothers. They already had four others; the wife of my former husband, as well as their mother's mother and her two grandmothers. In this old Virginia family that Zandy had married into, my image on photo paper would be a hopeful sign. In my convoluted needy thinking, I would somehow be part of their family or at least present for the boys to see.

On this visit, I spied a few framed photos crowded together on the living room bookshelf. There was one family grouping in which I was included. I looked closely, feeling a warm glow. It was of my happy but weary son, his wife, her in-laws, my former husband and his wife, and me. Me, as in "my arms and hands." I am holding my new

I Frame My Friends

adopted grandson Ethan at the airport on his arrival from Korea. I had no information on what day or time they would arrive back in the States. I was warned by a relative, via their house painter, not to try and meet them as they were returning "sick" and did not want any greeters.

There comes a time in our lives when desire and love combine to bring forth compassion from others. I phoned many airlines. Finally, a big-hearted airline official helped: "You just might want to be at such and such airport on…" and he gave the date and time of arrival. Since I did not know their gate number, I hung around the luggage carousels, with camera, flowers, cigars, balloons, and a cold cup of coffee. It seemed to take forever. I prayed I would not miss them. I prayed that my information was true.

Then, very slowly, the whole troupe came walking toward their luggage. I surprised everyone! No one was sick. Zandy was thrilled to see me, and never questioned how I could have been there.

"Here is my son," he said and leaned fondly toward his wife, who was carrying Ethan. We all took turns holding the baby, taking photos of each other. In this photo, now in their living room, my head is totally hidden behind Ethan's bewildered little face. But, I was there and he was in my arms. We are together on the family fireplace mantle.

* * * * *

Years ago, I was the overnight house guest of my older son Adam. His wife was extremely fond of her mother-in-law, the "other grandmother" who is married to my former husband. How could I not notice a colored photo of this special couple? In fact, there were three photos of them in the identical exact pose and frame (8 x 10, dark wood) displayed prominently in three separate rooms. My ex-husband and his wife were posed in the formal way that photo studios are adept at: sedate and stiff, smiling into the distance. She did look nice. Perhaps it was their silver wedding anniversary portrait?

Was I oversensitive, or were my hosts trying to tell me something?

What a treat! I was assigned to share the fairy-princess-bedroom with Meadow, my granddaughter, then six. Among all of her pastel and brightly colored stuffed animals and books and girlie things was one of the three formal photos in its dark brown frame. The happy couple was staring right at us, front and center, from atop Meadow's white dresser. I turned them around as we climbed into bed. Once settled I realized they were facing the mirror and reflecting back at me. When Meadow fell asleep I snuck out of bed like a guilty child and I socked it to them. I put them to bed for the night, face down in Meadow's sock drawer.

* * * * *

Cousin Frieda, with her sweet North Carolina drawl, is one of my favorite thirty-eight first cousins! We were toddlers together in the 1930's under the same tender care of Grandma Roslund... and she came north from North Carolina each high-school summer — and I found her jobs and dates. I felt honored to be a bridesmaid in their Chapel Hill wedding, on the day they both graduated, she a nurse and David a doctor. We were thick and we were family... from my view. Perhaps I took our friendship more seriously than she; the relationship was a bit lopsided, but I paid no attention, so strong was my devotion toward her.

My cousin Frieda Bryant Bruton (left) and I in Michigan, 1938.

We all traveled together to China fifty years later. I was welcomed along on their trip. "Ready, set, smile," said the courteous Communist guide. Frieda and David, with their three children, their spouses, and eight

I Frame My Friends

grandchildren, posed with the Great Wall winding up into the distance behind them. We all smiled broadly when they mentioned their Christmas card. I was snuggled up on the end of the second row, enjoying the happy thought that my Chinese Good Luck was including me on their holiday card.

In my mailbox that 2006 Christmas was a letter in Frieda's writing... a fancy small cursive that I would know anywhere. With my heart held high, I ripped open the anticipated "family photo of the year" and their photocopied family news. When had they posed a second time? Was it PhotoShopped? No! but I was not there.

* * * * *

I introduced my Uncle LeRoy to Ted Kennedy at Dulles Airport, when it was first built and rarely used. Mr. Kennedy was alone, waiting to meet his wife and I was meeting Uncle LeRoy, arriving to escort me to Zandy's wedding. Because Mr. Kennedy and I were the only two standing there in a vast, empty hanger-type space, I pretended out of respect that I did not know who he was. I waited until Uncle LeRoy was nearly in front of us, walking in his familiar gait, fresh from the farm and literally having just milked his cows, wearing his new two-dollar haircut.

"Uncle LeRoy, I want you to meet Mr. Kennedy." Mr. Kennedy was quick. He offered his handshake in a flash and Uncle LeRoy grasped his hand in turn, stunned. On the way home, I explained to Uncle LeRoy that I always tried to arrange for a politician to meet my important visitors. Later, I wrote for a photo of Senator Kennedy and in the return mail received a note and autographed picture for LeRoy.

Years later I phoned Cousin John, who lives in the farmhouse left to him by his dad, my Uncle LeRoy. John was driving home from the pickle factory and answered his new cell phone. It carried the old farmhouse's phone number. Strange and sad.

"Your dad's photo of Kennedy? Still on the piano?" I asked.

He parked the truck, slammed the door, let out his barking dog, and I listened to his footsteps take him into the room with the old upright piano... never moved from its spot in the one hundred and twenty years the farmhouse has stood.

John said, "Well, let's see. It's back in there somewhere, maybe, but I don't see it."

Could he hear my silent disappointment? Waiting.

"Oh yeah, over on the end. There it is, behind all the others. Dad, me, Lori, all of Marilyn's boys, just family. It's still here…. Hey, you gonna put your story in a book?" he asked.

* * * * *

It is hard to choose whom to write about. There are many more friends who I would like to share with you. There are more I could frame. I am blinded with tears, both joyful and sad, at the memories of them. They are stand-ins for family and merge at times into being them.

Meg Irish and Sharon Roslund, 2012.

LIFE

Yes, you can go home again

I could see from the street the spot where I had buried her – 67 years ago, at least – and she was over 50 at the time.

Should I knock? Who lives there now? In a burst of instant inspiration, I hopped out of my cousin Tim's car and ran up the familiar steps of 410 Walnut Street in Alma – my lifelong favorite address.

Dora Fisher answered the door and didn't hesitate a moment ushering me in when I said, "I used to live here."

Stepping into the past was like swimming in a warm pool of sweet memories, surprisingly pleasing. The dreaded dishwashing chores, the time wasted vacuuming an already-clean rug, and the cold winter mornings when dad stoked the coal furnace and I sat huddled on the register waiting for the house to warm, dressing for school on the bumpy metal grate, faded.

There was Dad's scratchy maroon chair in the corner where he read aloud the Detroit Free Press's funnies...Mandrake the Magician. There was Mother's sewing machine in the corner of the little side room, where she sewed my ballet costume making me a boy dancer. I wanted to dance as a girl, but Elsie got the part. She was better at her pirouettes.

The black phone on the wall – number 313, a party line. I could still hear its two short rings in 1946 to tell the sitter my little brother Dan had been born at Wilcox Hospital.

And upstairs in the back unheated bedroom was where I secretly made a puppet show with a cardboard box stage and plastic dolls dangling from white kitchen string tied around their wrists and necks.

In fourth grade, Miss Crum let me show it to the class and to all the other classrooms at Lincoln School.

Sharon Roslund

Especially sweet, out the dining room window I could still see Kenny's house where my fifth-grade crush gave me the incentive to do a watercolor of his house, counting and painting every single clapboard. On the windowsill sat my smelly fish bowl.

"Would you like to see the upstairs?" Dora asked.

By now we were friends and I said, "Let me show you the bathroom!"

It was still down the hall on the right but the white claw foot tub was gone. In its place was a 1960s square model.

"I am replacing it when I can," Dora said, "and getting a claw foot tub." Full circle goes the tastes of man. We laughed!

It was time to break the news.

"Dora, there is a treasure in your side yard. I will show you the spot. At the end of the War, I bought a 1880s porcelain doll in a junk shop in Shepherd. Maybe she cost $3. I was acquiring a sense of history and a taste for the mystery of archeology, so I secretly buried her in a shoebox to dig up someday when I got old.

The time has come. You own the land so you have inherited her. Find her if you can and she is yours!"

This took place Nov. 25, 2011.

An Invitation (to the Big Party)

> *You Are Cordially Invited*
> *to*
>
> ## The Big Party
>
> *Your presence is kindly requested.*
>
> **STARTING TIME YET TO BE DETERMINED**

There is no starting time? That seems a bit rude.

I'm preparing to attend the biggest party I have ever been invited to or have ever given. I feel physically fine, so it is easy to delude myself. But, why should I feel like I am so special that I would be the only one not going? Denial can be a comforting friend.

There is so much to do! Although there is no definite date, I don't have time to waste. Forget about what to wear. That hardly matters. Someone will help with that at the time. It is all the "stuff" I have to attend to. I had better be a good sport; attendance for this party is mandatory. Did I mention that? Rather off-putting, to be forced to attend a party. But, if good manners are in your blood, you feel compelled to be a gracious guest and make a good impression. So... I am starting to shed possessions.

The easy part is the piles of paper. Paper dolls, love letters, folders by the box-load. In the heaviest ones, sagging and bulging, are the black-and-white photographs from eight decades. Sharon Bray, my best friend, and I were in fifth grade when she got a "photo kit" for her birthday. It was better than any science-class project that the senior high kids ever dreamed of. We thrilled to see the skinny guys we had crushes on and had taken pictures of appear under the blankets, as photos on paper. This draped underworld was our darkroom. That would have been the exact time for Sharon's mom, only twenty-eight years old, to march into her bedroom without knocking, yank off the covers, and say, "Stop, girls! This hobby you are starting tonight will weigh your life down. Wait and see. You will stop developing your own pictures, start using the drugstore at two cents a print, then years later start ordering 'doubles,' and way before you are old and wrinkled, they will bury you!" She could not have known, being so young herself, but she might have wisely added: "And who is going to want them?"

Who is this? I ask myself as I sort them into piles. Who really wants this photo of second cousins my Dad never met, with the greeting written in Swedish. And here is Grandma holding one of her twelve babies, but which one? Mother, a perfect beauty in her flapper dress, had climbed high up the windmill ladder to flirt with Daddy below... not yet her husband. They are all deceased now. Their souls have moved into another dimension, unless they have reincarnated already, but certainly dead to this world. Gone. Memories to me. But to whom else?

I always wanted to be the family historian. But the family I intended is not around. Some are not even related. Do my son's sons, adopted from Korea, want photos of Caucasian Swedish immigrants pitching hay, or German Great Grandpa Archie butchering a hog? If I take five hundred hours and make photo books from these pictures for my grandchildren, who barely know me, will they care? A few of my cousins will. Tracy for sure! Should this be part of my preparation? I look at my heart and say *maybe*.

An Invitation (to the Big Party)

My friend Bryan and I were sitting at a sidewalk cafe. "What about it, Bryan. This dying deal?" In rebellion, I consciously used the word *die*. I had just phoned my insurance company to learn how to correctly fill out a beneficiary designation form. I said to the woman who answered, "I am preparing for my death." She corrected me: "Don't you mean to say *if something happens to you*?"

"Don't you use the word *die*?" I asked, surprised she was avoiding the term.

"Oh no, we are trained when speaking on the phone with customers, to not use the word *die* or even the word *death*. It is too morbid."

"But, it's part of your work," I said.

"Yes, I know." Her voice brightened. "We're allowed to say the word 'passed'."

"OK, Bryan, I'm ready for your thoughts on where we are headed next," I told him.

Without my notebook handy, I was ready to scribble Bryan's comments on my Starbucks paper cup. He and I are the same age, longtime friends and neighbors, and he had just witnessed my signature for my revised will.

"I want to be kind to my executor," he said. He was a portrait of kindness himself, quick to give me a ride or grab the check. "I just made a list of all my important phone numbers, user ID's and passwords. The most important numbers to me are for the Defense Finance and Accounting Service and my civilian retirement... Office of Personnel Management, the Social Security office and the Army Retirement Center. I want someone to stop my checks," Bryan added.

"That's smart," I said, remembering how my daughter's boyfriend had forged her name and cashed ten months of her SSI checks while she was in the hospital. She was responsible for paying all that money back.

Bryan continued. "I have saved two suits; one for Sunday mass, and one for my burial. My nifty grandson, who is starting life in New York City carted off the rest.

"Wait until you hear what they charge to drive your body to the morgue. It would be cheaper to call a cab... and have someone hop in and ride along with you," he added.

I listened about his possessions, his practical letting go, and wished I could be that casual.

I had to admit to myself, "I must stop going over the past."

Besides the material stuff I leave behind, what needs to be released is the pain. One does not want to attend a party in a negative mood. Who ever heard of dressing up and attending a party with a frown on your face? I don't want to see myself standing at the astral threshold in my favorite silk chiffon dress, scanty high-heeled sandals, eyeliner carefully drawn, feeling all scrunched up with a dismal expression and a resentful heart. That is not how I see myself making my grand entrance.

Clarity is at hand. It is not really about the stuff at all; the furniture, my unsold artwork, the junk jewelry, silk scarves, books, and the cabinets of old dishes. Those, of course, in time will go.

It is my psyche, the contents of my consciousness, that needs the preparation. Emptied, given away, traded in, bequeathed, and abandoned. I do not want to go in the condition I am in right now. I am beginning to suspect that folks with a clear conscience, saturated with loving thoughts, leave with less fear and trepidation. They have analyzed their thinking, and taken on some humility.

My Great Grandpa Meyers, a German immigrant, was passionate about dying. He lay on his narrow cot in his tiny bedroom on the farm, his face glowing from an inner light, "I've got my ticket. I'm going home!" he said joyfully. I was eleven; he was eighty-nine.

His funeral was held in the modest clapboard Church of God just a few blocks off Superior Street in Alma, Michigan. *Why is everyone in this whole church weeping?* I thought. Cousin Dolores played the upright piano while we sang hymns, "That old rugged cross..." and folks took turns speaking about love. God's love. Love for Grandpa Meyers, his love for them, and everyone's love for God. Even Reverend Tuttle was hidden behind his handkerchief and couldn't stop crying to read the Bible. "The Lord is my Shepherd, I shall not want..." The service stalled while everyone gathered strength... waiting in silence; to find some peace inside themselves.

If Grandpa was so happy to go, why couldn't they be happy for him?

* * * * *

Today I phoned Virgie, an old high-school friend, to ask her about her Big Party plans. She didn't even wonder what I was trying to be clever about. "I'm rather looking forward to it," she said calmly.

I still see her as that darling, rambunctious majorette who did fancier handstands and higher twirls than any girl in all of Gratiot County. Virgie was the cutest jitter-bugger in our class, sailing across the wooden floor of the old armory, with the jukebox blaring "In the Mood."

And now as she waits for a back operation, moving around with the help of a walker. I hear her saying with the even-mindedness of a saint, "I've donated my body to Wayne State so the doctors can study me. It's my second choice, because yellow jaundice ruined my organs. Darn, now they can't be used by anyone," she told me.

"Virgie, you're still organized. Like your locker in school."

"That's me," she said, laughing. "I picked out my favorite photo and wrote my obituary. All done. Best of all, I wrote a letter that my kids will read to everyone at my funeral."

Without a hint of self-consciousness, Virgie read it to me.

The letter said: "I ask that all of you take Jesus Christ as your personal friend and Savior. He gave me peace within my heart.... I have loved the Lord so much it hurt. I have cried with joy from the love He has given me. I hope and pray we will all be together and have eternal life in Jesus Christ — the Lord — Son of God. Love, Virgie." Jesus will meet her when she crosses over. That seems clear.

Yogananda says, in my own words, "Live well every day and do not worry about dying. Once you are dead, it is too late."

When I ask the young about their plans, they are thinking "now." However, some older people I question are thinking about the Big Party, perhaps unconsciously, but still they must be. They tell me what is on their "bucket list": paddling down the Amazon, visiting their place of birth (even though there is no physical building standing), finding the history of their "real" father, writing a book (of course) and parachuting into Higgins Lake.

I would much rather take a trip to see Machu Picchu or visit Shanghai again. "Yes, please, set me a-sail on an emerald blue sea, with a Big Band orchestra, a chocolate milk-shake bar, and an international passenger list of writers, artists, actors, and yogis."

A tougher choice would be: "Yes, would you be so kind as to reserve me a month at an ashram on a mountain top, or in a cave; in silence, to ponder, meditate and visualize my daughters-in-laws in white light, forgiving them for keeping my grandchildren to themselves." Help me forgive. Help me give up attachments. This is my real work and preparation before the Big Party.

In India, I once visited the huts outside Kolkata, where the families truly seemed peaceful and were non-collectors of stuff. They pull down a hammock to sleep at night, and hang it back up by day. They die close to home among their kinfolk and are cremated. Their ashes are blown away in the wind or sent down a river. They do not crowd the earth with buried boxes.

I am meeting this solution halfway. My compromise is cremation and sharing a small plot, in a Michigan cemetery, of urns filled with ashes, with my father, mother and eventually, my daughter Amy. We are downsizing from Great Grandpa Meyers, who is just a few yards up the row and Grandpa and Grandma Sandy, also in their caskets, just across the grass. It was my mother, with my assistance, who started the cremation trend when Dad said to me, "What shall we do?"

I, without having ever asked Mother said, "Oh, Mother would wish to be cremated." I felt it in my heart. In her last year, she had read "Autobiography of a Yogi" and learned about reincarnation and Hindu philosophy. Dad looked shocked, fell silent, but humbly agreed. Later, he, Uncle Quenten, and many more Swedish relatives followed suit.

There is hope. It sits next to faith. I have always visualized living for ninety-four years. If that is God's will, that might still put me in the position to be like my Grandpa Meyers, leaving this earth with a grandchild by my side. The Berlin wall came crashing down, and Nelson Mandela was released from prison. Miracles happen hourly.

Maggie Soule's Cabinet

There it stood, its claw feet planted precariously on the gravel at the edge of the corn field. Its presence was powerful, as if it glowed with happiness from the breeze blowing across its oak surface after one hundred years inside the stuffy Michigan farmhouse. The cabinet was nearly six feet tall, with elegant curved glass enclosing oak shelves and a mirrored back.

I stood alone near the edge of the crowd, my sandaled feet, white and pasty from city living, clutching my bidder's card. It read "#70," which unnervingly, and quite accidentally, corresponded to my age.

"Do I hear two hundred dollars? Eh, do I hear two hundred? Two hundred? Will ya' give me two hundred?" the auctioneer bellowed at the crowd of Gratiot County farmers, dark tan from the shirt collar up, snow white like my feet, from the collar down.

There were few old-style farm auctions left in Michigan in 2005 and the folks were there to buy the 1920's quilts, the chipped dishes with pink roses worn from a million suppers of fresh green beans and corn on the cob, the 80-acre parcels, the two falling down farmhouses, the tractors and plows and corn husker, and even the 1965 Mustang that had been parked in the barn, tires rotted but otherwise sound, waiting for the gas station kid to buy it and haul it away.

A few had come to watch and see who carted off what and the price it sold for. Some lovingly sorted through the boxes and piled-high tables and counted their money out carefully. A sprinkling of antique dealers and junk shop owners grabbed hungrily at what they knew would bring a smart profit, adding in their heads as they gave a nod or raised their cards.

I was there like a returning soldier, after decades away, feeling the comfort of black dirt and corn fields, my own country roads, and the voices of relatives I had known since birth and could recognize in the dark. Like the cabinet, I was soaking up the perfect sunny day and feeling the sweet breeze wafting across the pancake-flat fields.

I am young, really, I thought. Perhaps I could kid myself a little longer. If I ignored mirrors and didn't look down at my wrinkled and brown spotted hands, I was only seven. If I could erase the in-between years when life tossed me bitter lemons, I could feel again that sense of not yet wounded youth.

I once had fourteen uncles. Even on this day, I still had four living. Three of them were right here on farms nearby. And I could still claim myself as the younger niece.

Uncle Bud had led the way to the auction in his pick-up using Tarvia roads, avoiding the gravel ones. I followed him in my red Nissan truck with its Virginia license plate proudly proclaiming "Roslund." Uncle Kenny wandered through the crowd. Cousin Dolores checked out the crocheted pot holders.

I'm not a stranger here, I thought. *That lady dresses like Aunt Bonnie. That old man in coveralls reminds me of Grandpa. Oh, and there is my mother, from the back.*

As I stood there on the Soule farm, my reverie took flight. I looked across the field directly into the past. It was less than a mile to my Grandma Roslund's farm and I could *see* the year 1921... Grandma's cluttered noisy farmhouse, alive with five boys and two girls. There's Grandma in her house dress, a feed-sack apron covering yet another pregnancy, out in the barnyard, scattering feed to the chickens. The ground is dotted with weeds and chicken manure, rakes, and an old plow. Cries and giggles come from the house.

Grandma was named Hulda and Grandpa was named Oscar and they had just arrived in Michigan from Illinois. Tired of sharecropping, Hulda and Oscar had traveled up with other Swedish immigrant families and bought their own eighty acres. Oscar was just turning fifty and painstakingly building his dream. Life was hard, simple and exhausting, with few distractions. A friend was a comfort and there was Maggie Soule, tall, big-boned with long straight black hair down to her waist and exactly Hulda's age, thirty-seven.

*Grandma Roslund lugging a pail across the barnyard.
Photo by Agnes Roslund Bryant, early 1920's.*

For any woman, the luck of finding a girlfriend for life and one close by is rare. Maggie had grown up in the county just a quarter mile down the road from Hulda's farm... exactly where I was standing. Hulda and Maggie shared the same birth year, 1884, the same wedding year, and each had given birth to her first child, a son, in 1905. Uncle Herman, the first of Hulda's twelve children, was the same age as Maggie's only child, Clifford. Unknown to both Hulda and Maggie, the name Clifford spelled doom.

Maggie Soule's family in front of their log home. Front row, seated, left to right: Emma, 1886-1959; baby Edna, 1882-1964; Maggie Presler (Soule), 1884-1971. Back row, left to right: Lula Belle, 1880-1961; Barbara Ellen, 1875-1960; Maggie's mother, Amy Presler, 1850-1922, and father, George Presler, 1848-1928; Milton Presler, 1878-1967.

My thoughts returned to the present and out of the corner of my eye I caught sight of the auctioneer. He was approaching the cabinet that I had no intention of buying. I admit I had been admiring its beauty and graceful lines for at least two hours. It seemed odd that all the rest of the furniture parked in the yard was made of unattractive wood Formica veneer and peeling beige plastic. It didn't seem to fit. Without thinking, I fumbled for the #70 card buried in my purse. I had no plan to bid, or at least I didn't let myself think I did, but I wanted it handy for some reason. I suddenly found myself pushing to the front of the crowd just to see better.

Suddenly, my heart threatened to pound out, as though I was in a car race, going faster than I could steer. Uncle Kenny was somewhere in the crowd and Cousin Dolores had gone home. Where was Uncle Bud? There was no one to confer with, as usual. *What was I doing?* Was I trying to hold on to something by getting my first china cabinet at an age when others were giving theirs away, downsizing and simplifying their lives? I was getting entangled in the middle of my history... no, maybe in the end of my history.

If I were to buy this cabinet what would that do? Who would I even leave it to?

I raise my #70 card again and again, in a panic of dizziness, not even hearing clearly what I am paying. I am into the race; I have forgotten the money; I just want the cabinet. Suddenly the auctioneer's huge finger points directly at me like Uncle Sam in a World War II poster and booms, "Sold!" The man bidding next to me has stepped aside. It's mine.

"How much did I pay?" I gasp. "Four hundred and seventy-five dollars!" *My entire July's social security check!* Surprisingly, the crowd cheers for me. Maggie's great-granddaughter Denise Burkholder walks over and says, "You bought Grandma's cabinet. I remember it in her parlor."

"You mean it was Maggie Soule's cabinet, really?" I exclaimed, joy seeping throughout my suddenly more youthful body.

"Didn't *you* want it?" I asked, guiltily. *Shouldn't it stay in your family?*

"No, not at all. I'm glad you got it." Denise smiled and hurried away.

Uncle Bud strode up from the back of the crowd, laughing. "I see you got yourself a beauty! Come on, let's go! I need some coffee."

Uncle Bud settled into his recliner with a hot cup of coffee and Daisy, his dog, at his feet. He was five-feet-eight, with a tan, sculpted face, large ears, a strong square chin, and a good amount of gray hair on his head, which rounded up to a peak. At eighty-six years old, his arms were muscled, taut and firm from chopping wood and building

And It's Only Monday

projects, and his legs were strong and lean from hiking at a fast trot four miles up and down uneven trails in his woods, every morning before breakfast. He was not as handsome as some of his brothers, but he out-glowed them with his warmth and enthusiasm.

Uncle Bud Roslund and Daisy... in the middle of telling tales and drinking coffee.

I sat opposite, in a large overstuffed chair, facing Uncle Bud head on, so I could read his lips and hear better. He yelled, as he could not hear well, either. "Once upon a time... in Sweden." Daisy switched her tail and sighed. I leaned closer, pen in hand. We knew our arrangement well, as this was one of many of our "interviews."

"Of course you know, Mama told me often that they were very poor back in Sweden. Her mother Hanna was an only child who married her first cousin, Gumme Erickson. Gumme was a dentist and a farmer of sorts. He was large, most likely fat, and he was stern. His heavy drinking haunted Mama."

I knew that to be true first-hand. I had visited Sweden, where my Grandma Hulda grew up. I saw the old farm near Blekinge and the rocky ground. Their place was similar to most of southern Sweden; rugged and hilly. Definitely poor dirt for farming. That explains why the immigrants came mostly from southern Sweden; in the north the land was kind to the farmers and they remained content.

Uncle Bud claimed that Grandma Hulda was a teen-aged cow herder. She studied, she ran, she sang, and she day dreamed. She was petite with a pretty face, framed in dark hair, and a dimple in her chin. She ran the cows down to a pasture before school and then retrieved them later. They kept the cows overnight to milk them and then she would drive the cows in the morning to where the next good grass was.

My Grandmother Hulda, age eighteen, in Sweden.

Great Grandmother Hanna, who told Hulda, "I'd rather see you in your grave."

"Mama told me she jogged the three miles to school," Uncle Bud said. "My brothers Everett and Herman teased her, 'Oh Mama, you couldn't run three miles!' But she insisted, in her feisty manner: 'I did!'"

"I used to go out on a rock in the river and sing, too," Hulda told her son Bud. "And daydream of going to America." Grandmother Hulda was nineteen years old in the spring of 1904, when she left Sweden.

* * * * *

Hulda, at age nineteen, told her mother Hanna goodbye for the last time. I can imagine Hulda crying in anguish, "Oh, Mother! Oh, Mother! *I love you.* I am <u>so</u> torn." She knew she would never see her mother again. Hulda sailed on a ship to America, passed the test for immigrants at the New York Port of Entry, and traveled via train on to Chicago. Her sister Tilly welcomed her, got her a job, and wisely threw a single's party where Hulda met her future husband, Oscar.

After the wedding, working as sharecroppers in rural Illinois and seven children later, Hulda and Oscar headed for Michigan. In 1921, they arrived at their farm in Gratiot County.

Maggie Soule was already living there, just down the narrow muddy road and around the corner. Their friendship clicked!

"Your farm was all tamarack trees when I was a girl. They had to clear it to farm. It was almost a swamp," Maggie told Hulda soon after they met, wanting to share what she knew. Uncle Bud said, "Maggie was tall and big boned, compared to Mama, who was five feet at most. Maggie had long black hair down her back and it was rumored she was 'a little bit Indian,' not round faced like her sisters. My brother Everett — your Dad — was quite amazed when he met Maggie. He ran home at high speed, 'I just saw my first Indian!'"

I remember the time I saw my first Indian, too. Just like my Dad, I was thrilled! This colorful mother looked like she was stepping out of a Wild West movie, with her baby in a papoose on her back as she left the gas station in Needles, Arizona, on Highway 66. That was the time Dad drove us all out to California right after the war.

What a shock! The land was purchased sight unseen, from a slick salesman who came to Illinois to charm the sharecroppers and convince them they were getting good farm land. "Michigan looks just like Sweden," he told them. "You'll be pleased."

The eighty acres Grandpa Oscar so blindly purchased from Charlie Harrier had been a swamp and it was still wet... it needed to be drained even more. The swamp had been full of tamarack trees that turned golden and lost their needles each fall. The good news was the wood made wonderful wagons and houses. It was both lightweight and strong.

That was Uncle Bud: endlessly enthusiastic. He was a cross between a professor teaching a hungry student and a lecturer... thrilled with this assignment.

"They had to drain the ground and Papa had to pay a 'drain tax' in 1926. Two-foot diameter glazed clay tiles were laid out on the ground and that 'took the creek away'. They installed them level with the creek and had to dig some of the creek bed out to lay them.

The tiles were then covered with dirt. We farmed right over it," Uncle Bud told me.

"We were paid five dollars a day for a man, wagon and a team of horses. By hauling gravel to spread on the muddy dirt roads, we worked off the drain tax. They took it off our property taxes. The drain tax was one thousand dollars in 1926."

One tradition my family followed, as families do over much of the world, was naming someone after another. My mother always said, "Naming a child after someone you care about is an honor." My mother Verneal's best friend June named her son Dan Neal (as close as she could get). Mother was very pleased. Sadly, Dan Neal did not live long. It seemed a special loss to Mother because he bore her name. I named my gleeful, chubby blonde daughter after my German grandmother, Amelia, as soon as she was adopted. Grandma was so pleased I had "taken in an orphan." It is most probable that Maggie was delighted in the same way when my Grandma Hulda named her new baby Clifford, after Maggie's son. So, when little Clifford Roslund died within six weeks, it was especially heartbreaking for them both.

My father Everett was twelve and recalled when his baby brother Clifford passed away. He told me, "I remember my father was seated, hunched over the kitchen table in the morning, when we all came down from upstairs. He spoke softly, 'I heard angel wings in the night and Clifford was taken away.' I had never seen Papa cry before." My father cried himself when he told me about that morning. Clifford Grant Roslund. Born and died in 1921. The name was doomed.

Maggie was a comfort. She never missed a chance to help Hulda, in spite of her many miscarriages. Maggie's husband Clay was a quiet, stoic man who solemnly took the tiny souls outside behind the barn and buried them. The death of Hulda's baby Clifford added another heartsore disappointment. But Maggie was filled with more than enough love and having only one child, she lavished all the rest of it on Hulda's children and her neices and nephews. Hulda, following baby Clifford's death, had four more sons in a row: Quenten, 1922; LeRoy, 1924; Kenneth, 1927; and Walter, 1929. Hulda needed all the help she could get, and Maggie's love spilled over into action. Uncle Bud remembered, "Maggie and Clay came and picked me up from the hospital after my appendicitis and took me home."

*****

Roughly built, crude cupboards that groaned under chipped unmatched dishes stood at one end of Grandma Hulda's kitchen. Maggie was prosperous by comparison; her dishes were delicate, some edged in gold, and they matched.

Agnes, Hulda's oldest daughter and close in age to Clifford Soule, enjoyed the treat of walking down the road to Maggie's home for coffee and cake with her mother. (And perhaps to get a peek at Clifford?) Maggie's farmhouse was simple and humble, yet because of careful saving and just the three of them to house and feed, they appeared well-to-do.

"She had it *fancy*," recalled Aunt Agnes, "with fine china and linen cloths." When Aunt Agnes got married, she saved up in order to buy a china cabinet just like Maggie's, something she had always wanted.

The Soules found many ways to help the Roslund family. Clay hired my Uncle LeRoy to drive the team when they pitched hay. Clay "set the fork," which was lighter work for a small man than pitching. LeRoy drove the team of horses and Maggie did the heaviest work, pitching the hay. "I made five cents a day," bragged Uncle LeRoy. "Not bad for a six-year-old."

Selling milk was another important source of income and the women helped with milking. Maggie wore overalls; Hulda wore a dress and apron. But, there was no heavy, rich milk for the kids. Grandpa Oscar needed cash too much to keep any for his family, not even for the youngest.

Maggie separated their milk and sold the cream. Her leftover skim milk was considered pig food; "slop," good only for the hogs. Uncles Quenten and LeRoy were sent by Hulda to Maggie's house with an empty pail between them to bring back Maggie's free skim milk. But first, before they trudged back home, she and Clay often sat down and played a game of Pedro cards with the youngsters.

My Dad remembered when Maggie's Good Samaritan spirit was sorely tested in "The Fire." Like a giant earthquake or flood a neighborhood lives through, this event was spoken of with sorrow and awe for many years, even throughout my own childhood.

* * * * *

It was a bitter cold morning and Clifford, age twenty-one, Maggie and Clay's only son, was renting a farmhouse with his young wife Ester, and their four-month-old son Charles, across the field from my grand-parents, Hulda and Oscar. The *Gratiot County Herald* on January 18, 1928 read:

> Thursday morning about 8 o'clock, while Mrs. Ester Soule was outside feeding the chickens, Clifford Soule started to fix the fire in the stove. The fire was very low and he poured some kerosene from the can into the stove and an explosion resulted that blew the bottom out of the can, sending the flaming oil all over Mr. Soule's clothing and throughout the room.
>
> He ran outdoors, a seething mass of flames, where his wife wrapped him in an automobile robe and he rolled on the ground and into water puddles. The flames however, were not extinct until his overalls, pants and underclothing had been burned off his limbs. His hands were burned clear to the bone, his arms and legs badly scorched, while the rest of his body and face were not so seriously injured.
>
> After aiding her husband, Mrs. Soule rushed into the burning house where baby Charles was asleep in the bedroom. After gathering the infant into her arms, she escaped through the window which had been blown out by the force of the explosion. The house and contents burned to the ground in less than twenty minutes.

Uncle LeRoy was three years old and remembered it clearly. "Standing on the East porch with Mama and Quenten, we looked across the field and watched the house burn down."

At the same time, Hulda, Ed and Bud were trudging down the icy road to Mull School. Uncle Bud recalled proudly, "I was the first to see the blaze. 'Fire!' I shouted. At the age of nine, a fire was a big event. Even for adults. There were no fire engines or telephones in the county. If a house caught fire, there was no stopping it. We watched the fire walking backwards, as we couldn't be late for school."

Grandma Hulda went to the Saginaw Hospital with Maggie to visit Clifford before he died, two agonizing weeks later. He had lived twenty-one years, nine months and twenty-seven days, stated the *Herald*, which didn't round off any of his time on earth. Maggie and

183

Clay hung a wreath on their farmhouse door and laid their only child on an army cot in the parlor. The neighbors came on foot, horseback and car. Uncle LeRoy remembered: "Mama took my hand and led me into the parlor to say goodbye. Death was for everyone. It is for everyone today also, but some do not know it. Maybe only when it is too late."

Maggie celebrated Christmas just once with her newly enlarged family. As often happens in life, a dream that finally comes true can shatter before it is hardly realized. She was finally a mother-in-law and a grandmother. In her devastation, Maggie found solace in Baby Charles, her grandson and only surviving blood relative. He is "my little gold mine," she told friends, referring to the fact he would "inherit it all." In time, my Grandma Hulda would have thirty-eight little gold mines, many of whom delighted in her great affection for them.

Despite this enormous loss, Maggie was a doting aunt; she hosted dinners and birthday parties at her farmhouse for her two sisters, Belle and Edna, and their children. She gave to everyone, and like a good Christian, who attended the Methodist Church at Beebe, she followed the teachings of Jesus, "Do unto others, as you would have them do unto you."

When my daughter Amy was a teenager and should have been in high school, she was living in the state mental hospital. At Lord and Taylor's one day I turned a corner in the Junior Dress Department to find Amy's best friend trying on a prom dress with her mother's help. The mother, brushing her daughter's hair from her eyes, said, "That looks beautiful on you, Sweetie."

I fled the store as though I had seen a murder. When it happened at Garfinckel's a few months later with a different mother/daughter, I wanted to give up shopping. Not once in all the years with any of my children did I get to help them dress for a prom or even a simple date. I was haunted in all directions... but it was a small thing compared to what Maggie endured.

How did she bear it? Even now, with no child of her own, Maggie's willingness to give her friend Hulda a hand never lessened. They stayed close friends — but I have often wondered how? I believe it was because Maggie never shut Hulda out, and my grandmother didn't hide out of guilt for having what her best friend had lost. Maggie shared her grief and Hulda joined in. My grandparents included Maggie and Clay in their family fun.

Uncle Bud was deep in sobering thought when he told me, "We survived by sticking together. Our community was loving. It salved the hurt, soaked up the pain and we all needed each other then. It was nice. We were close. It's not that way today," he ended with a touch of sadness.

The very next Fourth of July (in 1929) after the fire, "everybody," meaning Maggie and Clay and all the Roslunds, adults and kids, piled into a big farm trailer and drove fifty miles to Bass Lake for a picnic, on gravel roads at best. They couldn't sing "God Bless America" that day, as it wasn't performed until ten years later. But they might well have felt its sentiments.

Growing up, I had my own "God Bless Grandma" moments. I do not recall Maggie, but she is in photos of events we both attended, where I am out of the camera's range: weddings, picnics, and Swedish Aid coffees, where Grandma and the old ladies in black gabardine and clunky shoes gossiped in broken English mixed with Swedish. I ignored all of those old people. But during the many gatherings, Maggie and I must have talked, or at least smiled at each other. Perhaps she hugged me.

*****

Among my many memories of growing up, is Grandma and my fish.

It was summer time in her kitchen. My glistening minnow swam in a circle at the bottom of the enamel pan that sat on her kitchen table. A hot breeze blew through the screen-less window, bringing in the poignant smell of cow manure. Flies buzzed overhead and zoomed smack into the overcrowded fly paper dangling above the kitchen table.

"It's a pretty one," Grandma said to me, as she bent over to take a closer look at my fish. "Yaw, its colors shine," she said in her strong Swedish accent.

It wasn't the fish but the fact it sat on her kitchen table that thrilled me. I had hung over the cement parapet above Bush Creek holding a tin can tied to a long white string. My eight-year-old patience paid off when a fish finally swam into my snare. With a quick jerk, I pulled the can straight up and there it was. My catch of the day!

At home with my parents, fish were off limits in the house. So was anything that might be dirty or messy. Grandma, I was certain, would have let me lead a muddy pony into her kitchen if I had had one.

Grandma Hulda's funeral was in Michigan in 1966; she was 81. Maggie's funeral was in 1971; she was 87. They were both buried in Emerson Township Cemetery, down the road from their farms. There, with tombstones at their heads, lie Hulda and Oscar, Maggie and Clay, and the *three* Cliffords.

Being respectful of his father, Baby Charlie, Maggie's beloved grandson, whose auction I attended, named his *own* son Clifford. This great-grandson of Maggie's, Clifford L. Soule, born in 1953, was discovered by his mother behind a shed at Maggie's farm, shot to death. Although his mother never believed the sheriff's report, he had taken his own life. He was forty-eight.

Rest in peace, dear ones. All three Cliffords.

* * * * *

The auction was over and Maggie's cabinet, resting flat on her back in my pickup, allowed the tailgate to close with an inch to spare. She was ready for her seven-hundred-mile ride to her new home in Virginia. Three road men from Guatemala, El Salvador and Mexico, just happened to be working out in front of my house when I arrived. They graciously accepted the job of carrying her inside.

"Si, Señora," they said, laughing as they lifted her up in the air like she was an acrobat lady they were twirling, and as though she couldn't break.

The Roslund Clan

Introduction

The past is often ignored by children. A bore. But not all children are alike. I watched my Great Grandfather Justus Meyer live to be eighty-nine and the fact he was "old" made him intriguing. He peeled an apple super thin... all in one continuous strip, turning it so it never broke. To cool his coffee, he poured it into a saucer and slurped. He got on his knees each morning at Grandma's, and led us all in prayer. He let me sit on his lap while he rocked by the west window, reading his Bible and watching the sun set on the flat fields. No one else that I knew did any of these things.

So, old age and facts that would change with time were important to my young mind. I decided to keep notes about my life. I was obsessed. I wrote down the price of bread (12 cents a loaf for white at the neighborhood store on Woodward Street), the weather, town news, what Mother did, how my friends acted — for five years. It was my most serious and private project. I did not know how I would use this information. I would like to say I figured I might write about things someday, but I am not sure I was thinking that far ahead.

Then I grew older and the vicissitudes of life crowded in, one of which was boys. My sentiments and impressions of life, along with my faint romantic yearnings, were logged into my diary of "current facts." But too soon, I allowed myself to "go steady" with a popular, idolized guy. His dad was a local professional, high on our town's status list and rich by Alma, Michigan's standards. Lex was captain of the football team, and *he* thought himself to be quite important. *I* thought he was merely cute. I realized that I suddenly came into his sight at the same time we moved from Walnut Street to the higher stratosphere of Wright Avenue, near his house.

My teenaged opinion of people's character was developing. Lex took me to the Alma Country Club to play golf, as "they" were members. I had never touched a golf ball, and after nine rounds of his critical suggestions, I never wanted to play again. And I didn't. Not until decades later, at our 50th high-school reunion at the same country club, when I hit one round with the old gang. Lex kept on playing, I know, as he boasted years later to me that he was hitting balls with his neighbor, Clint Eastwood.

Sedate State Street held several mansions and Alma's two hospitals. One crisp fall evening before the final dissolution of our relationship, we met at the top of this street where it ended in a field. Standing there, with his blond crew cut, looking handsome and sly, Lex said, "If you want to prove you love me, you will burn your diary." I felt sick to my teenaged stomach. "Burn it?" I wanted to die. "Did you bring it as I asked?" Lex asked, his hard look erasing what remained of his charm. "Yes," I nodded and pulled it from my coat pocket. He built a small bonfire in the field and I sadly tossed my diary (or did he?) into his fire. No, _our_ fire.

Could there be anything worse for my writing career that was still fifty years into the future? Not the extinguished diary, but the lack of self-esteem and not doing what I believed in. That moment's fire of regret still smolders.

At the 50th high-school reunion, I learned from La Deana, an old classmate, "We should have traded tips back then! I joined Lex on a golf date and never played golf again either!" This helped me understand how much Lex liked to control and how little he cared for me. If I loved to write and collect facts and memories almost as much as I loved art and photography, he must have found destroying my diary a powerful experience?

To make up for giving in, I got a second chance to stand my ground at the Spring Prom. Fitting his sense of entitlement, this handsome hunk asked my father to "borrow" a brand new, yellow Lincoln Continental convertible, to drive us to the dance. My father,

The Roslund Clan

who sold new and used cars, said "Yes," without even consulting me. It was a man's world in the 1950's. Even I could see he was using Dad. I faintly suspected the car was far more enticing than I was.

My sophisticated wrist corsage, a lovely wilting gardenia whose scent mingled with the refrain of "Because of You" by Tony Bennett, filled the air... all the way up to the gymnasium's ceiling. I felt a true touch of romance as we danced, feeling the swish of my taffeta formal, as Lex guided me across the floor, under the basketball hoop, and dipped me. Once we danced the starry, starry night away in the high-school gym, sipped the last of the Koolaid punch, said goodbye to the chaperone/parents, Lex drove me home. Inside the garage, he turned off the ignition to the snazzy car, the new leather seats giving off a tantalizing fragrance, and said: "To prove you love me, you have to have sex with me. Now. Tonight." I shook my head. "Otherwise, I will break up with you," he said. *After he had the nerve to borrow my Dad's car?* I thought.

Definitely, he had the idea that I was not only a fool to burn my writing, but also that I would now give him my body! "No thank you, Lex," I said politely. Although, what I really thought was: *Oh, there go our darling crew-neck sweaters-to-match we wore together on chosen days for study halls and auditorium events. Poof! One, a set of pale baby blue, the other a grey. Twelve dollars for a sweater is a lot to pay, to never be able to wear it again.* He stopped speaking to me the next day.

So, I could blame my teenaged angst, my poor judgment, my burned up diary, my shaky self-esteem, and my straggly hair (Mother always said that) on the skill of my writing, but I will not. I have an unquenchable desire to record the past. Here are the best stories of the Roslund clan I could dig up from my kin folks, our friends, and anyone else who knew anything or thought they did. And some are mine.

*****

The Roslund Clan of Emerson Township, Gratiot County, Michigan, began with my Grandma Hulda and Grandpa Oscar. As in the Bible, they begat and begat... until eventually they produced my eight uncles and two aunts. Since all their children married, that added more aunts and uncles, who in turn begat my thirty-eight first cousins!

It all began in the Old Country of Sweden where Hulda and Oscar were born. My Grandma Hulda was nineteen years old in the spring of 1904 when she left Sweden.

Hulda's family was poor. Her daddy was a dentist… and a farmer of sorts. He was large (most likely fat), and he was stern. His heavy drinking haunted her. Her parents were first cousins. Their land in Blekinge, like most of that part of southern Sweden, was rugged, hilly, and rocky. It was poor dirt for farming. Hulda was a cow herder. She would run the cows down to the pasture and then retrieve them at day's end. They kept the cows at the barn overnight to milk them and the next day she would drive them to where the next good grass was.

Will I see Mama again? Hulda wondered. She didn't want to even think about the answer. Those she knew who went to America never returned. She had not seen her sister Anna Matilda (Tilly), two years older, since she had gone to Chicago three years earlier. Tilly and her future husband, Andrew, finally, and with great generosity, sent Hulda steerage. "You will love America!" wrote Tilly. It had been Hulda's dream to go. But now that it was at hand, she felt a mix of trepidation and joy. Crying one minute, laughing the next, "I am going to America!" she sang, a thrill going through her small frame.

The day arrived. Hulda and her mother Hanna left the little rocky farm near Jamshog, Blekinge, and started down the dirt road toward Karlshamn, a seaport at the southern tip of Sweden. Hulda was dressed in her best black high-button shoes, a long black skirt and a fashionable black velvet bonnet, edged in rose crepe. Her only possessions were stowed in a heavy wooden box.

"I'll walk you as far as the gate," said Hanna, taking Hulda's hand tightly with one hand while gripping firmly the heavy basket of food with the other.

It was four miles to the end of the lane, where the old wooden gate enclosed the cows and marked their parting spot; keeping the cows in, her mother in, her past in.

Every few yards as they walked, Hanna pleaded, just as she had done for months: "Hulda, don't go." "You're too young to travel alone." "You're my youngest." "We'll never see each other again. Don't you realize that?"

Then, from the depths of her anguish Hanna spoke words that Hulda never forgot and that haunted her for the rest of her life: *"I'd rather see you in your grave."*

It is hard for me to believe that Hanna was so anguished that she put her own feelings before her daughter's future, wishing her dead to keep her close, rather than wishing her a good life in America. But a mother's love can be a tragedy of selfishness. And even when well meant, love can do strange things. Through my own experience with motherhood and friendships, I understand the longing of this ancient Bengali chant: "In this world, Mother, they do not know how to love me. Where is there pure loving love? There my soul longs to be."

Hulda and her mother, with tears stinging and throats aching, found the last mile almost too painful to endure.

All Aboard

"Goodbye, Mama." Hulda grabbed the basket that Hanna had packed tight with cheese and hard bread, hitched up the wooden box with its rope handle and rushed away. With her mother's last words ringing in her ears, Hulda found her way to Karlshamn and waited for her turn to board the ship. She stood with the cold wind whipping the lonely line, and was finally directed to the lowest level in the hold.

Once settled, she pulled from her pocket a small piece of paper showing Tilly's address printed in English. Her second independent decision of the day was to guard this paper. She closed it in her hand, vowing not to open her fist again until she reached Chicago.

For twelve days Hulda slept on a wooden shelf in steerage, far below deck, never once allowed up topside to see the silvery moon or span of sea.

The poor in steerage were barred from leaving their assigned space. One small lantern gave them light. Their cramped quarters reeked of seasickness and exhaustion. Lice kept company and multiplied in the same clothes she wore for the entire trip. Hulda didn't consider opening the tightly nailed-shut box. Her father had thought the 14 x 14 x 27-inch dimensions of the box were the perfect size for a young woman to carry. *Yes,* she mused as she ran her hand over its smooth surface, *Good old Papa.* He was a big man as dentists go and was known to immobilize his patients by sitting on them while pulling their teeth. She was touched that her father had built the box for her with his own hands.

Grandma Hulda told me herself, "We were down in a hole and it was so crowded we couldn't move. It stank! The only food I had was in my basket. I carried Tilly's address with me in my closed fist and never opened it the entire trip... not until I got to Chicago. I was petrified of not being able to find her. I didn't know any English." Hulda's tightfistedness may have been an exaggeration, but it remained a part of her story forever.

It always struck me as something more than coincidence that, exactly fifty years later, in 1954, just like Grandma Hulda, I also was nineteen years old and saying goodbye to my mother. But I was not sailing alone to a new country. Dad was driving me to college and instead of building me a box, he let me fill the entire back seat and trunk of his Buick with my belongings. In that same manner, I continued to collect more stuff over my lifetime than Grandma ever did. Instead, she collected more people.

Grandma Hulda passed through Ellis Island like an exhausted but surprised student who had dreaded a final exam for weeks and then left the classroom realizing she had given all the right answers. Now there was New York City, spawning train tracks in all directions. Hulda luckily took the right one to Chicago, and she always claimed that she didn't open her hand until she saw her sister running toward her. "Oh, Tilly," she cried. Her left hand ached from the weeks of clenching it. Now she could let go.

"Get out of those clothes! Horrors!" Tilly was a take-charge big sister and she relished having Hulda with her to fuss over and care for. She had been lonely, too.

Sisters Hulda and Tilly, Chicago, 1905.

"None of that 'Old World.' You're getting an American hairstyle, modern clothes, and a nice job as a maid in a dentist's home."

"We know dentists, don't we?" They laughed together.

"Nothing too complicated; just scrubbing floors, sewing, washing, ironing, watching kids, cooking, gardening and keeping the clocks wound," Tilly said.

Hulda frowned.

"But, here there are no cows to herd," Tilly soothed.

Hulda wondered. She realized she had liked taking the cows out to pasture, sleeping in the summer grass under the midnight sun, and dancing barefoot round the maypole at the midsummer festivals. She loved singing with her girlfriends, the other cow herds. She wasn't going to be an American cowboy but she certainly had been a Swedish cowgirl.

Tilly said, "One more surprise. I'm throwing a single's party in your honor! All the Swedish men I can find are coming."

Hulda didn't say a word. She knew Tilly wanted the best for her and believed that her life would be easier if she married.

* * * * *

Hulda meets Grandpa Oscar

Hulda was about to meet her future husband, on a blind date of sorts.

There was no time to waste. I can imagine the scene. I can smell the coffee.

Tilly worked as a seamstress. She was extremely skilled at altering clothes, she had found Hulda work, and now she was playing Cupid. The two sisters put on their best dresses and did up their hair; double-checked the coffee cakes they had baked, saw that the coffee was boiling on the stove, and gave each other an excited hug. Everything was set out on a Swedish lace cloth and the room soon filled with laughter and grateful voices, excitedly speaking their native language.

"Vilken del av Sverige kommer du ifran?" a young woman asked, smiling hesitantly. (What part of Sweden are you from?)

"Nar anlande du?" A man asked flirtatiously. (When did you arrive?)

These were some of the many young and lonely immigrants who knew no English... longing to start life with someone. Then Oscar Nilsson entered the room, wavy haired and dashingly handsome, with a mustache and quiet shy charm — and only one seeing eye. His one blind eye only made him mysterious, I imagined. I would like to write that he was debonair and sported an eyepatch, but one has never been mentioned, nor have I seen him in a photo with one.

"Oscar's been around," Tilly whispered to Hulda. Tilly had heard that Oscar had come from Tingsgarden, Sweden, twelve years earlier in 1893, and restlessly wandered around the United States trying out stone masonry, farming, and odd jobs. But had he? He supposedly showed great respect by earning money to make a return visit to Sweden to see his widowed mother in 1898. *That is a very good sign when a man respects his mother*, Hulda reasoned.

Oscar was now thirty-one and a confirmed bachelor — until he laid eye on Hulda. His quiet nature balanced her warm, outgoing friendliness. Grandma told me later, "I met Oscar at Tilly's party, got mad, threw a shoe at him, and married him." What a Cinderella thing to do! I cannot imagine what he said to her that made her mad enough to marry him. It just has to have been a past-life rekindled friendship.

Hulda and Oscar Roslund wedding photos, January 27, 1905.

Eight months after Tilly's party, in borrowed finery, their grand wedding photos appear to show a wealthy American couple. It had to be magnanimous Uncle Magnus (Martin), Oscar's brother, a well-to-do Chicago tavern owner (and behind the scenes whiskey manufacturer), who dressed them in fancy wedding clothes, paid a professional photographer, and rented a horse and buggy for the festivities on a cold Friday, January 27, 1905. On the surface, Oscar and Hulda had a fine and fancy start.

But their son Randolph, my Uncle Bud, grew up believing Tilly came to their aid. He remembered, "Tilly and her husband Andrew were again generous, providing Hulda and Oscar with wedding clothes, etc." But Tilly did not marry Andrew until a month after Hulda and Oscar married and it is doubtful that a hard-working seamstress would have extra money. Someone treated them to a romantic start and I vote for Uncle Magnus.

I wrote this little poem for them:
> *The embroidered lace blouse, hairdo and flowers;*
> *Smart suit and hat, and soft gentle showers,*
> *All melted into a hard and cold existence.*
> *Frozen farm furrows, skim milk and slop,*
> *Cows in the cold barn, would never stop.*

Often the sons in Sweden take a new last name when they are grown. Oscar dropped his father's last name of Nilsson and adopted the name of Roslund. No one recalls who said this, or if there is a bit of truth in it, but the story goes that Grandpa Oscar saw a Swedish billboard advertisement of a prosperous Swede with that name. If that was true, he made the change to Roslund while he still lived in Sweden. I cannot say.

Oscar Nilsson, age 17, Sweden.

Growing up, I heard many tantalizing stories about my Grandpa Oscar. Speculation abounded. Tales came and went over the years, with everyone taking a stab at what they imagined or thought they knew about his earlier life. The truth is elusive. Perhaps he left a wife back in Sweden during those missing years from age twenty-one to thirty-one. Did he leave behind children? My Uncle Arthur, his third oldest son, imagined his father's darker-than-Swedish complexion (Grandpa always looked pale white to me) meant that he was the son, or at least a descendant, of southern European royalty. "No," other uncles insisted, "Papa was the true son of the King of Sweden!"

"Oscar's brother, 'Magnus' Martin Nilsson, whose wife Marie was supposedly from the McCormick (Deering Tractor) family, worked for

The Roslund Clan

Al Capone at a speakeasy in Chicago," said my Uncle LeRoy's son John (my erudite cousin from Ithaca). "Oscar was afraid of Martin's criminal connections." "Oscar poured cement to build sidewalks in Chicago." Cousin John also said, "Oscar returned from Sweden for the second time (date unknown), but was worried they would not accept him with only one eye, so he jumped overboard and swam to shore in New York." *Maybe he took the ship further north and dove overboard in Canada?* Whatever the reason, there is no mention that I could find in the Ellis Island records of Grandpa Oscar's second arrival in America.

The Swedish Royal Family

The most elaborate stories that we cousins created on Sunday afternoons at our grandparents' farm were inspired by the portrait of the King and Queen of Sweden in its ornate fake gold frame, which hung in Grandma Hulda's parlor. We could pick out King Oscar in his beard and mustache, with Queen Hulda in her crown and lovely pearls. The nine boys standing around, weighted down with medals and braid, were our uncles and the two seated women our aunts. We cousins believed without a doubt that the photo had been taken just for our family.

* * * * *

The truth is: Oscar was not from the Swedish royal family. Oscar was born Oskar Nilsson on December 6, 1872, in Tingsgarden, in a home

And It's Only Monday

with a sod roof, which is now a small museum. I visited at Summer Solstice in 2008 and listened to the locals give a little talk in the long, dark building... speaking slowly in English with a heavy Swedish accent. All the men sounded like Grandpa Oscar. I wandered through the low, dark, connecting rooms... trying to imagine at what exact spot my great grandmother gave birth. Outside, in celebration of the solstice, everyone danced around the Maypole and then gathered in the meeting hall for coffee and cake, and I saw again the same scene I had experienced back home as a child. Chattering grown-ups, loudly speaking Swedish over each other, and drinking cup after cup of coffee. It was boisterous, unrefined and jovial.

Oscar's father was a poor farmer who, on the first day of 1886, was killed by a strike of lightning. He was fifty-eight and Oscar was only thirteen years old. I visited Grandpa Oscar's church (in Ostra Ljungby) that 2008 summer and put flowers on the gravesite of his parents, just inside the gate of the churchyard. It was a humbling day when I could honor, in person, my great grandparents: Grandpa's mother, Gunilla Olsdotter (born June 22, 1830, in Ostra Ljungby), and father, Nils Hansson (born March 14, 1828, in Walinge, Malmohus Lan). I attended a concert that evening in Grandpa Oscar's church, and hoped I was sitting in a pew he might have sat in as a boy.

It was said that Oscar had tried to keep the farm together after his father died, and had attempted blacksmithing, until he was also struck by fire, this time by a wayward spark as he forged a metal tool. Not enough to kill; just enough to blind one eye. If this is the correct order of events, then perhaps that was the "last straw" in his rough, young life and Oscar decided to make a daring change.

Grandpa Oscar came to America the first time through Ellis Island on May 30, 1893, when he was twenty. The Chicago World's Fair had just opened earlier that month, on May 1, and he always claimed he had attended. I believe this to be true... but there is nothing in writing, of course. How could he not have gone? He was an adventurous, single guy out to see the world! He would have experienced the first Ferris Wheel, along with Helen Keller and

The Roslund Clan

Alexander Graham Bell and twenty-seven million others. A pretty heady beginning in America.

However, when did Grandpa Oscar go back to Sweden and return to the States the second time? What did he do from ages twenty-one to thirty-one, when he finally met Hulda? Did he really visit his mother? Did he return to Sweden and marry and have children in that missing decade? His daughters Hulda and Agnes were never sure themselves of their mysterious father's past adventures. He kept his secrets.

* * * *

Hulda and Oscar began their married life as sharecroppers. They lived in Paxton and Ludlow, Illinois, in the rural area of Champaign, south of Chicago. From 1905 until 1921 they farmed and started their very large family of twelve children: Herman, 1905; Agnes, 1907; Everett, 1909; Arthur, 1911; Edvin, 1913; Hulda, 1917, and Ernest "Bud" Randolph, 1919.

I imagine Grandma writing home to the "Old Country:"

1905 — "Dear Mama, Merry Christmas. Enclosed is a wedding photo of Oscar and me, taken January 27. Our first son is here, little Herman. Are you upset that Norway split from Sweden? Now we are half the size. It's shocking!"

1907 — "Dear Mother, I learned that they have started a new holiday in America called Mother's Day. Good! I am a mother again and singing lullabies to Agnes, just like you did for me."

1909 — "Dear Mom, Everett was born! 'Another son to help with chores someday,' Oscar says."

1911 — "'Anna Karenina' is playing at the movie house in Chicago. I wish I could see it. We mainly play cards and drink coffee with other Swedes. Arthur was born."

1913 — "Edvin arrived. More help for the farm. Oscar is counting."

1917 — "Dear Mama Hanna, we have a second daughter. Oscar insisted she be named 'Hulda.' Buffalo Bill died. He was a famous man, who Oscar saw in person at the 1893 World's Fair."

1919 — "American women are cutting their hair short. Called a 'bob.' I won't do it. Surprise, another son, our fifth. He is Randolph. We call him Bud."

1920 — "Lots of news. Alcohol has been banned and they labeled it Prohibition."

*****

My grandparents' neighbors in Illinois were also sharecropping Swedes and they all knew they were trapped. Land in 1920 was selling for five hundred dollars an acre and that meant their destinies were cemented in sharecropping or renting a farm for the remainder of their lives. The times were harsh and discouraging. Then, as if by magic, three land agents appeared from Alma, Michigan, with enticing news. Like cunning foxes, they made their pitch, "Land! We've got cheap land!" They painted a glowing picture of rich farm land for sale in their county, never mentioning it was nicknamed "starving Gratiot" county. "You will love it; the climate is similar to Sweden," they claimed. That part was true.

These hopeful, hardworking and naive pioneers would come to populate the entire northeast part of Emerson township (one of five townships in Gratiot). There were the Swedes: the Oscar Roslunds, Ole Weburgs, Gus Bloomquists, the Elmer Andersens, the Pearl Glads, the Martin and Arvid Andersons, the Hartwick Ostlunds, the Frank Carlsons — and one Dane, Jens Fosgard. From 1920 to 1922 they made their move by train and automobile. Some families rented their own boxcar to transport their possessions of clothing, furniture, and farm equipment. Others shared one to split the cost. A member was chosen from each family to travel with their livestock.

My Uncle Herman, age sixteen, was selected to watch over the Roslund ark. He said, "When chickens laid their eggs, I dashed back to the caboose and the train's cook fried them up for the crew." Jerry Dewer, reporter for the Gratiot County Herald, wrote in 1953, "We would have liked to have seen Herman trying to milk a cow while the car bounced its merry way in a swaying fashion over its metal highway."

The Roslund Clan

Before the move to Michigan, Hulda and Oscar held an auction to sell some of their livestock, horses, and household items to help finance the trip.

I imagine Hulda taking a moment to dash off a letter to her mother in 1921: "Mama! We are moving to Michigan. We are buying a farm! I am expecting a baby again."

Farm Sale Poster

The small print reads:

As I am going to move to Michigan, I will sell on the Mrs. F. E. Johnson farm, 4-1/4 miles straight west of Ludlow, on Friday February 18, 21 commencing at 12 o'clock sharp.

One roan mare 8 years old, wt. 1400; one black horse 6 years old, wt. 1300; one brown mare 13 years old, wt. 1200; one black mare coming 3 years old, wt. 1200; one gray mare coming 2 years old; one black mare 5 years old, family broke; two work horses.

Farming Implements

One Little Giant corn dump, 38 ft., good running order; three cultivators, 1 new; two gophers, one sulky plow, one Emerson gang plow, 14-in., used 2 years; one walking plow, one potato plow, one 8-ft. binder, cut 150 acres; one new John Deere corn planter, 160 rods of wire, one Peoria endgate seeder, used 2 years; one Bradley 10-ft. disc, new; one spader disc, one cutaway disc, one 4-section iron harrow, one 4-horse International kerosene engine, one new Holland No. 6 grinder, one pump jack, one new Peter Schuettler wagon, one Weber wagon, one South Bend wagon, 100 rods of hog wire, three spools barb wire, two water tanks, one Star tank heater. two oil tanks, hog oiler and troughs, chicken coops, smoke house, 5x5 ft.; two sets work harness, 1 good as new; one set double driving harness, one set single harness, dozen good collars, some halters, hand corn sheller, cistern pump, 30 gallon jar and other jars.

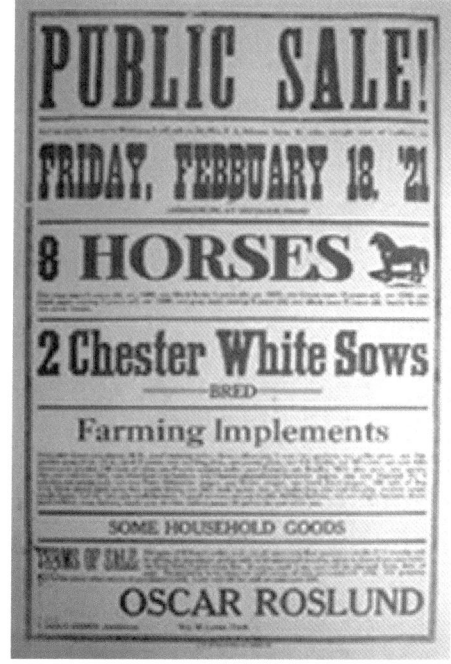

SOME HOUSEHOLD GOODS

Terms of Sale

All sums of $10 and under, cash; on all sums over that amount a credit of 11 months will be given, by purchaser giving note with approved security, notes to draw 6 per cent interest from date if paid when due. If not so paid, 7 per cent will be charged from date of sale. No property to be removed until terms of sale are complied with. All property left on the place after sale is at purchaser's risk. 2 per cent off for cash on sums over $10.

Col. S. S. Denny, Auctioneer Wm. M. Lateer, Clerk

Whoa! You darn car!

Grandpa Oscar was forty-six years old in 1917, when he got his first car. He had three years of limited experience before they headed north. It is likely he seldom drove his car. He had driven a team of horses, every single day, for over a decade. It's possible — and would not have been unusual — for Herman, age twelve, to have done most of the automobile driving; he drove his mother, my Grandma Hulda, to do her shopping in Paxton, a small town nearby.

Now it was 1921 and Grandpa Oscar would celebrate his fiftieth birthday year by driving the family to Michigan and taking possession of his first land purchase! Herman had already gone ahead on the livestock boxcar. Oscar gingerly got behind the wheel of their Model T Ford. He had never driven a long ways before. Hulda and the other six kids piled in. Straight through downtown Chicago they puttered. All his life he had driven a team of horses and yelled "Whoa" to bring them to a stop. Oscar yelled "Whoa" again, his life-long mantra for "stop." They headed straight into a trolley.

"A policeman swung his Billy club and stopped the runaway car," said Cousin John, obviously on the receiving end of his father's incredible story. His dad, my darling Uncle LeRoy, a storyteller with an amazing imagination, was born two years after the move to Michigan and probably never even saw a Billy club. It was a touring car, not enclosed... and now it was useless. The eight Roslunds were forced to continue by train.

Herman, with the family cattle and possessions, arrived first. The train let him off in Breckenridge, Michigan, and Herman drove the herd out to their eighty acres. They needed a wagon and a team of horses to move their possessions. Could these have been in the boxcar? No one ever said.

My Uncle Kenny remembered hearing that his mother and the other kids arrived on a later train. Grandma Hulda disembarked at the same Breckenridge depot as Herman, then walked five miles down the narrow dirt road to their new place at the southwest corner of Van Buren Road and Baldwin Roads in Emerson Township, farmland in all directions, as far as one could see.

They must have been relieved to finally arrive, and were probably pretty impatient, too. Big sister Agnes was twelve; Everett, eleven; Arthur ten; and Edvin, nine — all old enough to run on ahead and lead the way. I can imagine little Hulda, three, and Bud, two, tagging along behind with their mother. Because she was expecting another child, Grandma Hulda probably couldn't carry Bud very far. They arrived late at night — only to find moonshiners in their farmhouse. Horrors!

"Mama was stubborn... in a good way!" Uncle Bud said, when he and I discussed their arrival. Hulda dragged her brood further down the road to stay with a neighbor. They weren't going to sleep in their new house with drinkers; the memory of her father's habit always lurking in the back of her mind. Again, Grandpa Oscar was not mentioned in this particular story... neither what he was doing nor where he might have been at the time. Perhaps he was feeling overwhelmed. Or discouraged over his ruined car. Or, better yet, I would like to imagine that he was basically invigorated by their safe arrival and went off to find some of his farmer men friends to share stories with over a cup of coffee and a cigar.

Moving to the new farm

Maggie Soule was already living in Emerson Township, just down the narrow muddy road and around the corner from Hulda and Oscar's new homestead. She was born there in a log cabin the same year that Hulda was born in Sweden. They were both thirty-eight years old when they met. Maggie's only son, Clifford, was the same age as Hulda's oldest child, Herman. So much in common. Their friendship clicked!

"Your farm was all tamarack trees when I was a girl. They had to clear it to farm. It was almost a swamp," Maggie told Hulda soon after they met, wanting to be of help and share what she knew. Uncle Bud described her to me: "Maggie was tall and big boned, compared to Mama, who was five feet tall at most. Maggie had long black straight hair down her back and it was rumored she was 'a little bit Indian,' not round faced like her sisters. Your father Everett was quite impressed when he first met Maggie and ran home at high speed, yelling, 'I just saw my first Indian!'"

I remember the time I saw my first Indian, too. Just like my Dad, I was thrilled! This colorful mother looked like she was stepping out of a Wild West movie, with her baby in a papoose on her back as she left the gas station in Needles, Arizona, on Highway 66. That was the time Dad drove us all out to California right after the war.

How my Swedish grandparents drained the swamp

The eighty acres Grandpa Oscar so trustingly purchased from Charlie Harrier was mostly swamp and it was still wet, exactly as Maggie had told Hulda. It needed to be drained. The swamp had been full of tamarack trees that turned golden and lost their needles each fall. That wood made wonderful wagons and houses. It was both lightweight and strong. Earlier owners had already timbered it off.

My Uncle Bud, Grandma Hulda's seventh child and fifth son, was one of my main sources of stories from those long-ago days. His memory was sharp, his interest keen. He loved to share his knowledge with me and I was delighted to write it down. For decades, I visited Michigan and recorded the stories told by my uncles and cousins. But out of all of them, it was Uncle Bud who proved endlessly enthusiastic and talked up a storm. He was a cross between a professor teaching a hungry student and a lecturer... thrilled with his assignment.

"They had to drain the ground and Papa [Grandpa Oscar] had to pay a 'drain tax' in 1926. Two-foot diameter glazed clay tiles were laid out on the ground and that 'took the creek away.' They installed them level with the creek and had to dig some of the creek bed out to lay them. The tiles were then covered with dirt. We farmed right over them. County men came to do the work, wearing overalls but no hats," said Bud. I regret not inquiring why he pointed out their lack of hats. Was that uncommon?

"By hauling gravel to spread on the muddy dirt roads, we worked off the drain tax. It nicely came off our property taxes. We were paid five dollars a day for a man, wagon and a team of horses. The drain tax was a thousand dollars in 1926," Uncle Bud told me.

Gravel was to bring good fortune decades later to Uncle Herman, whose land happened to almost be a gravel pit. This God-made commodity helped make the new Michigan Route 127 from Alma north to the Straits, in the 1960's... and it helped Uncle Herman's prosperity considerably. They used his gravel and dirt to build up the overpasses over Michigan Avenue, Pine River and the railroad tracks.

Horses to high school...

My father Everett and his buddies, Ray Griffith and Howard Presler, met at Mull School early in the mornings and rode the farm's work horses to St. Louis, stabled them, and went on to high school. Everett could only get a horse when Grandpa Oscar wasn't using one in the field. In winter, with the icy roads edged in snow banks, the boys rode to town regularly. Otherwise, Everett walked the five miles.

"I had just one pair of shoes, of course," my Dad explained to me. "And at the end of each school day and my ten-mile round-trip hike, I cut new cardboard soles. The next morning, they were ready to go again." Uncle Bud remembered him doing that. My Dad also learned to darn. He taught me how and when he was eighty, he mended the holes in the toes of my canvas sneakers.

Food...

I couldn't get enough of Uncle Bud's stories. "Tell me about the meals. Your food."

And It's Only Monday

At that, he reheated the pot and, like good Swedes, we had another cup of coffee... which reminded me of how my addiction began. Grandma Hulda scolded me, "If you want to be a good Swede *you must learn to drink coffee.*" So, I did. But *yuk!* In my college dorm room I made colored water with instant Maxwell House, increasing its strength over time. Finally, I went with Dad to the farm and reported, "Grandma, I did it! I'm now a Swede!" Laughing, she handed me a cup of her strong black brew. "Show me!" she said. Coffee is one of my treasured connections with my Grandma.

Uncle Bud continued his reminiscing. "The neighbor women helped each other with the cooking. There was no refrigeration, so they killed a chicken and ate it the same day, quick and fresh! Add biscuits and gravy, or mashed potatoes laid on top of a bowl of gravy. Delicious! Or, we had a choice of white beans, navy beans, green beans in season, butter beans, lima beans, or baked beans with ham." Uncle Bud was on a roll. "Papa had a smokehouse and they rubbed the meat with curing salts, all over the slabs of back, loins, chops," Uncle Bud recalled with a sigh. "Pork? One hundred pounds! They [the families] would trade meat off among them so the hogs could be eaten fast. When we were lucky, we shot a rabbit. There was seldom a wandering deer."

Grandpa Archie Sandy (right) and Ed Morford, butchering a pig, early 1920's.

Uncle Bud also recalled, "Mama [Grandma Hulda] was friendly to strangers and once invited a salesman to dinner. He started to eat all of our pickled herring (called *sil* by the Swedes). Mama snatched it away from our greedy guest. She wanted some for the rest of us."

"Nobody was fat!" Uncle Bud added. "No meat even on a crow. You had to have barn cats to keep the mice down. But no fat cats, either."

* * * * *

I remember in 1943, when my Uncle Wally was a teenager and I was eight or so, my Grandma leading me through the ice-cold parlor that she *never heated* and into her bedroom. There, she opened her bottom dresser drawer. Among her corsets and nightgowns were cookies. Swedish *spritzels* if I was lucky. But whatever kind she offered me, they tasted like "forbidden fruit." I felt guilty for poor Uncle Wally. He was left out of this secret. Sometimes she hid the cookies from him out on the sun porch in her crochet basket. Wally was a typical starving teen-ager, endlessly on the prowl for her sweets.

"Pike! They swam to our door!"

Uncle Bud loved our interviews. He never tired of trying to recall the smallest detail.

"Your father Everett graduated from St. Louis High School in St. Louis, Michigan, in 1927, when the bridge over the creek in front of the house was still made of planks. There, with a three-pronged pole (or pitchfork) he and my brothers speared five- and six-pound pike out of the creek. As the little kid brother, I was charged with the job of dragging them across the lawn and up to the house. The creek was two to three feet wide and ran along behind the outhouse, perpendicular to the road. The pike spawned and came up from the still clean, pure Pine River and down Bush Creek. Papa and Mama cleaned the fish, cut them up, and laid them in a wooden barrel: a layer of fish, then salt, then fish, more salt, on and on to the top," he said. Uncle Bud never told me what all that salted pike actually tasted like and I never heard my father rave about any salty fish they consumed; only the "shit-in-bull" dish with meatballs that Grandma made. Mimicking a Swedish accent, the Uncles and Dad said that phrase so quickly, with an exaggerated pronunciation, that I never caught on to what they were actually saying until I grew up.

Bud wasn't the only uncle to tell me a fish tale. On another trip to Michigan, I drove out to my Uncle Kenny's farm and, pen in hand, got him talking. We always visited by the front door next to the wood stove, with a cup of Aunt Violet's coffee. The back un-used parlor, like most farmhouses in the county, was used only on Christmas morning. The gifts were opened around the tree and near the oak china cabinet, another fixture in any farmhouse. Ornately framed family portraits hung on the wallpapered walls. Uncle Kenny was son number eight, born in 1927.

"When Wally and I got hold of a shotgun, we went out to the ditch, where the pike were swimming. I had the gun and fired at one. Water went up in the air and scared us to death! I had shot its head right off!" he said.

Windmills

Grandpa Oscar may have lost an eye and bought a swampy farm, but he was lucky in one regard. The farm came with a windmill. Most farmers did not have one.

Uncle Bud told me, "The windmill pumped the water into the house... and there was a tank in the kitchen with one spigot. Cold. There was one dipper in a pail of water for thirteen of us to drink from and everyone did. You coughed all winter long, because if one kid got a cold or a sore throat, everyone caught it. Round and round it went."

Other not-so-blessed neighbors had to pump water up from the ground with a metal hand pump, an activity that was magic to me as a child. My other set of grandparents, Archie and Amelia Sandy, over south of Alma, had a hand pump until they got electricity in 1947. The pump's handle was so heavy and stiff that I had to jump on it with all my weight to ride it to the down position to force the water up and out. Like all well water directly from the ground deep below, it was cold and delicious! We pumped it into a wooden pail and carried it to the house.

The Roslund Clan

Uncle Bud recalled how Grandma Hulda sent two of her kids at a time off with a pail to the neighbors. "It was a privilege. Mostly a boy's job... Two of us kids carried one bucket between us." The little boy came out in Bud when he reminisced. He still swelled with pride, even as an old man, when he remembered his chores. "We carried water by the pail as far away as Bernice and Ed's, nearly a mile, and to the Shaffers."

The horses got their drinking water from the horse tank, which sat near the windmill and quite close to the house. A pipe ran from the windmill to the tank to fill it. Water was diverted from the pipe that sent water to the house and was sent to the horse tank instead. The flow was controlled by some sort of braking mechanism no one has been able to explain to me. (They did need to keep it fresh and running.) I never recall seeing anyone try to swim or play in the tank.

Outhouse

A few yards away from the horse tank sat the outhouse, which served as the family's combination toilet and library. I was always proud to say I knew all about "outdoor facilities," as if I had lived as a pioneer on the prairie or something. It could feel like the Wild West when it was snowing out there or cold rain blew in. Some of my in-town girlfriends had never used an outhouse, so I thought my grandparents owned something special. It never occurred to me that some misguided souls were perfectly happy never to have had to use one.

"How did you clean the outhouse, Uncle Bud?" I asked; a point I had never cared to know about before.

"Ha! For sure we *never* moved it. Just tipped it over! Papa, Everett and Herman shoveled out the s--- up from 'the hole' into a wagon and spread it in the fields as manure." Uncle Bud added with a laugh, "Once LeRoy threw a bucket of water through the broken outhouse roof on me. I was quick; raced out and beat him up!"

The outhouse had a more revered meaning for me. It was my first interior-design job. When I sat out there, summer and winter, the breezes blowing through the wide cracks, and the Sear's catalogues stacked to use (and to read, along with a few old Swedish

And It's Only Monday

papers) boring me to death, I dreamed of fixing up the place. Sweet Grandma said "yes" and let me tack as many coloring-book pages as I wished all over the walls. Such freedom. Such trust. She left them up until they blew away.

Thinning Beets

"It had to have been 1928, when I was nine and your dad, nineteen," Uncle Bud said. "After high school, Everett went down to Detroit 'to make good.' It didn't work out. What a come-down for him. I can still see us out there on the northeast corner with the hoe. Now he was back on the farm with his little kid brother, me, out in a darned old beet field, thinning beets. I was pretty happy in his company but way too young to understand how he must have felt, having to come back home and all."

My father Everett enjoyed looking spiffy and being neat. He told my mother Verneal that the frayed collars on his dingy white shirts embarrassed him growing up, but he would never hurt his mother (Grandma Hulda) by telling her. He understood. He was tender with his many little brothers and helped my Grandma out. circa 1925.

My father Everett was valedictorian of his high-school class. He truly loved learning; he was wild about school — especially literature and French class. And dancing. Dad danced the Charleston with magic in his feet, his hands crossing his knees at lightning speed, even when he was in his seventies. But, his buddies from school were off to college and now he was thinning beets. Not out in the garden eating worms exactly, but still out there.

Uncle Bud went on, "Everett blocked the beets with a short-handled hoe, thinned them so they were twelve inches apart. I came along behind and made sure there was only one beet in each spot. Two beets and they would not grow well. I had to crawl on my

210

hands and knees. It was a quarter mile up a row... or eighty rods up and eighty rods back. Then it would be noon. We did four rows a day. It took four days to thin an acre.

"Everett used his Detroit stories to entertain me as we hoed. He had worked at the Fisher Theater as an usher. He told me, 'All I did was say "up the aisle and to your left" a thousand times. One lady said, "I don't want to go to the left." Everett replied, 'I don't care if you don't want to. I don't care if you have brass tits, you have to go to the left!'"

Uncle Bud thought that was hilarious. He must have been very impressed with his big brother's bravado to remember that story so clearly seventy-five years later. A young man showing off to his impressionable kid brother can last a long, long time.

That small risqué word still embarrasses me. I do not recall hearing my father swear... or say dirty words, except for "he's a pot-licker!" or a "nincompoop," which obviously was not a good thing to call someone. Swearing was not common among the uncles. And certainly not the aunts. I never once heard a lady of any sort say a swear word of any kind.

When it came to beets, though, my Grandma Hulda's "beet baby" story topped Uncle Bud's, in my view. She was helping pick the beets, felt a kick or two, went into the farmhouse and gave birth to another son, and returned to the beet field to work a few more hours. On my honor, this is true! Everyone said so. Figuring from the birthday dates and what sort of beets were being harvested, it was most likely Uncle LeRoy. I always knew he was special... the type who's always ready to get on with things and enjoy life.

From mud to gravel...

"Gratiot County was full of muddy trails," Uncle Bud told me. "When it rained, it was impossible to drive a car on the roads. Nothing but mud.

"The County started to spread gravel for the first time on the road we lived on, all over the township and most of Gratiot County around 1929. Everett and his high-school buddy Howard Presler (whose aunt was Maggie Soule) each had a team of horses and a wagon. (A team is two horses). Everett and Howard, both twenty years old, sat together up in the front wagon so they could talk, and put me in the rear wagon, holding the reins. I didn't really steer anything as my team of horses just followed the wagon ahead. But I sure was thrilled. It was a big responsibility, in my estimation, for a youngster. There were twenty-five to thirty teams hauling gravel at the same time. We did two loads a day, one in the morning and one in the afternoon. That was about all the horses could manage." Uncle Bud added, "We walked 'em, not trotted 'em."

Uncle Bud continued, "We started at the gravel pit site (which was on land Bud ended up buying years later). Four men worked on each side of the wagon and shoveled the gravel by hand into the wagon. Those men stayed there and continued to shovel all day long. Once the wagon was filled, four horses were tied to the wagon to bring it up out of the deep pit. The wagon was then reattached to a team of horses to be hauled the six-and-a-half miles," Uncle Bud concluded. "We drove past Beebe to the half-mile road."

"A boy my same age, nine, named Keith Richardson, fell off a wagon one afternoon, right into the gravel pit. Dead. He had died of a sunstroke," said Bud. I heard some lingering sorrow in his voice.

Grandpa Archie Sandy and Great Grandpa Meyer with their horses, a precious commodity, circa 1925.

Arsenic and Queen Anne's Lace

Grandpa Oscar didn't just plant, weed and harvest. Selling what he grew was equally as important. His crops in the 1920's and 1930's were beets, corn, cucumbers, string beans, potatoes, pumpkins, squash, peas, and lima beans. His pumpkins, squash, and sweet corn went to a cannery in Edmore; the peas went to the Roach and Company canning factory and the lima beans, which were thrashed like peas, went to the town of Owosso.

Uncle Bud recalled, "We picked our string beans by hand and dragged a gunny sack behind us as we picked. They went to the Libby-McNeill canning company. Tiny cucumbers brought the best price but were hard to pick. They went to Libby in gunny sacks and they paid us by the pound. Sometimes we took cucumbers and string beans to Alma all mixed together."

Uncle Bud had started on his "farm report," and there was no stopping him. I took notes as fast as I could write... and gulped coffee in between.

"We had to hoe to cultivate and that was hard work. There were no pesticides! The potato bugs were the worst and the cutworms were terrible. We mixed arsenic powder into water, put it in a sprinkling can, and walked up and down the rows."

Uncle LeRoy also contributed his recollections about farming. At one time, Clay Soule (husband of Grandma Hulda's neighbor and best friend Maggie), hired LeRoy to drive the team when they were pitching hay. Clay "set the fork," which was lighter work for a small man than pitching, LeRoy drove the team of horses and Maggie, by far the strongest of the lot, did the heaviest work, pitching the hay. "I made five cents a day," Uncle LeRoy boasted. "Not bad for a six-year-old." It was 1930.

All along, I can imagine Grandma keeping up her correspondence with her mother in Sweden:

1921 — "Mama, we made it to Michigan and now own a farm. But our baby son Clifford only lived a few weeks."

And It's Only Monday

1922 — "Dear Mother, I wish I could show you. The Michigan ditches are filled with wonderful wild flowers! The Queen Anne's Lace is beautiful here, too, except you call it 'dog biscuit' in Sweden. Quenten is our newest son."

1927 — "Oh Dear! Mother, I am more a mother than ever. Quick in a row, I had LeRoy in 1924, and now Kenneth in 1927. I wish Papa would stay away from me."

1929 — "Mama! I just had my last baby, I hope. I gave him all the rest of the names I could think of: Walter, Earl, Clarence, Henry, Elmer, Junior, Jence, Peter, Oscar. We call him Wally."

Thrashing

As a child, I loved the excitement and holiday feel of thrashing days, running around and watching, but I never analyzed how it worked. I was curious about the process of thrashing and asked my sheep-raising cousin, Tracy, son of my mother's sister Bonnie, to explain it to me. He described it as "the action of removing the seed from the pod of peas or dry beans, or removing grains of wheat from their seed heads."

Everett Roslund on Thrashing Day. Photo taken by his sister Agnes.

214

Thrashing was hard work. First the men cut the wheat with scythes like the Grim Reaper uses, and other men gathered the cut stalks up off the ground and stood the bundles into standing "shocks." Along came a wagon pulled by a team of horses and more men piled the shocks into the wagons and drove them to the rented thrashing machine near the barn. One man ran the machine while other men threw the bundles off the wagons into the machine, where the stalks were shaken up. The chaff, as well as dust and grasshoppers, were blown away. The grain came out a chute, where more waiting men "bagged it off," usually in hundred-pound bags. The leftover straw was used to bed the animals. Nothing was wasted.

The population then was far smaller. "You knew all your neighbors. We traded help, not just for thrashing, but for hoeing corn, beans, and sugar beets," Bud said.

Thrashing especially demanded a lot of manpower, so the farmers all helped each other and took turns at one another's farms for Thrashing Day. I never wanted to miss that! My mother's mother, Grandma Sandy, five miles over from Grandma Hulda's farm, always let me stay over when they were thrashing. I was tantalized by such a crowd of tanned, strong farmers in their coveralls, rough and rugged, shouting orders over the roar of the thrashing machine. Barn-raising days were just as much fun.

Grandma Sandy, with the help of Aunt Bonnie, my mother's sister, and other farm ladies, set up a long table out in the yard and covered it with her ironed, white linen tablecloths. She used her best dishes. They cooked for days to prepare and at noon on the big day, the sweaty, dirty, exhausted men sat down to a feast. Grandma Sandy was loved for her chicken and homemade, thick noodles and famous among the farmers for her fancy table settings. It might have been that her German mother, who died when Amelia was eleven, had ingrained in her a clean, crisp style. Grandma Sandy once told me she had at first lived in a log cabin with Grandpa Archie and to make it nice, she covered the ceilings in white sheets. Of course! That is where my mother Verneal must have gotten her exasperatingly neat habits.

And It's Only Monday

Barn Raising Day - June 11, 1916. A festive event; practical and social. Everyone came to build the new barn. Grandpa Archie and my Great Grandpa Meyer in turn helped all of them build their barns. I count forty-three men and six boys. Did I miss anyone? Where were all the little girls?

The Roslund Clan

My Grandma Amelia overlapped her white, starched and ironed linen tablecloths for the dirty and sweaty (but grateful) men. She used her best dishes. Nothing was too good for her guests. If they were lucky, they got her fresh chicken and thick home-made noodles. I see seven ladies serving nineteen men, with room for more. Maybe this is a second seating? At lower left is a well-dressed gal in a hat, curled up in a buggy seat. Far out under a tree two women are chatting.

And It's Only Monday

Above left: My Grandma Amelia Meyer Sandy, age twenty-seven, and Grandpa Archie Sandy, age thirty-one, in front of their log home, east of Breckenridge, Michigan. (1913) This is where my Grandma stretched white sheets across her ceilings for neatness and cleanliness: a good German daughter! My mother Verneal was born here and regularly found arrowheads on her way to school. The area once was heavily populated Indian territory.
Above right: My mother Verneal, age three, with her doll Dorothy, 1916.

Off to market

Uncle Herman, Maggie's son, Clifford Soule, and Lolly Stacy hauled beets for the Michigan Sugar Company from the "pilling station" where they piled them up, to the St. Louis Sugar Factory where they made both white and brown sugar. Alma had a sugar-beet factory also. I can attest to the fact that the odor and soot were awful to live near. When I was six and World War II was raging, we lived three blocks downhill from the St. Louis Sugar Beet factory. The smell was bad and our combs were black with soot from the tall furnace stacks spewing smoke round the clock, as well as from our house furnace that Dad shoveled coal into every morning.

The Roslund Clan

Uncle Bud was more into peas than beets.

"We mowed peas and lima beans like we mowed hay. We pitched them, vines and all, onto a wagon. Then we hauled them to the Pea Vinery to be thrashed. My very first job was at the Pea Vinery in Beebe, with stationary thrashers. After they had been thrashed, we shoveled the peas into wooden boxes called 'lugs' that weighed twenty- to twenty-five pounds each. The vines went into a pile. We stacked the lugs, and trucked them in a Model A Ford truck to the cannery. I think it was in Owosso," Uncle Bud said, trying to remember.

He also recollected that this would have been sometime in the early 1930's, just as the Depression was rolling in. Then he grew tense, leaning toward me from his chair like he wanted me to understand at a deep level what he was about to say. "The (pause) Depression (pause) was (pause) bad. Farm life was endless drudgery."

Do not fear hard work

The kitchen stove had to be fed wood and corncobs constantly, for boiling water and cooking. The washing machine had a scrub board with a hand ringer. Aunt Margaret, Uncle Wally's wife, lived with

On the county line between Midland and Gratiot, from left to right: my Great Great Grandfather Henry Meyer, Great Great Grandmother Elizabeth Meyer, Grandmother Amelia Sandy and her father, my Great Grandfather Justus Meyer, 1905.

Grandma Hulda in her old age and so knew many of Grandma's stories. She said that Grandma Hulda told her, "I had to get so much done and there was never enough time. I would iron until two or three in the morning and Oscar would yell at me, 'Come to bed! What are you going to do, sleep all day?'"

Hulda was always up early to make pancakes, send assorted kids off to school, gather eggs, feed the chickens, slop the pigs, clean out the chicken coops, help milk the cows, make butter, garden, can food for winter, mend and sew, and work in the fields along with the men. Hulda told Aunt Margaret, "When I married, I thought I would have an easier life." In spite of a life that must have come as something of a disappointment, Grandma Hulda told her kids many times, "We were put on this earth to work. Don't be afraid of it."

Grandma Hulda certainly did not fear it. She did the family washing and there was a mountain of it! To dry the clothes, in addition to the clothes line, she threw them over the field fences and bushes or laid them flat out on the grass in the sun. I saw her do this and I have proudly carried on her ways. My clothes dry on the deck's wooden railing at my home, twelve miles from the White House, and have dried that way for nearly forty years.

Cousin Frieda emailed me from North Carolina about her six-week stay at the farm in 1942, when she was six. "I can see Grandma now, walking across the big driveway area carrying a heavy bucket full of chicken feed. It would be late evening and the chickens were coming home to roost. She would go into the chicken house, clucking and cooing and talking in a sing-song way to the hens, as they flew up into their nests. There was a rickety, old chair leaning against the wall. Sometimes she sat there, visiting with the chickens, just to rest and not have to go right back into the house to do the never-ending chores."

A chicken can be a fine-feathered friend. When Grandma Hulda plucked a chicken for dinner, she saved its feathers. The chicken had given eggs for years to feed the family and now it would be eaten for dinner. Most important of all to me, the hen gave her own feathers for making pillows. I covet mine. I have eight feather pillows from my two grandmothers that I sleep with. My inheritance was not sterling silverware or diamonds; but feathers to dream on.

When it came to chickens, Grandma Hulda was something of an entrepreneur. She once traded a chicken for a magazine subscription. It must have been an egg-laying one that continued to give; I surmise a year's subscription to a magazine was worth more than just one chicken dinner.

Not everyone in Alma struggled with hardship. At the same time that Grandma Hulda and the immigrant women of Emerson Township were grappling with survival, Sarah Wright and Louisa King lived in State Street mansions in Alma with their nannies and servants. Out on Michigan Avenue, Rose Ruggles lived on her seventeen-acre estate on Pine River. I am certain the farm women and the high society ladies never knowingly crossed paths. It is possible, though, that the elite might have eaten an egg from one of Grandma's chickens.

A day of rest

Grandpa Oscar had his own ideas about the Sabbath. He never worked on Sundays. The Swedes published two papers in Chicago, the Chicago Blade (1877-1949) and the *Furbundets Veckotidning* (1916–1934). No one knows for certain which one he read, or if it was the one that came by mail monthly or weekly. I think it must have been weekly, as every Sunday afternoon Grandpa would take his cigar and read the paper out loud by the bay window. *He never read silently.* He would put a toothpick through the end of his cigar so he could smoke it all the way down. My cousin Ike recalls watching Grandpa burn his lips, so entranced was he in the paper and reluctant to waste even a bit of his precious cigar.

If it was nice weather, Grandpa Oscar sat out under the big tree and read to the older kids. Everett, Herman and Agnes could understand some of what he read… but he made no attempt to teach any of his children Swedish.

"We were to be real Americans and speak good English. Only English!" said my Uncle Bud, who often wished that he had learned

Swedish. The teacher in Ludlow, Illinois, told Herman, "We speak English. We *don't* speak Swedish." Grandma Hulda and Grandpa Oscar's first real English lessons came from Herman, as he was the oldest and the first to go to school. Agnes and Everett no doubt added more words to their vocabulary when they traipsed home from school each day.

Oscar and Hulda kept their charming Swedish accent to the end of their days and I loved to hear them talk. I believe everyone new to our country should learn English. However, I think all immigrants should continue speaking in their unique tongue as well; and teach their children. The lucky offspring will be naturally bilingual. An accent is like a unique badge or a different haircut or style of dress; it completes the person... and no one should cover up the speaking part of themselves.

The one-room schoolhouse

Mull School was called a "one-room schoolhouse," but in reality had *two* rooms. It sat at the corner of Van Buren and Bagley Roads, just a mile from Grandpa Oscar's farm. Everyone was taught in one large room, from Beginners through Eighth grade. There was an advantage to be able to listen in on each other's lessons. A single teacher managed this remarkable job of educating about forty students.

There was a back room (perhaps an addition built in later years) for bad-weather days when the students couldn't go out. A big black stove sat at the front of the classroom. Corn cobs and chunks of coal were tossed in by the teacher and older students. A teakettle of water sat heating on it all day long.

Cousin Elaine recalls, "We sat on a long board bench with no back when it was time for our little class to be with the teacher. She always had a yardstick in her hand to touch the blackboard, especially for the numbers in arithmetic class. We also sat up front when we learned to read and she wrote out those sentences as famous as Shakespeare's, like 'See Sally run' and 'Jump, Spot, jump!'"

I can say that many of us, for over twenty-five years, entered the same main school door facing Van Buren Road. This group includes my father, uncles, aunts, visitors like my cousins Frieda and Marie from North Carolina and Richard from St. Louis, and even me. Uncle Wally took me to school with him. I thought it was so much more interesting than in town, where they shut you up in one room, only with kids your own age. Everyone, if they listened and wished to, could learn from each other's lessons. On the Bagley Road side, you could enter beneath the school bell tower, where a long rope hung down from the bell above. Only the teacher and tall kids could reach it. It divided the space between the girl's toilet on the right and the boys on the left... an 'outhouse' inside the building with a board with a hole cut in it. "There was no flushing," Cousin Elaine emailed, "Just a long drop... but I remember hearing the pee or poop fall a long ways down if there wasn't toilet paper from someone else already on top of their droppings. I do not remember where we might have washed our hands. It was a foul smelling, small area."

So it was a good thing that a second door separated the 'indoor outhouse' from the large classroom. Cousin Elaine could not imagine they ever cleaned out the toilets, but I am sure during each summer recess, men came to do that job.

Just once, I followed Uncle Wally and his friend to the schoolhouse in the summer time. Wally was tall and gangly, zesty and full of mischief. I think he climbed through an unlocked window and let us in. I was mesmerized by the stacks of colored paper and pencils, ready for school to start. *Temptation!* Was it like candy? No, I did not like candy much. Better yet, it was art supplies in abundance. I still can see myself stealing a sheet of paper from the shelf, along with some colored pencils, knowing it was wrong, and sitting down to draw, my second misdemeanor of the day. (Our break-in was the first.) Then I heard the bell ringing. Bong, bong, bong! Wally was swinging on the bell rope. I left my unfinished art, my heart pounding, weighted with guilt, and we all raced out to hide in Uncle Ed's cornfield. We were never apprehended.

There were certainly enough kids to fill a schoolhouse! Uncle Bud could see them clearly in his old grey head like it was yesterday.

"The surrounding families were the Anderson's, who had nineteen kids." Bud changed his mind, "No. I think it was twenty-one! There was 'Big Andy,' the oldest, and then they ran out of names and there was 'Little Andy.'" He spoke seriously, intending no joke, and continued his list.

"Hulda and Oscar Roslund, we had eleven, not counting Clifford; Brink, a Dutchman, had fourteen; the Manns had nine, the Preslers... Let's see: George, Paul, Howard, and three girls. Yup, they had six. Carmans were riffraff trash and moved away. Also, the Sanders and the Siefkies had lots and lots of kids! It was the sign of the times, with no birth control. It did make for plenty of home-grown farm hands."

Concerning those notes above, verbatim from Uncle Bud, he admitted to a little prejudice. "We looked down on the 'Hunkies' (Hungarians), the Polish, Czechs and the Mexicans. The Mexicans brought marijuana up from Mexico and would sit out under a tree in the middle of a field, at their noon break, and have a smoke. I have no memory of any Blacks in the 1920's. Until high school, there were very few."

Cousin Elaine, daughter of my famous Uncle Ed and his manure-spreading tractor, recalls the migrant workers near their farm, next door to Mull School. "What I remember mostly about the pickle pickers was that they lived in the Beebe area in small little homes that all looked alike and always seemed to have their doors open, with lots of small children standing in the open doorways, just looking at us when we drove to Beebe's meager grocery store. Sometimes there were little waves (from the children)... but I remember everyone looked dirty, I'm sure from working in the fields, and little ones probably played in the fields where their mothers worked. Probably no running water in any of them. They had outside toilets." That was from Elaine in the 1940's. I picked beans with the migrant workers in 1950, outside of Alma, and they too lived in small unheated shacks lined up in the fields, with no running water.

* * * * *

Grandpa Oscar was a serious man and his main aim was to feed everyone and work the farm. Thus, he needed all of the farm hands he could get. Grandma Hulda, however, wanted all of the children to go to high school. Grandpa Oscar expected them to help. The only farm hands he could command were his own children. He had no choice. Their labor was essential for the farm to succeed. That's why the education of his oldest son, my Uncle Herman, ended after eighth grade. The teachers said to Grandma Hulda, "Your Herman is smart!" But Grandpa was stubborn. What else could Herman do but comply? None of Uncle Herman's children can recall him ever speaking of this with resentment. He understood. That was life.

In contrast, my father Everett, the second oldest son, fought and won against Grandpa Oscar. I never heard a word about what went on or how this happened, but he went to high school in St. Louis. After that June ceremony, however, there was no obvious thing or person for Dad to fight against to get his larger dream: college. I do not believe poverty alone was to blame. It appears there were no educational counselors to advise students in finding scholarships or loans. Dad was on his own and his disappointment never faded completely.

Saving the farm in 1934: It was a good year

Uncle Bud explained, "Grandpa Oscar was already fifty years old when he 'bought the farm.' Not the colloquialism for dying, but literally purchasing a farm. The Depression hit ten years later and Grandpa Oscar couldn't make the payments. He was sixty-four by then, with eleven kids, although some no longer lived at home. It was just awful that Mr. Anderson with his nineteen kids (no, twenty-one kids!) lost his farm. The banks took it." I could see Uncle Bud still was saddened by this.

"Charlie Harrier wanted to foreclose on Grandpa Oscar, but when Roosevelt became President he passed the Emergency Farm Mortgage Act and that stopped the foreclosures. This gave Grandpa time to refinance." Joy filled Uncle Bud's face as he relived their good fortune. "I always loved Roosevelt for helping save the farm! I remained a Democrat my whole life and secretly split ticket votes. The interest rate for the Land Bank was three percent and Mama wanted to pay off the mortgage before she died," Bud said. I do not know if she did.

Getting on the county: 1934

Appendicitis struck the family like a plague! Four in one year. Grandpa Oscar had his appendix removed at St. John's Hospital; daughter Hulda, age seventeen, went to Pompeii to have her appendix out, which was like Dr. Hall's hospital in Beebe: small. At nearly the same time, the family was surprised to receive a letter from their son Art. While working for the California Conservation Corps in the Sierra foothills, a long way from civilization, he felt an ache in his right side. It was "ride or die." The road was rough and winding, so he had to steady his Indian motorbike like a pro. He cautiously sped the fifty miles on his motorcycle to the Bakersfield Hospital; holding his side, swallowing the pain, praying like crazy. He survived with a harrowing story to tell — and a very large scar.

Now it was Uncle Bud's turn for surgery. He was the fourth in the family that year, after Grandpa Oscar, Hulda and Art. Appendicitis was a serious thing in those days. Uncle Andrew, married to Aunt Tilly, had died from a ruptured appendix seven years earlier.

"There was not a dime left for me," said Uncle Bud. "Maggie and Clay Soule hitched up their team of horses and drove me to the county seat in Ithaca, and they got me 'on the county.' That's welfare."

Dr. Wilcox had just come from Ford Hospital in Detroit to Dr. Carney's "hospital," a house in Alma. Uncle Bud remembered groaning on the table with his left leg cocked up and he heard their conversation. "His left leg laying up like that? That's appendicitis," said Dr. Carney to young Dr. Wilcox. After the operation, they put Uncle Bud on a cot in the hallway. The hospital was crowded.

Grandma Hulda came, "May I take my son home?" she asked, as Bud jumped up off his cot. "Just keep him still," the doctor ordered. He was fifteen years old. "I refused," bragged Uncle Bud.

The stitches came out one week later. Uncle Bud said he defied the doctor's rules because in his gut he felt that to "get up and get going," made him stronger. That is what doctors, of course, advise today, eighty years later. Uncle Bud said, "They told my sister Hulda to stay in bed two full weeks and she got weaker and weaker." Still the smart aleck kid brother.... feeling wiser than his sister.

Electricity comes to Gratiot County

In the barn in winter, straw or bean pods and horse manure were piled up to keep the cold out. The sheep ran loose all over the yard in the day time, and slept in the barn at night. The buck sheep would come up to the living room window of the farmhouse and peer in. Once Grandpa Oscar brought a mirror to the window and held it up. "The sheep bucked right into it!" remembered Uncle Kenny.

"For our first seventeen years at the farm, we lived without electricity," said Uncle Bud. "Grandpa Oscar carried a kerosene lantern to the barn and hung it on a post to milk the cows and feed the animals. He was extremely careful and always remembered to carry it out when he left. Some folks feared electricity because the wires could fray and catch fire. There were many fires that burned houses and barns to the ground because there were no telephones and no fire trucks close by.

"In 1936, when the Rural Electrification Act was passed, you could either put lines into the county then or you would lose your franchise (the right to do so). Again, Roosevelt was our hero," Uncle Bud told me.

"In 1938, Helgo Rassnusson, a handy Swede, wired our farm. He was a farmer, not an electrician, but he could read English and so he simply read the book of instructions." Uncle Bud said this as proudly as if he had done the job himself. "Helgo wired the farmhouse with one bulb in the center of the ceiling in each room, as well as one wall receptacle, the big yard light on the windmill, and wires for one light in the barn. We still had to use lanterns for going to the hay mow. We were billed two to three dollars a month, as a minimum amount, whether we used it or not. Usually we paid three dollars."

Trading horses; trading tractors

East of Leonard Refinery, outside of Alma, was a fox farm with big, long cages.

"It was a good place to get rid of your dead horses; feed them to the foxes," said Uncle Bud. "Papa, Boots (Uncle LeRoy), Herman, and Ray Nelson traded horses with the fox farm.

"When Grandpa Oscar butchered a beef cow, he sometimes would trade it for a horse and maybe a little money, too. Once Grandpa Oscar traded a horse for beef with a neighbor who changed his mind. His neighbor returned for his horse, but the poor animal had just died from a heart attack in his harness. Perhaps the collar was too tight?" mused Uncle Bud. "Whatever, the neighbor got only one-quarter of a beef.

"Ethel Thomas had a hardware store in Breckenridge and she, too, was a trader. She sold farm implements in exchange for horses. Uncle Herman traded a team of horses for a new red F14 Farmall Tractor in 1938, when he lived in Ashley.

"Grandpa Oscar had an F12," Uncle Bud continued. "One time a gentleman from the 'St. Louis Community' came out to trade tractors, around 1940, just before the War started. Uncle Kenny wanted Papa to get a bigger one. Kenny was thirteen, a strong-willed teenager, and wouldn't quit nagging Grandpa Oscar. 'Get in the house, you damn kid,' Grandpa Oscar said.

"The salesman couldn't arrange that, because the difference to trade would cost Grandpa Oscar three hundred to four hundred more dollars, which he could not afford, and didn't want to do anyway. He just wanted a tractor with a starter on it. It was a Farmall BN and had a power lift and was the same size as the old one. He did not get a bigger tractor. Kenny lost!" Uncle Bud said with a certain satisfaction, traces of sibling competition still alive fifty years later.

Then he added, a little guiltily, as if he shouldn't tell me, "Papa always raced the motor and slipped the clutch when he drove."

I believe it was a Farmall A tractor that my Uncle Ed owned. If any Uncle (and I was rich with uncles, having fourteen of them) did me a favor, it was Uncle Ed. I was fifteen years old and no one trusted me to drive their tractor, even though the *boy* cousins my age, such as Richard, had been driving for seven years! As the cliché goes, Uncle Ed was 'outstanding in his field'! He laughed and good-naturedly gave into my pleas.

"OK. Here ya go!" he said as he pointed to the metal tractor seat, showed me the starter, and sent me out into his field to spread manure. I can still see him standing there in his coveralls, arms crossed, grinning like Tom Sawyer.

Automobiles

"Grandpa Oscar got his first car in 1917. Herman was twelve then and drove his mother to Paxton, a small town nearby, to shop. Mama would then get behind the wheel and drive it around town," Uncle Bud once told me. Of course, that was before Bud was born.

I do not believe it. Never did I, nor my cousin Richard, ever see Grandma Hulda drive a car. She sat daintily on the passenger side with her purse on her lap.

"Who knows who was driving, but Grandpa Oscar's car hit Harvey Mann's horse in the head and killed it," Uncle Bud added with a slight chuckle.

Social life in those times, the 1920's and 1930's, consisted of getting cleaned up, driving to town on a Saturday night to sell some eggs or milk and pick up staples, and visiting with all the other farmers who were in town doing the same thing. I used to go along, riding in the back seat of Grandpa and Grandma Sandy's car. They parked their black car (all cars were black) on St. Louis's Mill Street (two wonderful blocks of exciting activity), facing the sidewalk, and from the front seat of their old Model T, they looked at everyone walking by. That is when I learned the art of people watching.

Uncle Bud recalled a trip to town one Saturday in 1928. Grandpa Oscar was driving their Model T in downtown St. Louis when Grandma Hulda turned around and asked four-year-old LeRoy, "Where's Quenten?" LeRoy took his time, thought for a moment, and finally said, "Oh, he fell out back there." They circled around and found where Quenten stood waiting, as happy as though he had just tumbled off their horsehair settee. In my memory, he always had a jovial presence.

Decades later, I remember Uncle Quenten had a pet chicken named Lucky. Lucky's mother dutifully sat on her clutch of eggs, but when they hatched, only one survived... our heroine. Aunt Wanda, Uncle Quenten's wife and a fantastic cook, brought the tiny chick into their kitchen and placed her in a box with a light for warmth. Lucky was a survivor and her name was fitting. She was happy with her home in the kitchen, as it was Grand Central Station for the cats and dog who padded in and out. She must have felt she was just like them. Lucky loved cat food. When she grew up, she would jump on Cousin Ike's bike handlebars to go for a spin around the barnyard, or

Lucky the chicken with Zandy and Uncle Quenten Roslund, 1988.

hop into his red flyer wagon to be hauled around. When she became more independent, Lucky came to the front door — or whatever door she chose — to be let in. Lucky would then help herself to some cat food, cluck a little, get petted, and walk back out. She was a lady and never messed the house; she politely performed her bathroom duties out in the yard. Her gift to the family were beautiful blue eggs. A rare bird.

Cousin Frieda and I named this uncle "Silly Quenten" because he grinned a lot, teased and spent time with us. I believed Frieda to be his favorite, as he pushed her around in a wheelbarrow more than me. Frieda had an advantage. The summer she turned six and came up to the farm with Aunt Agnes, she was adorably petite, with long braids, a sweet Southern drawl, and a new talent. On command from her mother, she tap danced in her under panties for our admiring aunts and uncles, grandparents and cousins. I remember standing on the sidelines and watching, unsure of my feelings. I suspect it was my first hint of jealousy. I also felt a touch of embarrassment for her, as I recall thinking she should be wearing a top.

Dancing at the lake under the stars

The same year Uncle Quenten toppled off the back end of the car, Everett (my Dad), Howard Presler and Alford Peters took Grandpa Oscar's Model T Ford, which had a cloth top, to Bass Lake's Pavilion on a Saturday night. It was a favorite spot in the 1920's, where dance bands entertained. The Charleston was hot! Dancing was their favorite entertainment. (Maybe necking, too?)

Dance bands on a soft summer night on a Michigan lake mesmerized me, also. I was so sentimental that on my sixteenth birth-day, Mother volunteered to serve a candlelight dinner for my date Lex (him again) and me and another couple (Marilyn Hoard and Jim McHugh, who later married and never divorced) at our Wright Avenue home. She loved cooking and baking and setting a beautiful table, just like her mother. We then went dancing to the last notes of Guy Lombardo's fame, which was in the throes of fading as fast as the sun dropped behind Crystal Lake's Pavilion. I didn't care. It counted to me that Guy Lombardo used to be famous. I grabbed drama whenever I could.

Back to my Dad as a wild nineteen-year-old. He accidentally drove the car into a ditch at Bass Lake that Saturday night. It promptly turned upside down, trapping my father inside. "I had to hold my head up regularly to breathe and not drown," he told me years later. *Was he teasing?* He liked to kid me because I would believe anything. I now wonder. Some of the guys raced back to the farm and summoned Grandpa Oscar, who brought his team of horses to pull the car out. No one was seriously hurt, but the car remained in the barn for a very long time.

Uncle Bud related to me, "During World War I, the tires were made of canvas, not rubber, and you could get only five hundred miles to a tire. When balloon tires came in, in the 1920's, Everett couldn't wait to try them out, which he did when we went huckleberry picking. 'They are supposed to be good on sand,' Everett said." Uncle Bud sighed. "He was wrong."

Another time, Uncle Kenny and his friends were out driving in Grandpa Oscar's 1937 Pontiac and came across Route 46 on Beebe Road. Uncle Kenny told me, "When I got across the highway, we saw a car with a flickering little light. I slowed down, luckily, as I had no idea it was a train. I was fourteen or fifteen." Another time, in 1942 or 1943, Kenny recalled, "I was walking home from school and stopped at Kouchrarah's, where they were loading hay. They offered me a drink… a swig of turpentine."

I can't think that was really true, as much as I love my uncle. Perhaps I should have asked him to give me more details.

Cooning melons

Sometime around 1936, Grandpa Oscar wanted to catch the neighbor kids who were stealing his melons. He decided to hide at dusk in his own melon patch.

"I will get a rock and throw it and find out if it's a cow!" He yelled out his intentions loudly so the kids who were hiding in the patch could hear him. The rock thunked into the dirt near them. They were scared of Grandpa Oscar and started yelling, "Wally, Wally, save us!" After Grandpa had had his fun, he brought them up to the house and surprised them with all the melon they could eat.

Bill Burnham raised melons especially for the kids to "coon." He drove a big Packard and kept it locked. At that time, no one locked his car — and if you did something different around the county, you were considered odd. He was also odd to raise melons purely for destruction. Maybe he was nicely odd. It would have been similar if Mr. Burnham had raised angle worms just so he could throw them into the creek to treat the fish.

"Cooning was great entertainment," said Uncle Bud. Cooning was the act of sneaking into a melon patch and grabbing some... to eat or just to throw and smash up. Or steal and carry away. "All in fun, nothing malicious!" he told me.

Six "Sad Little Cousins" (1912). Left to right, Tilly's children Evelyn and Rudy, and Grandma Hulda's children Agnes, Arthur, Herman and Everett. We know they traveled by horse and buggy to the photo shoot somewhere near Chicago. Why so sad? Were they bored having to sit absolutely still and wanted to run outside and get out of their Sunday clothes? Or maybe they were hungry! Or did the photographer order them not to smile or giggle as portraits were quite solemn in those days?

And It's Only Monday

Hulda's sister Tilly dies

Tilly was Hulda's beloved favorite sister, her closest relative and only family member in America when she arrived. Tilly and Andrew had paid Hulda's steerage to America and introduced her to Oscar. In early 1905, Hulda married Oscar and the next month Tilly married Andrew.

It can happen in our lives that we are given love and support to such a degree by someone that we wonder if we can ever repay them. Grandma Hulda may have wondered that about her sister Tilly; *How can I ever thank you, dear Tilly? You have done so much for me.* Now the time was here.

Tilly and Andrew's two children were not in perfect health. Rudy suffered a hearing loss and wore hearing aids. Evelyn was struck with infantile paralysis when she was two that affected her left leg. At age eighteen she had a major experimental operation that transplanted some muscles from behind her left knee to the front. She had to wear a brace on that leg the rest of her life to keep it from going backwards too far. However, the surgery did allow her to walk without pain and to drive a car.

It was a tragedy how Hulda's sister Tilly died.

At the time, Tilly's husband, Uncle Andrew, was out of town. She must have thought it was not a practical time to have another child. But the midwife's botched abortion

Evelyn's birthday, August 20, 1917, the year before Tilly died.

234

The Roslund Clan

took her life. Evelyn and Rudy were suddenly without their mother. Little Evelyn was only eight years old; Tilly just thirty-eight. After Tilly's death, Andrew hired a family, Emil and Selma Magnuson and their pretty daughter Mabel, to move into his home and help raise his children, as he continued to travel for his work. They stayed until Evelyn was eighteen years old. To Evelyn, Selma was very kind, but it was not enough. She needed her "Aunty on the farm" for love and support. Grandma Hulda became her "second Mother" and Evelyn visited the farm every summer. She and her same-age cousins, Agnes and Everett, became very fond of each other. Agnes loved to play dress up with Evelyn... and pose for photos. Agnes always played the bride and wore her mother Hulda's wedding dress. In every photo, Evelyn is the groom. Always the groom, never the bride?

Above left: Grandpa Oscar with his bride Grandma Hulda in her wedding finery, 1905. Above right: My Aunt Agnes, playing the bride in her mother Hulda's twenty-year-old wedding dress, while Tilly's daughter Evelyn (Grandma Hulda's niece) plays the groom. (Roslund farm, circa 1925.) Both women would be widowed when they were in their forties. Agnes was forty-seven when Walker died and Evelyn was forty-one when David passed away.

Perhaps Evelyn's leg brace was more appropriate for wearing pants, but she could have hidden a braced leg under the dress. My heart reaches out to Evelyn, probably because of my high-school ballet lesson recital in Alma. I was forced to play the part of "the boy," which I hated, and Elsie McClure (her again!)... pretty, confident and a cheerleader no less, played my dancing partner as the girl. That is why I feel sad for Evelyn, always appearing dressed as the man at the make-believe wedding. Strange how we impose our own experiences on to someone else's life.

"Evelyn's health did not stop her from playing the accordion like a professional and singing beautifully when she was older," Uncle Bud said. "She would play for us at the drop of a hat." Evelyn did lament that she always thought Mabel Magnuson was prettier than she was and could walk so gracefully.

Evelyn married David Nilsson at age thirty-three. Sadly, her newfound happiness did not last. It was another heartbreak in her life when her husband became mentally ill and Evelyn had to move David to an asylum.

Evelyn's daughter, Karen Nilsson Goetz, said that as her mother lay dying in 1986, when she was seventy-eight, Evelyn relived in detail the agonizing scene of her mother Tilly's death. Evelyn told Karen, "My mother called me into her bedroom and there was a lot of blood. She told me to run to a nearby neighbor for help."

The neighbor came and closed the bedroom door so Evelyn could not witness all the commotion. Tilly called out, "Evie, Evie," as Evelyn was waiting outside the bedroom door. Tilly begged, as she lay bleeding, to see her daughter. Little Evelyn was outside, screaming and pounding on the bedroom door, trying to reach her mother. Sobbing, she cried out, "Mama, Mama." Did the neighbor think it best to keep them apart? The door stayed closed.

On her own deathbed, Karen said her mother told her she was happy and at peace. Evelyn believed she was going to see her mother Tilly at last.

Tilly's husband Andrew

Uncle Andrew was an artist. He did fancy scrolling in plaster for movie theaters throughout the United States. He was also a good Samaritan. It was his desire to help others that found him out in Washington state, helping new Swedish immigrants find work, when Tilly died.

Uncle Andrew was also a Coca-Cola addict. Uncle Bud witnessed proof of his addiction when Bud was six and attended Uncle Andrew's funeral in La Grange, Illinois, in June 1924. Herman, nineteen years old, drove the family down for the wake and service. The automobile was a Durant Motors "Star Car," with disc wheels in back and spoke wheels in front.

Uncle Bud sneaked down into the cement basement in his Uncle Andrew's brick house and was amazed (even decades later in the telling) to see all the walls lined with cases (some empty and some full) and bottles by the thousands of Coca-Cola... then made with cocaine. Andrew was fifty-six years old when he died – and not from a cocaine overdose. Appendicitis claimed him in just one day, just eight years after Tilly died, when he was about to marry his second wife. Now there was even more reason for Evelyn and Rudy to go summers to the farm; they were orphans.

A Radio!!

Uncle Bud was my reporter again. "When we came up to Michigan, there was no electricity and we had no radio. Cousin Evelyn drove up from Chicago (circa 1930) in her car, still single at thirty and working, and brought us a large radio in a big cabinet. And batteries. The antenna sat on top and had a big frame with little nails on it and she wound up the antennas framework to pick up a signal. We would carry it around the farmhouse and turn the antenna, trying to get better reception. We took the batteries to town to have them recharged.

"The radio expanded our world overnight! We were thrilled. We listened to WLM... music from Cincinnati, WGM Chicago, WJR Detroit, and KNOX in St. Louis, Missouri. We felt wonderful! It was a

And It's Only Monday

far bigger step than getting a television set years later," said Uncle Bud, his countenance melting into a big smile as he recalled those magical, musical nights. "Our favorite was 'Amos and Andy,' five nights a week at 7 P.M. We stopped everything. They were two black men... and 'Queen Lightning'," Uncle Bud added.

Other visitors from Chicago also came to the farm. My father Everett told me how he and his siblings felt the sting of rejection from their Uncle Magnus, Grandpa Oscar's brother.

Magnus drove up with his wife Marie (Mary) and four offspring, Gurlie, Nils, Geynor and Mimmie.

They were a lovely sight; four beautifully dressed, clean and perfectly groomed, well-educated children. As the farm cousins stood in shock, probably dressed in patched and faded hand me downs, some barefoot, they watched the fancy car full of high-style kinfolks drive into the driveway, circle around with their noses held high, and drive right on out and back to Chicago. They never stopped.

Magnus may have lived a more comfortable life but not nearly as long. Oscar died at ninety; Magnus lived only to seventy.

The children of Grandpa Oscar's brother Magnus Nilsson and his wife Marie, who sped with their parents in and out of the Michigan farmyard without stopping, and headed right back to Chicago. Left to right, standing, are Gurlie and Geynor; seated are Nils and Mimmie.

Circa 1898.

Riding the Rails

Uncle Art and my father Everett planned to jump the rails together and head "Out West." Grandpa Oscar often yelled, "There's the road. It's wide. Go!" He knew they hated farming and wanted to leave. The brothers were truly at the crossroads of their lives, choosing their future, sealing their destinies, standing by the railroad tracks in the dark that night.

"Ready, set... go!" Uncle Arthur jumped. My father did not. As the train rolled away, Art shouted out in anger and raised his fist in the air. But they each knew in their gut that they must be true to their own selves. Art rode, hungry and cold and exhausted, for 2,300 miles, and jumped off near East Bakersfield, California, near the giant rail yard.

Uncle Art had made the same trip before. He and Augie Forsgard had gone out – but they came back. Augie took a job in a meat plant in Detroit. Now Uncle Art was headed West – alone this time. He "rode the rods," and was known as a railroad bum. It was dangerous. The "bulls" (railroad police) had Billy clubs and tried to force them off. Underneath the box cars were rods, and hanging on them cost many men their legs or their arms. Thank heavens, Uncle Art got there safely.

He walked across a field and knocked on the door of the first house he came to. Mrs. Price, a pleasant woman, invited Art in and let him sleep on a cot in her hallway. When Art later took a job with the Civilian Conservation Corps, he sent money from his pay to Mrs. Price to save for him to buy an Indian motorcycle. In time, Uncle Art met a lovely school teacher with a convertible: my sweet Aunt Gladys.

My father turned back from the railroad tracks toward home. He married my mother, Verneal, the gal he took one look at in the Breckenridge Post Office and said to himself, *I want to marry her.* She was sixteen. It took five years for her to accept his diamond... a humble one-eighth of a carat, that I wear proudly today.

Fifty years later, Uncle Art's son, my cousin Nels (who graduated in the same 1954 Class at Van Nuys High School with actor Robert Redford) took his dad for a ride to visit some old haunts and to thank Mrs. Price. Uncle Art knocked on doors until he finally found a woman who knew of her, but it was too late. She had died. Uncle Art said, "Mrs. Price was a wonderful person."

The woman replied, "That's your opinion."

Business

Uncle Herman, the oldest of the Roslund boys, settled in Michigan, just like all of his brothers did, except for Arthur. Always a smart entrepreneur, Herman had many escapades in business. He ran a restaurant in Detroit that went bankrupt, early in the 1930's. Grandma Hulda saved the coffee mugs as souvenirs. "That's from Herman's restaurant," she said proudly and often, pointing to one in her kitchen. They were extra heavy with thick sides and held eight ounces... a true cup of coffee. Later Grandma gave me one and I am drinking from it now as I write. When Uncle Herman closed down his Advance Laundry business in Hazel Park, he and Aunt Billie moved back up to Gratiot County in the late 1930's and never left again.

Uncle Herman and Aunt Billie ended up living at Grandpa Oscar and Grandma Hulda's out of necessity for a short time in 1932. They were at the farmhouse when their second child, Martin, was born in the front parlor. According to Uncle Bud, "It was a beautiful morning and all us kids were sent down the pasture to 'watch the cows.' I was reading 'The Bobbsey Twins'."

Aunt Billie had been hemming draperies, while sitting on the edge of Grandma Hulda's bed, when her labor began. This is where Uncle Bud's story veers off the path.

"My brother Ed and his wife Bernice lived just up the road, so Bernice took Billie's draperies home to finish hemming them on her machine. Everyone was close, everyone helped everyone," Bud said wistfully, with a touch of regret that it was not the same today. What I just quoted from Uncle Bud was six years off. The fact that Uncle Ed and Aunt Bernice were not married yet, nor had they purchased their farm a mile away, does not really matter. The substance of the memory does; Bud recalled how loving and helpful everyone was to each other. That is timeless.

Fun and mischief....

"We were poor, but did not know it. We made our own fun!" laughed Uncle Bud. "I remember when my brothers, Kenny and Wally, took two tame cats, tied them together and made a harness with twine. Turned 'em loose!"

The barn cats had a better life, especially at milk time. I saw them sit, patient and perfectly still, not far from a cow being milked. They opened their mouths wide, while Uncle Wally, Grandpa Roslund or my Grandpa Sandy, gave each cat her due. They all were good shots. They could squirt the milk far and straight.

Grandma Hulda Roslund holding cousin Richard and Grandpa Oscar Roslund holding me among the hollyhocks out on their farm, 1936. Note Grandma's small waist after having twelve babies!

I do not remember how Uncle Wally's experiment ended. I saw him take a cat up to the hay mow and drop it from that tiny window near the peak of the barn roof. *Would it land on its feet?* was Wally's question. He also wanted to double check to see if it had nine lives. I cannot remember if I peeked to see how the cat landed, but it must have been fine. I loved cats.

May Day

Cousin Elaine remembers this as her favorite time at Mull School.

"We had a tall pole in the second room of the schoolhouse, which we used in bad weather. The pole had used crêpe paper tied to it. We went over and under the streamers to a song as we went round and

And It's Only Monday

round. There were a lot of streamers, so lots of kids did it at the same time... two circles of kids going opposite directions," she told me.

* * * * *

Summer time

My North Carolina Cousin Frieda and I had as much imagination as our uncles. One sunny summer day, we spotted the steep roof of the storage shed with its wooden shingles that sat between the horse tank

Standing, left to right: Marie Bryant, LeRoy Roslund, Quenten Roslund (holding dog). On horseback: Wally Roslund and two summer visitors, circa 1935.

and the outhouse. Wouldn't it make a great slide? We were experienced. We had sailed down snowy hills on our bottoms and had slid down school playground slides. We climbed up to the peak of the roof (who knows how we did that) and shouted, "OK! Together! One, Two, Three… Yikes…!"

For miles away the neighbors thought Grandpa was slaughtering pigs; the squealing was the same. Aunt Agnes and Aunt Hulda came running. Agnes threw Frieda over her lap and Hulda threw me over hers. They plucked splinters out as we sobbed and screamed for mercy.

In the summer time, we all met at the farm for ball games, tag, climbing the windmill, jumping in the hay mow, and eating homemade ice cream, which everyone took turns turning… and Grandma's angel food cake. It took a pint of egg whites to make a good cake. As Grandma fried eggs in the mornings, she saved the whites. No one could compete with her delicious, light-as-air, fine-as-fairy-dust cakes — although the daughters-in-law tried. No one denied that Grandma made the best! At least not in public. It took me years to understand the politics of a silly cake.

Archie Sandy and son Ronald, 1910.

Out at Uncle Herman's Farm Market, between St. Louis and Alma on Michigan Avenue, and next to his house, he and his wife Aunt Billie raised twenty-five cows. Cousins Richard and Martin, the whole family really, milked them twice a day. That was before they got a "milking machine."

I remember one day we were all playing Cowboys and Indians. A cow had died and was lying in Uncle Herman's field, deteriorating, so we took advantage of this prop. Sitting on the poor thing, riding on its back, we yelled "Hi ho, Silver! Away!"

That same day I got my first electrocution lesson. Cousin Martin, the gang leader, enticed his brothers and sister and Uncle Wally to hold hands in a line and placed me on the end. With a big grin on his face, Martin grabbed the electric fence. The current went down the line, bypassing without harm the offenders in the middle, and shot with a jolt... into me!

The parlor

My sister Linda and I were not allowed comic books. Uncle Wally not only took me to visit Mull School with him, but he also shared his comics. They were mostly coverless, grungy, and torn. It was a sneaky secret, and a wicked deed to read them, which added to their intrigue. Superman, Jughead, Archie, Dick Tracy and Mandrake the Magician were my favorites. My sister Linda was five years younger than I, and as often happens among siblings in the same family, she got a completely different message. They were not "sinful" to her, just an unnecessary expense in our family budget. She got her fill of comic books at Uncle Herman's house, but without the guilt.

Chinese Checkers was a specialty of Grandpa Oscar.

"He beat everyone... except maybe Jens Fosgard," said Uncle Bud. Grandpa sat down and taught Linda and me the first three winning moves of Chinese Checkers. It helped me all my life, as long as I didn't have to make that fourth play.

Linda's most powerful memory was our many hours in Grandma Hulda's parlor, playing the organ chaotically, pumping the big pedals, pounding on the keys, and jostling for who could sing the loudest. We competed for the organ stool, with its cast-iron legs and walnut seat. It could spin us like a top! It was a real treat when Cousin Dolores sat down at the organ and produced sacred and beautiful music, as she often did on Sundays in church. She was our family musician. She also sang solos, heart-rending hymns, at the Church of God.

Abandoning religion for the occult, the cousins crowded around the Ouija board, asking scary questions and getting amazing answers from the moving planchette. This game had just come into vogue again when World War II ended.

My sister Linda told me, "I didn't know whether to hide under the card table or run out of the room. I was scared! I wanted someone to protect me." I seem to have totally missed her feelings, and am sorry now that I was not better wired into my big-sister role.

Regular card games went on at the kitchen table or wherever a card table was free. Grandpa Oscar also loved euchre. Grandma Hulda, I recall, sat alone when I visited and played solitaire. It looked boring and a waste of time, so I vowed when I was still small to never learn; nor to ever try a cigarette, either. I have kept both vows to this day, but I wish I had more to brag about.

Fake news

This is fourth-hand, but Cousin Marilyn, daughter of my Uncle LeRoy, was told by her father that his brother Kenny told a genuine reporter at the "Emerson News" that Uncle Wally fell in the river and Uncle Art saved his life. The woman reporter was very impressed and published the story in the newspaper. None of it was true. Uncle Kenny seemed conveniently unable to recall this incident.

This may be confusing, but try having nine brothers and two sisters who tell their thirty-eight kids what they think they remember and those offspring pass on to each other what someone else said they said, if they remember it right.

But Uncle Bud seemed to have no trouble remembering how to celebrate Halloween. According to him, "That was the best night to gather your friends and move a neighbor's outhouse into the middle of the road."

Hunting and shooting

Uncle Bud claimed: "The biggest day of the year was the first day of hunting season. (Papa, however, did not hunt.) The deer season started in earnest in Gratiot County when the Conservation Department loaded up deer from up North and dumped them out into the fields east of Ithaca. Today, you have to draw a number to hunt a deer in the game area.

"We made our own fun, and our own 'toys,'" Uncle Bud said to me one day, while we were riding to town in his pickup, with the windows down. He flew down those country roads faster than a teenager, even in his eighties.

"We were good at creating slingshots. We made them out of old rubber tires, which we had lots of. We made homemade arrows from wooden shingles. A stick with a string on it was a bow," Uncle Bud shouted at me as he drove.

He recalled another scene. "One day, on the top of the barn's cupola, sat a sparrow. Everett hit it." Bud bragged again about his older brother's skill, as though he had shot the sparrow himself, and just as he had praised the Swede who wired their farmhouse with electricity. He never seemed jealous; Uncle Bud was happy for others. He was an endlessly cheerful guy.

As for my father, Everett, he became a great marksman from his Dow Chemical security-guard training and later on, shot his quota of pheasants handily — and everyone else's quota, too, on hunting day, if they didn't get theirs and wanted him to.

Dad shot animals for us to eat, venison and pheasants, but never just for the sport of killing. Dad visited me in Virginia one winter. My house has walls of glass that birds see as the sky and fly into. One morning, a small wren hit the glass hard with a thud and then bounced into the snow on the deck. It looked dead to me. Dad went out and cupped it in his hands, brought it inside and held it awhile, and when it opened its eyes and fluffed itself up, Dad went outside, opened his hands, and the little bird flew off into the bamboo.

Dad had 'yellow jaundice' during World War II. Once he recovered, he continued to donate his O-negative blood as often as he was allowed. It was in high demand. Type O negative blood could be given to anyone, without a reaction. However, hepatitis could be passed through the blood. Dad continued to give for years, not knowing this. No nurse or doctor thought to ask him his history — or perhaps they did not yet understand?

Winter

Uncle Kenny told me, "A bunch of us would clamp on skates and skate across the fields because a whole section of the township was flat and frozen. We could skate almost to Breckenridge. We also went to Pumpkin Hill on Sundays and slid down on homemade sleds. It was the highest spot around!"

Because God built the hill, it still stands. Just go east on Van Buren Road from old Route 127, and just before Mull School at Bagley Road, make a right turn (south) onto Half-mile, Royce Road. Travel on Royce Road two to three hundred yards and over on your right (the south-west corner) is the famous hill that has thrilled hundreds of Gratiot County kids for more than a century. Recently, Cousin Richard and I tried to find it. It wasn't there. Or are we getting old and a little lost?

Many of my kin claim that Christmas Eve was the biggest night of the year. I agree. I remember crowding around the frosty window-pane with cousins Richard, Martin, and Uncle Wally, looking out at the dark sky, watching cars come down the road and turning in… but never did we see Santa. Time dragged. It seemed forever, like it does when you have high expectations of meeting an old friend and wish they would hurry. We looked and we listened. Santa never once, in all of those Christmases, allowed us to see him flying through the air. We never even got a glance at his reindeer.

But, at last! We heard big, rattling sleigh bells clanging! Santa himself barged into the outside parlor door, never used at any other time, shouting, "Ho Ho Ho!" He wore a ratty, old, white beard and droopy, red hat trimmed in cotton. A matted fur coat was thrown over his shoulders. He always had a deep voice, although it didn't sound the same every year.

"Ho Ho Ho! And how are you, little girl?" Santa said, as he poked his fat finger toward my tummy. *Thrill!* My heart jumped. He clutched an old feed sack that someone had filled with a piece of candy and a little gift for every single one of us — with our name on it! The dining table was piled with food, the room was loud with the mixture of all the voices of everyone you loved and who loved you. We sang carols around the organ, "O Little Town of Bethlehem" and "Away in a Manger" — and there actually was a manger, out in the barn.

Sons of Oscar and Hulda Roslund, from left to right: Walter, Kenny, LeRoy, Quenten, Randolph (Bud), Edvin, Arthur, Everett (my dad) and Herman, circa 1945.

Leaving the county

Uncle Bud loved adventure and he relished this story.

"In 1940 you could make fifty dollars as a 'drive away'... from Detroit to Los Angeles. You drove a brand-new Hudson Terraplane. They hired twenty-five drivers at a time, and I got one of the slots. They also took care of our food and lodging. Lodging meant sleeping in your car. You could only drive thirty miles per hour for the first five hundred miles. You checked the oil, and stayed five hundred feet apart from the other twenty-four cars, so as not to hinder traffic. We could drive closer together going through the towns.

"We took Route 66, but there were no motels in those days. There was a hotel in Oklahoma… a 'cat house'… rooms with baths down the hall. 'Hey, do you want some fun, girls?' we said. In the Army, before the war, Fort Lewis had beautiful cat houses… big, like a fancy night club," Uncle Bud continued.

"You could go in and buy beer. It was all servicemen. But the government closed the houses down before the draftees came in. The Army had tolerated it. However, the new draftees were more Christian and weren't rough and tumble, like the old Army types."

Later, when Uncle Bud was sent to France, he recalled, "The French girls weren't tough. They were 'nice' girls, and they invited you into their homes. In the United States, the prostitutes were the worst kind, with no morals."

Returning from the War: 1945

Uncle Bud recalled the end of the War as though he was still twenty-six years old.

"I was discharged at 3:00 A.M. from Fort Dix, New Jersey, in September 1945. I took a bus from there to the Philadelphia train station. We all went into a bar and they filled us with free drinks while we waited for the train. The next thing I knew, I woke up on the train, with my head on some pretty gal's shoulder. 'Some friends of yours put you on,'" she explained.

"I didn't even know them, but I had told those guys earlier in that bar that I had a ticket for the Red Arrow to Detroit. Nice guys! They dragged me half unconscious onto the right train and propped me up next to a sweet girl," Uncle Bud said.

"I caught another train to Lansing from Detroit and then walked to the 'Motor Wheel' on Route 27… where all the hitchhikers stood. I got into a car with two kids, neither a bit over thirteen years old, who drove like maniacs. Twisting the wheel, skidding, yelling, laughing. I was scared to death! After all that terrible war and what I lived through, I had hitched a ride with some really wild and crazy guys.

How did I get into a car with nuts like these? I thought, fearing I would die. *After getting safely through the war, now I get killed?* I begged out at St. Johns, where I knew there was another hitchhiker corner. A big semi-tanker truck hauling gas, with a sign on its windshield saying 'No Riders' screeched and slowed. It took him a city block to bring that rig to a halt. I hadn't even put out my thumb!" Uncle Bud laughed.

"Lo and behold... when I ran up to the truck, there was my old neighbor, Harry Shaver, age forty-five! He had recognized me. I had run around with Rolly Shaver and Dean Shaver, who were still in the Army. He drove me to the Leonard Refinery and ordered me to 'Stay in the truck. I'll take you home.' He then drove me to the Gulf Station that Everett ran on Superior Street in downtown Alma [in 2017 this is now the parking lot for the Church of God].

"Everett and I hugged! And that was not something Michigan men were used to doing. It had been three years since I had had a furlough. I vowed I would never leave town again," Uncle Bud exclaimed. He didn't. He married — and there's more to his story.

Uncle Bud's marriage

Uncle Bud took Aunt Elaine out on their first date in October 1945, in his brother LeRoy's pickup truck.

"It stunk terrible. LeRoy had just taken a cow to the stockyard... and the manure was awful," Uncle Bud recalled. "We went to the movies at the Strand Theater in Alma. We had met at the Gulf Station the first time... and after that, we never dated anyone else.

True quotes from a man in love: "We couldn't see past our noses except for the other one." "It was instant love between two people... and love the first night." "We got along so good." "It went like clockwork, we were meant for each other." "I never tried to analyze it." I wrote down Uncle Bud's words exactly.

"After that first date, I got better at arranging transportation. I borrowed Everett's car for our next date, and it smelled so nice. We were invited to the Midland Country Club dance, as Elaine's best friend was Eddy Lobdell's wife. He owned half of Lobdell-Emory

Manufacturing Company and they were members of the club. Elaine was maid-of-honor in their wedding," Uncle Bud told me.

"I gave her a ring at Thanksgiving. My Papa and Mama had dinner for us one night and we discussed our upcoming wedding date," Uncle Bud recalled. "They first said, at the beginning of dinner, 'October of the next year.' While we ate roast beef and mashed potatoes, canned beets and canned green beans, they kept moving the date up. From October to September, then August to July. By the time we ate our apple pie, it was pretty much settled. We got married on June 2, 1946." Uncle Bud reminisced with a grin.

He recalled how much he paid for everything, as anyone who grew up during the Depression always can: "I paid seven hundred and fifty dollars for my car, one hundred dollars for Elaine's diamond ring, and sixty-five hundred dollars (with three thousand dollars down) for our house.

"We were runners. Elaine could run like the wind. I could run faster backwards than my brothers Quent and LeRoy could forward," claimed Uncle Bud, with a wide smile. "I was fantastic at Pom Pom Pull-away. I could stop, dodge; very agile!"

Uncle Bud's energy remained with him until he was ninety. He would wear me out, walking four miles in the morning before breakfast, when I was seventeen years younger than he. He had planted trees all through the

A sign. The cross in Uncle Bud's woods remained for over two years, held together not by nails or glue... but by thin air, as though invisible angels hovered above, holding up the horizontal piece. Circa 2005

woodland and called out their names as we walked; birch, maple, willow, beech, butternut (rare, he said), walnut, white pine and peach. We were both in awe of the unexplained cross that appeared in his woods.

* * * * *

When Grandma Roslund died, there was a farm auction.

My Aunts Hulda and Agnes, her daughters, came to clean the place and prepare it for the sale. They got first pick... which meant Aunt Agnes took what she wanted and loaded it in her car; Aunt Hulda boxed the items that she liked and took them with her to California.

"The axles on Agnes' car were dragging on the ground," I heard several of her brothers (my uncles) lament many times through the years. But as good brothers with a heart do, they forgave her and drove down to North Carolina for visits. Men can be as sentimental as women. They came home, noted what they had seen around Aunt Agnes's house, and wished that they had something of their mother's. They said nothing to their sister. Their quiet acceptance kept the peace.

I know too well that "stuff" can make trouble. Dan, Linda and I struggled at one time over the possessions we each received, claimed or carried off from Mom and Dad's, but now it is fine. In fact, there is way too much of it.

Some of Grandma Hulda's sons returned home from the farm sale disenchanted. They said, "There was not a thing to bid on." I went to the farmhouse years later, before it was knocked down, and walked alone through the stripped-down hollow rooms.

Behold! The doorknob on the door to the upstairs! I knew that every single relative of our entire clan, everyone I loved so dearly, had turned that knob and gone up those stairs. It was a few feet from the window, where we had watched for Santa Claus, and the window where Grandpa Roslund got the sheep to buck at him. It seemed it had been left just for me. I felt like a gold miner who went back into the cave, one last time, to find a nugget that miraculously had been missed earlier. I managed to wrestle it out in one piece. It still turns beautifully as the knob to my own front door.

And, as the odd twists of life often turn out, my Aunt Agnes had saved the bonnet Grandma Hulda wore and the wooden box and basket she carried on the ship from Sweden, along with some of the priceless photos shown in this book.

When we all do our well-meaning-best, it all comes out in the wash! And, it's only Monday, which is Mother's and Grandmothers' wash day. And we have the whole week ahead!

May God Bless Us All.

The End

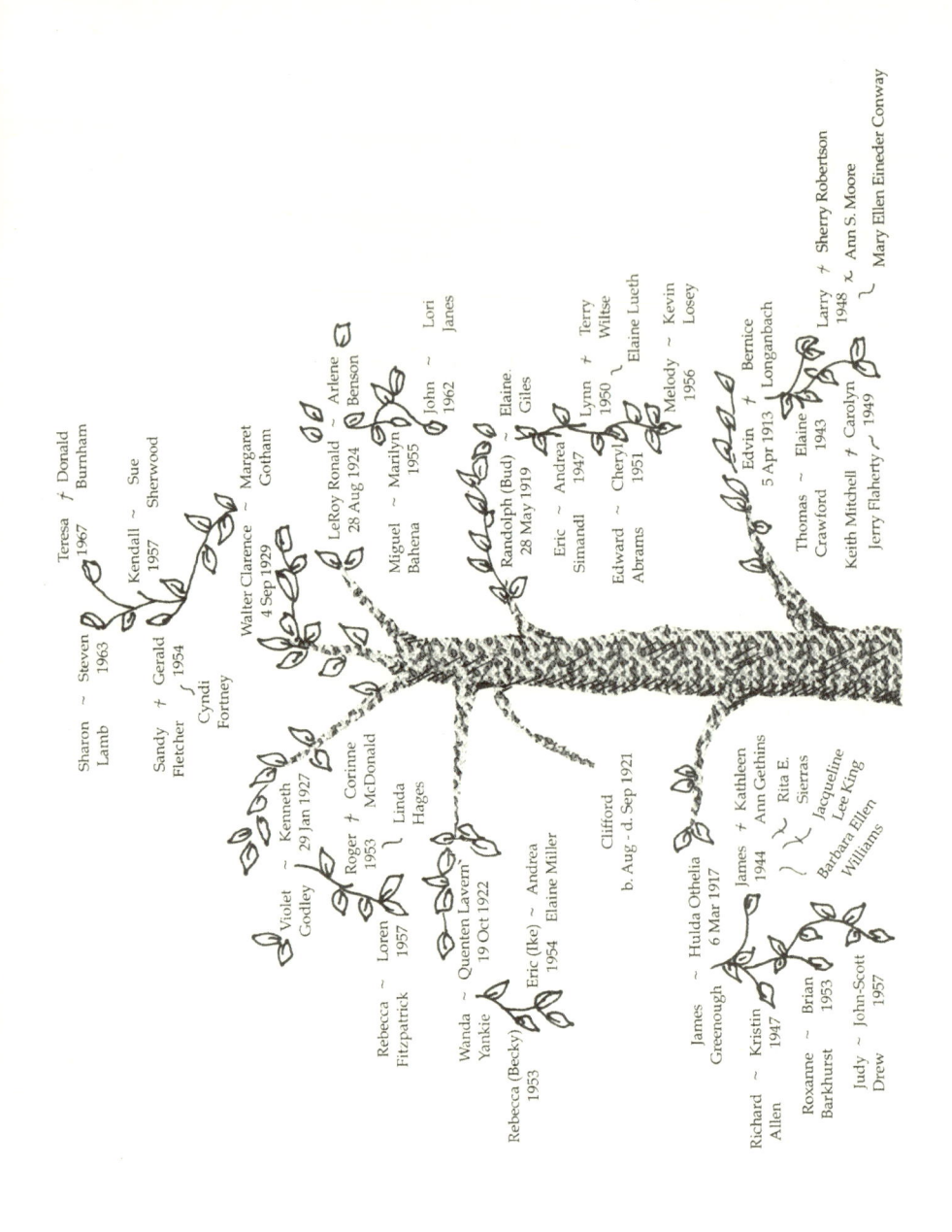

And It's Only Monday

Teresa ✝ Donald
1967   Burnham

Kendall ~ Sue
1957   Sherwood

Walter Clarence ~ Margaret
4 Sep 1929   Gotham

LeRoy Ronald ~ Arlene
28 Aug 1924   Benson

Miguel ~ Marilyn
Bahena   1955

John ~ Lori
       1962 Janes

Randolph (Bud) ~ Elaine.
28 May 1919   Giles

Eric ~ Andrea
Simandl 1947

Edward ~ Cheryl
Abrams   1951

Lynn ~ Terry
1950   Wiltse
       ~ Elaine Lueth

Melody ~ Kevin
1956   Losey

Edvin ✝ Bernice
5 Apr 1913 Longanbach

Thomas ~ Elaine
Crawford 1943

Keith Mitchell ✝ Carolyn
Jerry Flaherty ~ 1949

Larry ✝ Sherry Robertson
1948 ⚭ Ann S. Moore
     ~ Mary Ellen Eineder Conway

Sharon ~ Steven
Lamb   1963

Sandy ✝ Gerald
Fletcher 1954
       ~ Cyndi
         Fortney

Violet ~ Kenneth
Godley 29 Jan 1927

Roger ✝ Corinne
1953   McDonald
       ~ Linda
         Hages

Rebecca ~ Loren
Fitzpatrick 1957

Wanda ~ Quenten Lavern'
Yankie   19 Oct 1922

Eric (Ike) ~ Andrea
1954   Elaine Miller

Clifford
b. Aug - d. Sep 1921

James ~ Kathleen
1944   Ann Gethins
       ~ Rita E.
         Sierras
       ~ Jacqueline
         Lee King
       ~ Barbara Ellen
         Williams

Rebecca (Becky)
1953

James ~ Hulda Othelia
Greenough 6 Mar 1917

Richard ~ Kristin
Allen   1947

Roxanne ~ Brian
Barkhurst 1953

Judy ~ John-Scott
       Drew 1957

254

Roslund Family Tree

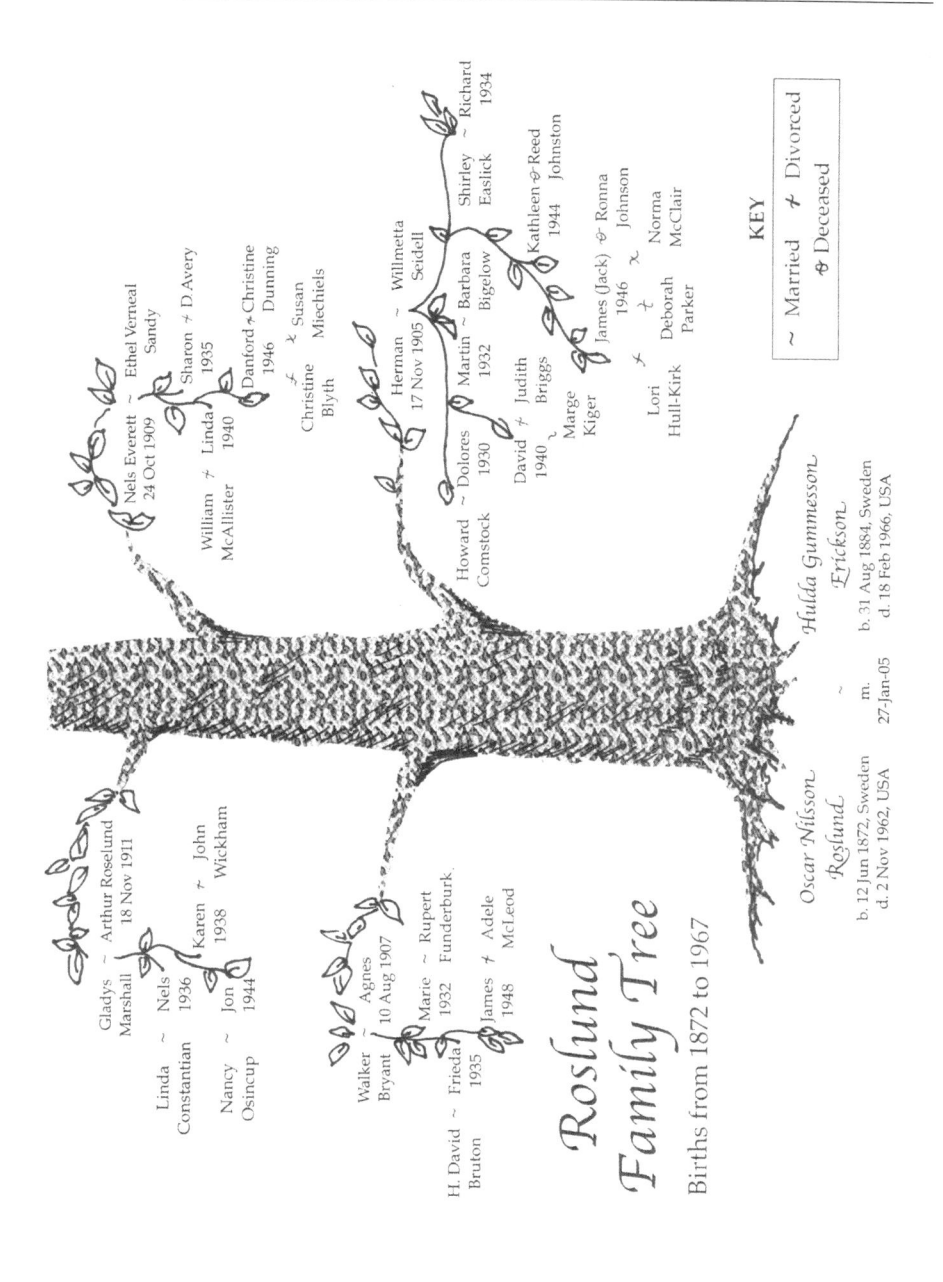

Births from 1872 to 1967

Oscar Nilsson Roslund
b. 12 Jun 1872, Sweden
d. 2 Nov 1962, USA

~ m. 27-Jan-05 ~

Hulda Gummesson Erickson
b. 31 Aug 1884, Sweden
d. 18 Feb 1966, USA

- Gladys ~ Arthur Roselund 18 Nov 1911
  - Linda Constantian ~ Nels 1936 Marshall
  - Karen ⊹ John 1938 Wickham
    - Nancy ~ Jon 1944 Osincup

- Walker ~ Agnes 10 Aug 1907 Bryant
  - H. David ~ Frieda 1935 Bruton
  - Marie ~ Rupert 1932 Funderburk
    - James ⊹ Adele 1948 McLeod

- Nels Everett ~ Ethel Verneal 24 Oct 1909 Sandy
  - William ⊹ Linda 1940 McAllister
    - Sharon ⊹ D Avery 1935
    - Danford ⊹ Christine 1946 Dunning
      - Christine ⊹ Susan Blyth ⚭ Miechiels

- Howard ~ Dolores Comstock
  - Herman ~ Willmetta 17 Nov 1905 Seidell
    - Martin ~ Barbara 1932 Bigelow
      - David ⊹ Judith 1940 Briggs
        ⚭ Marge Kiger
      - James (Jack) ⊹ Ronna 1946 Johnson
        ⚭ Norma McClair
        ⊹ Deborah Parker
      - Lori ⚭ Hull-Kirk
      - Kathleen ⊹ Reed 1944 Johnston
    - Shirley ~ Richard Easlick 1934

KEY

~ Married ⊹ Divorced
⚭ Deceased

255

Michigan Maps

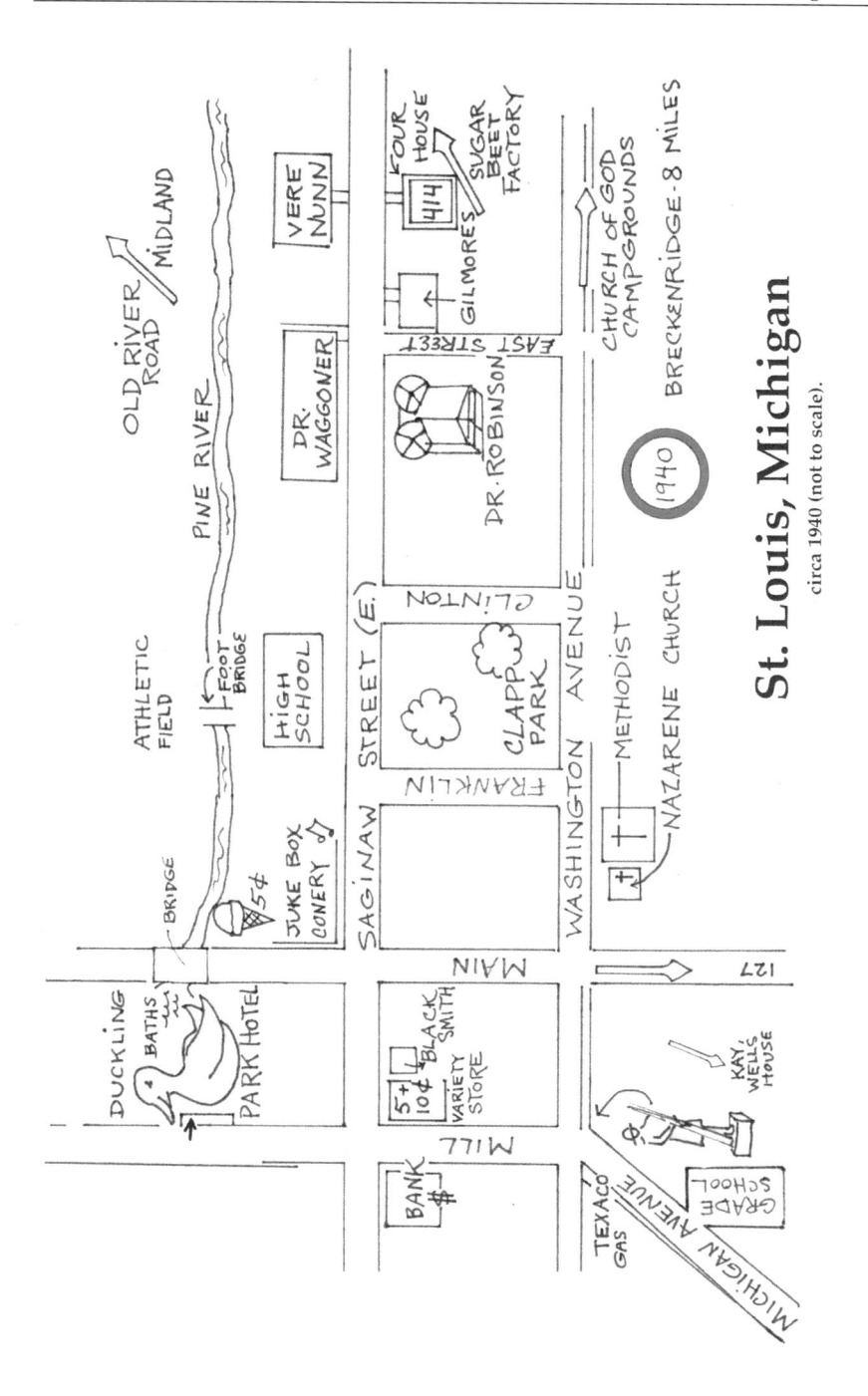

St. Louis, Michigan
circa 1940 (not to scale).

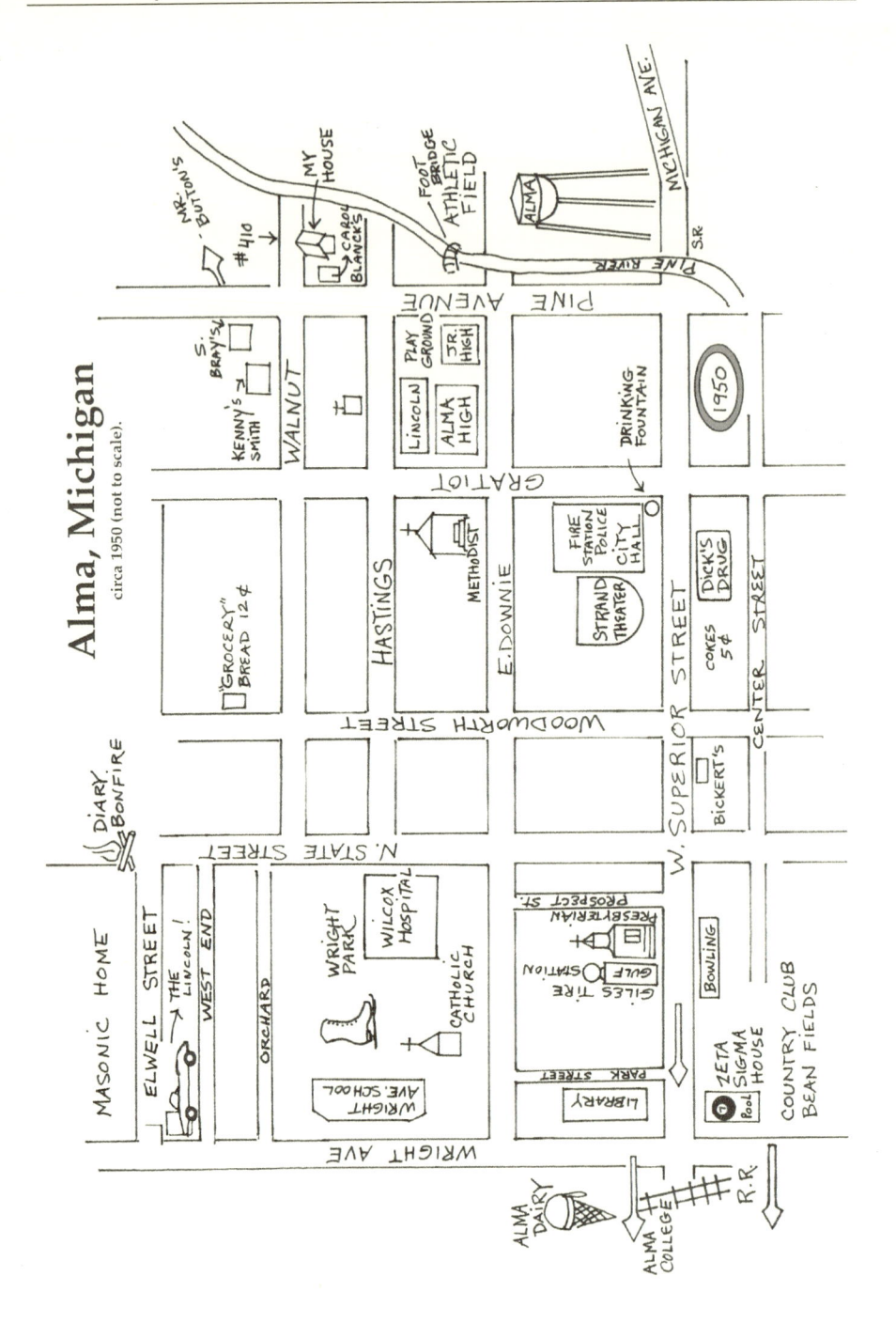

And It's Only Monday

Alma, Michigan
circa 1950 (not to scale).

Emerson Township

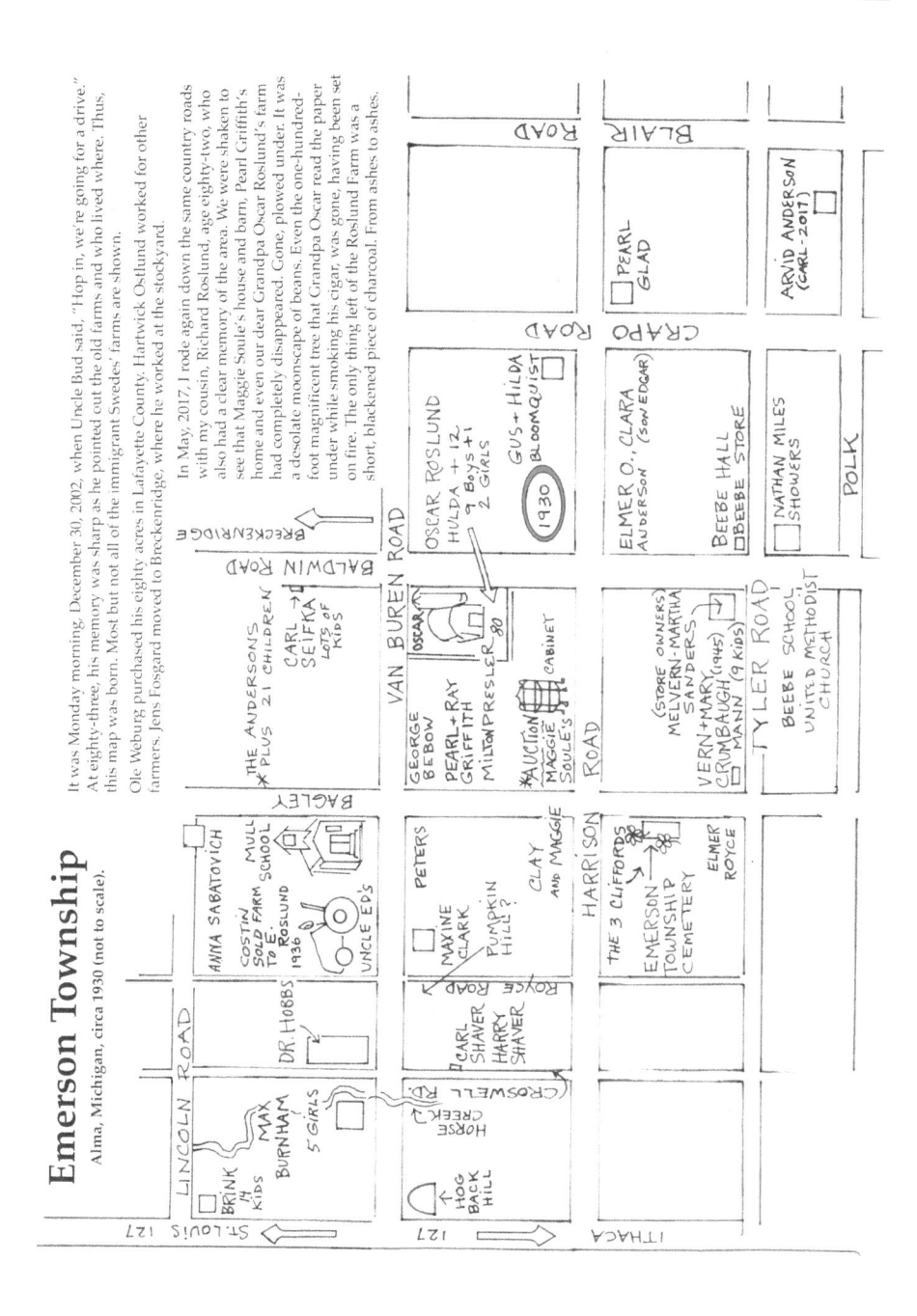

Alma, Michigan, circa 1930 (not to scale).

It was Monday morning, December 30, 2002, when Uncle Bud said, "Hop in, we're going for a drive." At eighty-three, his memory was sharp as he pointed out the old farms and who lived where. Thus, this map was born. Most but not all of the immigrant Swedes' farms are shown.

Ole Weburg purchased his eighty acres in Lafayette County. Hartwick Ostlund worked for other farmers. Jens Fosgard moved to Breckenridge, where he worked at the stockyard.

In May, 2017, I rode again down the same country roads with my cousin, Richard Roslund, age eighty-two, who also had a clear memory of the area. We were shaken to see that Maggie Soule's house and barn, Pearl Griffith's home and even our dear Grandpa Oscar Roslund's farm had completely disappeared. Gone, plowed under. It was a desolate moonscape of beans. Even the one-hundred-foot magnificent tree that Grandpa Oscar read the paper under while smoking his cigar, was gone, having been set on fire. The only thing left of the Roslund Farm was a short, blackened piece of charcoal. From ashes to ashes.

Michigan Maps